ZIMBABWE

Marxist Regimes Series

Series editor: Bogdan Szajkowski,
Department of Sociology, University College,
Cardiff

ZIMBABWE

Politics, Economics and Society

Colin Stoneman and
Lionel Cliffe

Pinter Publishers
London and New York

First published in Great Britain in 1989 by
Pinter Publishers Limited
25 Floral Street, London WC2E 9DS

British Library Cataloguing in Publication Data
A CIP catalogue record for this book is available from the British Library.

Library of Congress Cataloging-in-Publication Data
Stoneman, Colin.
    Zimbabwe : politics, economics, and society.
    (Marxist regimes series)
    Bibliography: p.
    Includes index.
    1. Zimbabwe—Politics and government. 2. Zimbabwe—
Social conditions. 3. Zimbabwe— Economic conditions.
I. Cliffe, Lionel. II. Title.
JQ2929.Al5S76   1988   968.91   88-25354
ISBN 0-86187-454-4
ISBN 0-86187-455-2 (pbk.)

Typeset by Saxon Printing Ltd., Derby.
Printed in Great Britain by SRP Ltd, Exeter

Editor's Preface

Since its independence in 1980, Zimbabwe has embarked on a series of major reforms aimed at the restructuring of the country's political, social and economic foundations. This book traces the history of these endeavours, examines the background to these reforms and evaluates the degree of their success and failure. Furthermore, it provides the reader with explanations and rationale for the adoption of what Zimbabwe's political elite sees as a Marxist programme of change.

The study of Marxist regimes has commonly been equated with the study of communist political systems. There were several historical and methodological reasons for this. For many years it was not difficult to distinguish the eight regimes in Eastern Europe and four in Asia which resoundingly claimed adherence to the tenets of Marxism and more particularly to their Soviet interpretation—Marxism-Leninism. These regimes, variously called 'People's Republic', 'People's Democratic Republic', or 'Democratic Republic', claimed to have derived their inspiration from the Soviet Union, to which, indeed, in the overwhelming number of cases they owed their establishment.

To many scholars and analysts these regimes represented a multiplication of and geographical extension of the 'Soviet model' and consequently of the Soviet sphere of influence. Although there were clearly substantial similarities between the Soviet Union and the people's democracies, especially in the initial phases of their development, these were often overstressed at the expense of noticing the differences between these political systems.

It took a few years for scholars to realize that generalizing the particular, i.e., applying the Soviet experience to other states ruled by elites which claimed to be guided by 'scientific socialism', was not good enough. The relative simplicity of the assumption of a cohesive communist bloc was questioned after the expulsion of Yugoslavia from the Communist Information Bureau in 1948 and in particular after the workers' riots in Poznań in 1956 and the Hungarian revolution of the same year. By the mid-1960s, the totalitarian model of communist politics, which until then had been very much in force, began to crumble. As some of these regimes articulated demands for a distinctive path of socialist development, many specialists studying these systems began to notice that the cohesiveness of the communist bloc was less apparent than had been claimed before.

Also by the mid-1960s, in the newly independent African states 'democratic' multi-party states were turning into one-party states or military dictatorships, thus questioning the inherent superiority of liberal democracy, capitalism and the values that went with it. Scholars now began to ponder on the simple contrast between multi-party democracy and a one-party totalitarian rule that had satisfied an earlier generation.

More importantly, however, by the beginning of that decade Cuba had a revolution without Soviet help, a revolution which subsequently became to many political elites in the Third World not only an inspiration but a clear military, political and ideological example to follow. Apart from its romantic appeal, to many nationalist movements the Cuban revolution also demonstrated a novel way of conducting and winning a nationalist, anti-imperialist war and accepting Marxism as the state ideology without a vanguard communist party. The Cuban precedent was subsequently followed in one respect or another by scores of Third World regimes, which used the adoption of 'scientific socialism' tied to the tradition of Marxist thought as a form of mobilization, legitimation or association with the prestigious symbols and powerful high-status regimes such as the Soviet Union, China, Cuba and Vietnam.

Despite all these changes the study of Marxist regimes remains in its infancy and continues to be hampered by constant and not always pertinent comparison with the Soviet Union, thus somewhat blurring the important underlying common theme—the 'scientific theory' of the laws of development of human society and human history. This doctrine is claimed by the leadership of these regimes to consist of the discovery of objective causal relationships; it is used to analyse the contradictions which arise between goals and actuality in the pursuit of a common destiny. Thus the political elites of these countries have been and continue to be influenced in both their ideology and their political practice by Marxism more than any other current of social thought and political practice.

The growth in the number and global significance, as well as the ideological, political and economic impact, of Marxist regimes has presented scholars and students with an increasing challenge. In meeting this challenge, social scientists on both sides of the political divide have put forward a dazzling profusion of terms, models, programmes and varieties of interpretation. It is against the background of this profusion that the present comprehensive series on Marxist regimes is offered.

This collection of monographs is envisaged as a series of multi-disciplinary textbooks on the governments, politics, economics and society of these countries. Each of the monographs was prepared by a specialist on the country concerned. Thus, over fifty scholars from all over the world have contributed monographs which were based on first-hand knowledge. The geographical diversity of the authors, combined with the fact that as a group they represent many disciplines of social science, gives their individual analyses and the series as a whole an additional dimension.

Each of the scholars who contributed to this series was asked to analyse such topics as the political culture, the governmental structure, the ruling party, other mass organizations, party-state relations, the policy process, the economy, domestic and foreign relations together with any features peculiar to the country under discussion.

This series does not aim at assigning authenticity or authority to any single one of the political systems included in it. It shows that, depending on a variety of historical, cultural, ethnic and political factors, the pursuit of goals derived from the tenets of Marxism has produced different political forms at different times and in different places. It also illustrates the rich diversity among these societies, where attempts to achieve a synthesis between goals derived from Marxism on the one hand, and national realities on the other, have often meant distinctive approaches and solutions to the problems of social, political and economic development.

University College   *Bogdan Szajkowski*
Cardiff

Contents

List of Illustrations and Tables

Maps

Tables

Figure

Preface

This book is intended to be a basic textbook offering an overview of Zimbabwe to a non-specialist, mainly student, audience, chiefly in the Western world. It is aimed at those who are generally interested in states with left-wing governments and/or those concerned with Africa. Accordingly, it seeks to provide a summary of information of an interdisciplinary kind and also a synthesis of much other work on the country, rather than reporting on any new research, even though both authors have done some specialist work on the country in recent years. It does seek to go beyond providing a catalogue of data in one particular respect, however. It offers some introduction not only to the particulars of the country but also to the literature and the interesting on-going debates about the character of the regime and the prospects of the country that have emerged in the last few years.

We have thought it appropriate to situate our discussion in the context of debates on Zimbabwe, and on Africa generally, for several reasons. First, is the intrinsic interest and sophistication of these debates, whose mainly African contributors are not always well known in mainstream Western scholarly circles. Second, is the fact that Zimbabwe is something of a marginal case in a general series on 'Marxist regimes'. The realities of political structures and style, policies, the economic system, and the general discourse in Zimbabwe bear little relationship to the familiar issues of analysis in non-African Marxist regimes, and the distinction in the political and economic systems with other African, but avowedly non-Marxist regimes, like Tanzania or even pro-Western, 'capitalist' Kenya, is so far from being clear-cut that the categories of Marxist and Africanist-single-party regimes, or at least Zimbabwe's position between them, are hard to distinguish.

It is with such distinctions and categorizations that the literature has been concerned, and this volume starts with a brief summary of the various issues that have been raised and tries to situate our approach in relation to these competing paradigms. The literature, and indeed our own perspective, is ambiguous, and this is no doubt in part a consequence of the very recentness of the emergence of Zimbabwe as an independent African state in 1980. It is too soon to reach a definitive assessment of the nature and extent of the change that then occurred from the white-settler-dominated economy, state and society. Nevertheless we sketch the dynamic of the forces that generated that change and the legacy of the earlier political economy in Part I of this volume, which also includes some assessment of the transition. One consequence of this history has been that 'race' has been a salient and politically explosive issue and thus has to figure alongside more conventional categories like class in our analysis of social structure and dynamics in Part II. The following section, Part III, offers an outline of the structures of government and party and of political forces, one that, given their short durations thus far, and the extent of changes in these few years, is necessarily tentative. The same can be said of our survey of the economy and its various sectors in Part IV, and of some of the regime's policies in Part V.

In preparing this text, we owe debts to several people and institutions. Lionel Cliffe benefited in being able to do background work on Zimbabwe in a concentrated way while spending a year as Holdsworth Senior Research Fellow in the Faculty of Economic and Social Studies, University of Manchester, and also from the usual but much-appreciated forbearance of staff, research students and secretaries in the department of Politics at the University of Leeds, while Colin Stoneman gained much from three years spent on a Leverhulme Fellowship from a base at the University of York. Some of the chapters have benefited from critical readings by Donna Pankhurst and Lloyd Sachikonye, but neither is responsible for our interpretation or any remaining errors. Yvonne Wilkinson has done a great job typing most of the manuscript.

LC and CS, September 1988

Basic Data

Official name	Republic of Zimbabwe
Population	8.6 million (30 June 1987)
Population density	23 per sq.km
Population growth (% pa)	2.9 (1987)
Urban population (%)	26 (1982)
Total labour force	2.5 million (1982)
Formal employment	1.05 million (1982); 1.06 million (1985)
Life expectancy at age 1	60.4 (males); 62.7 (females) (1982)
Infant death rate	83 in first year per 1,000 born (1982)
Ethnic groups	Shona 75% (of which Karanga 21%, Zezuru 17%, Manyika 13%, Korekore 12%, Rozvi 9%, Ndau 3%), Ndebele 19% (of which Ndebele 14%, Kalanga 5%), Tonga, Venda and Shangaan 4%, whites 1.5%, 'coloureds' and Asians 0.5%
Capital	Harare (previously Salisbury) — 656,000 (1982; probably over 1 million by 1988)
Land area	390,580 sq.km of which about 17% arable
Official languages	English, Shona, Ndebele
Administrative division	8 provinces: Manicaland, Mashonaland Central, Mashonaland East, Mashonaland West, Masvingo, Matabeleland North, Matabeleland South, Midlands
Membership of international organizations	UN (Security Council member 1983–4), World Bank, IMF, the Commonwealth, ACP (African, Caribbean Pacific countries of the Lomé Convention), Organization of African Unity, Non-Aligned Movement (chair, 1986–9), Preferential Trade Area for East and Southern Africa (PTA), Southern African Development Coordination Conference (SADCC)

Foreign relations	Diplomatic relations with most countries except South Africa (trade office), Namibia, Israel, South Korea and Taiwan
Political structure Constitution	Agreed at Lancaster House conference in London, 1979; radically revised 1987
Highest legislative body	House of Assembly: 100 elected members, of which 20 were reserved for whites on a separate roll 1980–7, but are now chosen by the other members. Senate: 40 members, of which 10 reserved for whites 1980–7. Proposed for abolition in 1990.
Highest executive body	Until 1988 the Cabinet, headed by Robert Mugabe as Prime Minister. Now Executive President with Cabinet.
Prime Minister	Abolished in 1987
President	From 1988 Robert Mugabe as Executive President (previously the Reverend Canaan Banana as ceremonial president)
Ruling party	ZANU-PF (Zimbabwe African National Union-Patriotic Front); from 1988 incorporating the former Zimbabwe African People's Union (ZAPU)
President and first secretary of the party	Robert Mugabe
Party membership	Open
Growth indicators GDP	1980–6: 4.3% 1982–6: 1.3%
Industry (volume 1980=100)	1986 = 114.5
Mining (volume 1980=100)	1986 = 99.4
Agriculture	1980–5: 5.3% per annum
Trade and balance of payments Exports	US$1,305 million (1986); 26% of GDP
Imports	US$985 million (1986); 20% of GDP
Main exports	Gold, tobacco, cotton, ferro-alloys, asbestos, nickel, steel
Main imports	Machinery and transport equipment, chemicals, petroleum products, manufactured goods

Destination of exports (%)	South Africa 10, UK 10, West Germany 7, Italy 5 (1986)
Source of imports (%)	South Africa 21, West Germany 11, UK 11, USA 4 (1986)
Foreign debt	US$2,143 million (end 1985); debt-service ratio 35% of exports of goods and services (1987 estimate)

Main natural resources   Gold, chromium, nickel, copper, asbestos, coal, iron

Food self-sufficiency   Self-sufficient in maize (the staple) with two years' stockpile in 1987; overproduction in dairy products; beef exported; one-third of wheat needs imported

Armed forces   42,000 (1986) of which about 1,000 in the Air Force; around 10,000 are involved in Mozambique in defence of the Beira Corridor. Paramilitary forces number about 38,000 (15,000 police, 3,000 police support unit, 20,000 militia)

Education and health

School system   7 years primary compulsory (5–12) (not yet fully implemented)

Primary	1979: 819,000	1986:	2,260,000
Secondary	1979: 79,000	1986:	546,800
University of Zimbabwe	1980: 1,873	1985:	4,742
Other tertiary	1980: 6,466	1985:	26,605
Adult literacy (%)	76.7 (1982)		
Population per hospital bed	443 (1984)		
Population per physician	6,800 (1986)		

Economy

GDP	US$4,944 million (1986)
GDP per caput	US$580 (1986)
GDP shares (%)	Manufacturing industry 30.2, distribution 13.0, agriculture 11.4, mining 6.9 (1986)
GDP expenditure (%)	Private consumption 58.5, public consumption 18.7, gross fixed capital formation 16.6, stock changes 6.4 (1985)

State budget (expenditure)	US$2,434 million (1986/87)
State budget (revenue)	US$1,836 million (1986/87)
Defence expenditure as share of state budget	15.6%
Monetary unit	Zimbabwe dollar (Z$1 = US$0.58 in 1988)
Main crops	Tobacco, maize, sorghum, cotton, sugar cane, soya beans, wheat, coffee
Land distribution (% of usable land including grazing)	50% communal areas (individual tenure rights with common grazing); 40% commercial (private free holdings); 10% former commercial holdings now resettled, of which 1% cooperatives
Main religions	Christianity (Roman Catholics the most numerous, but also Anglicans and many other protestant and revivalist sects); ancestral worship
Transport	
Rail network	3,400 km; links all the main towns and mines and connects to Botswana, Mozambique, South Africa and Zambia; 457 km electrified by 1983
Road network	85,000 km, of which 15% tarred, 54% gravelled
Air transport	8 airports, of which 3 international
Communications	Extensive telephone, telex and radio services, linked internationally via an Earth Satellite station
Oil pipeline	From Beira (Mozambique) to Mutare

Population Forecasting

The following data are projections produced by Poptran, University College Cardiff Population Centre, from United Nations Assessment Data published in 1980, and are reproduced here to provide some basis of comparison with other countries covered by the Marxist Regimes Series.

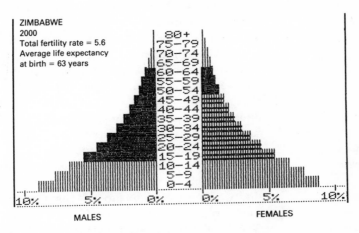

ZIMBABWE
2000
Total fertility rate = 5.6
Average life expectancy
at birth = 63 years

MALES   FEMALES

Projected Data for Zimbabwe 2000

Total population ('000)	14,730
Males ('000)	7,334
Females ('000)	7,396
Total fertility rate	5.65
Life expectancy (male)	61.0 years
Life expectancy (female)	64.7 years
Crude birth rate	41.3
Crude death rate	8.1
Annual growth rate	3.33%
Under 15s	46.3%
Over 65s	2.82%
Women aged 15–49	22.54%
Doubling time	21 years
Population density	38 per sq. km
Urban population	38.2%

Glossary

blacks and whites	These terms are preferred to *African* and *European*, the categories (along with *Coloureds* and *Asians*) used by the previous regime
chimbwidos	Young women who helped the guerrilla fighters
chimurenga	The liberation struggle
dare	Literally 'council' or committee, specifically the name of ZANU's high command in the 1970s
kraal	'Village' — the smallest unit/lowest level of administrative grouping, often consisting of small clusters of homesteads
lobola	Bridewealth payments by groom's family to bride's family on marriage (see also *roora*)
mujibas	Young men who helped the guerrilla fighters
pungwe	Political education meetings held by guerrillas, normally at night
roora	Bridewealth payments by groom's family to bride's family on marriage (see also *lobola*)
zsadu	'Ward' — the second level unit of local administration

Dollars: The $ sign is to be understood as referring to the Zimbabwe dollar (unless qualified as US$). The exchange rate with the US$ since independence is shown in the following table:

Average Exchange Rate (Z$ per US$)

1980	1981	1982	1983	1984	1985	1986	1987	1988
0.643	0.689	0.757	1.011	1.244	1.612	1.665	1.661	1.729*

* First half of year.
Source: IMF, *International Financial Statistics*.

List of Abbreviations

AAC	Anglo-American Corporation of South Africa
ACP	African, Caribbean and Pacific countries
AFC	Agricultural Finance Corporation
AMA	Agricultural Marketing Authority
BCG	Beira Corridor Group
BMATT	British Military Advisory and Training Team
CACU	Central Association of Cooperative Unions
CAs	Communal Areas
CAZ	Conservative Alliance of Zimbabwe (successor to the Rhodesian Front which ruled Zimbabwe illegally during the UDI period)
CFU	Commercial Farmers' Union
CIP	Commodity Import Programme
CMB	Cotton Marketing Board
CMEA	Council for Mutual Economic Assistance (Comecon)
CSC	Cold Storage Commission
CSO	Central Statistical Office
CZI	Confederation of Zimbabwe Industries
DMB	Dairy Marketing Board
EC	European Community
FLS	Front Line States (states actively opposed to white minority rule)
FRELIMO	Front for the Liberation of Mozambique
FFYNDP	First Five-Year National Development Plan (1986)
GDP	Gross Domestic Product
GMB	Grain Marketing Board
IDC	Industrial Development Corporation of Zimbabwe (sometimes IDCZ)
ILO	International Labour Organization
Lomé	The Lomé Conventions between the EC and the ACP countries
LSCF	large-scale commercial farms
MMCZ	Minerals Marketing Corporation of Zimbabwe
MNR	Mozambique National Resistance (also called Renamo)
NICs	newly-industrialized countries

NFAZ	National Farmers' Association of Zimbabwe (the CA smallholders' body)
NMS	National Manpower Survey (1981)
NRZ	National Railways of Zimbabwe
OCCZIM	Organization of Collective Cooperatives in Zimbabwe
PTA	Preferential Trade Area of Eastern and Southern Africa
RBZ	Reserve Bank of Zimbabwe
RF	Rhodesian Front (from 1980, Republican Front); *see* CAZ
SADCC	Southern African Development Coordination Conference
SSA	Sub-Saharan Africa
STC	State Trading Corporation
STF	Special Task Force
TMB	Tobacco Marketing Board
TNC	transnational corporation
TNDP	Transitional National Development Plan (1983)
TTLs	Tribal Trust Lands
UANC	United African National Council
UDI	Unilateral Declaration of Independence (1965)
UNCTAD	United Nations Conference on Trade and Development
UNDP	United Nations Development Programme
UNIDO	United Nations Industrial Development Organization
USAID	United States Agency for International Development
WHO	World Health Organization
ZANLA	Zimbabwe African National Liberation Army (ZANU's military wing)
ZANU	Zimbabwe African National Union — Patriotic Front (officially ZANU-PF)
ZAPU	Zimbabwe African People's Union
ZCTU	Zimbabwe Congress of Trade Unions
ZDC	Zimbabwe Development Corporation
ZIMCORD	Zimbabwe Conference on Reconstruction and Development (1981)
ZIMFEP	Zimbabwe Foundation for Education with Production
ZIPA	Zimbabwe People's Army (founded in 1976 initially as a common military front between ZANLA and ZIPRA, but after a split a faction within ZANU)
ZIPRA	Zimbabwe People's Revolutionary Army (ZAPU's military wing)
ZMDC	Zimbabwe Mining Development Corporation

ZNA Zimbabwe National Army (formed from ZANLA, ZIPRA, and the Rhodesian army)

ZNCC Zimbabwe National Chambers of Commerce

ZNFU Zimbabwe National Farmers' Union (organization of the small commercial farmers)

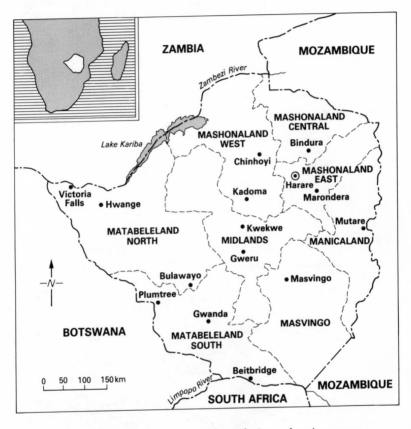

Map 1 Zimbabwe: provincial boundaries and major towns

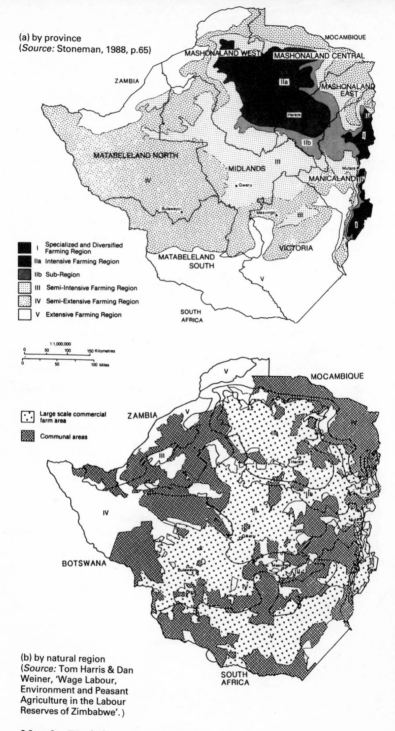

(a) by province
(*Source:* Stoneman, 1988, p.65)

MOCAMBIQUE

MASHONALAND WEST   MASHONALAND CENTRAL

ZAMBIA

IIa

MASHONALAND EAST

Harare

IIb

MATABELELAND NORTH   MIDLANDS   III

Gweru   MANICALAND

Bulawayo   Mutare

Masvingo   III

I   Specialized and Diversified
       Farming Region
IIa   Intensive Farming Region
IIb   Sub-Region
III   Semi-Intensive Farming Region
IV   Semi-Extensive Farming Region
V   Extensive Farming Region

MATABELELAND
SOUTH   VICTORIA

SOUTH
AFRICA

1:1,000,000
0   50   100   150 Kilometres
0   50   100 Miles

MOCAMBIQUE

Large scale commercial
farm area

Communal areas

ZAMBIA   V

V   III   IIb

IIL

Harare

III

IV   Gweru

BOTSWANA   Bulawayo   Masvingo

IV

V

(b) by natural region
(*Source:* Tom Harris & Dan
Weiner, 'Wage Labour,
Environment and Peasant
Agriculture in the Labour
Reserves of Zimbabwe'.)

SOUTH
AFRICA

Map 2   Zimbabwe: the distribution of land

Part I
History and Political Traditions

1 Approaches to the Study of Zimbabwe

There is an immediate anomaly that has to be explained in dealing with Zimbabwe as a 'Marxist regime'. It is indeed self-proclaimedly 'Marxist' — in fact when the ruling party was re-formed in January 1988 after the unity agreement between the two main former parties it reaffirmed its commitment to 'Marxism–Leninism'. However, it presides over an unequivocally capitalist economy, which it has not sought to transform in any self-consciously socialist direction since coming to power in 1980. Nor, arguably — and this is something which will be explored in this volume — does it have any coherent project for any such transition in the future. Moreover the party itself is an open, mass party, that has not sought to transform itself (like FRELIMO in neighbouring Mozambique) into a vanguard organization, and is seemingly, far from the Leninist model — another proposition to be explored.

In what sense then is the regime's self description objectively justifiable? Moreover, why should it make such claims — especially if they do not correspond to the reality? These are questions which must form the starting point of any such analysis, and will in turn determine the book's major theses and preoccupations.

Certainly some analysts and commentators see this self-designation as a sham. They point to the parallels with Kenya, which like Zimbabwe had been a settler colony, with a similar inherited economy and class structure. Indeed Zimbabwe has carried out an almost exactly similar minimum programme of social restructuring, limited to a very partial land redistribution from whites to blacks, to that carried out by Kenya in its first eight years of independence. During that period in the 1960s the Kenya ruling party proclaimed its commitment to 'African socialism'; the practice then and since has convinced many that the objective meaning of the adjective 'African' in that context can only be 'anti-'. There are certainly some analysts who see the Zimbabwe regime in the same terms. The puzzle for them is not so much why a ruling group bothers to dissemble in some way — some trendy and seemingly egalitarian ideological smokescreen is often thought necessary — but why Zimbabwe should choose 'Marxism-Leninism'. One speculative answer that has been offered is simply that it is the only label handy, 'African socialism' having been so discredited intellectually and the custom-built varieties like Zambian 'humanism' even more so.

One notable example of a text that would simply dismiss the Marxist pretensions of the ruling party is Astrow (1983), and certainly his is a generally well-informed book whose argument cannot be just side-stepped. He justifies his conclusions by categorizing the state in independent Zimbabwe as 'neo-colonial' and in the hands of a petty-bourgeois class, and argues that that outcome was an immediate result of a leadership group with that class background and orientation winning out through a complex set of struggles internal to the nationalist movement. But for him this outcome was more fundamentally 'overdetermined' structurally by the fact that the struggle was a national and not a class struggle, and that Zimbabwe's significant working class was never adequately mobilized, let alone the leading class in that struggle. It is in this latter dimension that the book is revealed as reductionist. It is obvious that for Astrow this outcome is entirely predictable not only for Zimbabwe but for all developing countries: national struggles are by definition not socialist. There is no prospect here of any two-stage transition through a 'national democratic reform', say, to socialism. Thus it is not Astrow's characterization of the present Zimbabwe regime that is questionable (indeed other analysts broadly agree), but his *approach*, which does not allow for any counter-factual possibility. Thus his own discussion of the particular nature of the national movement, however well-informed, is redundant to his essential argument: the Zimbabwe nationalist movement is neo-colonial *by definition*, and not as a result of particular experiences and internal struggles.

An influential volume by Zimbabwean scholars (Mandaza, 1986) in fact broadly accepts one part of Astrow's characterization of the regime, spelling out in a very frank way its conclusion that the class that has inherited state power is indeed 'petty bourgeois', and seeing the overall post-independence situation as 'neo-colonial'. However the outcome of the nationalist struggle is far from settled; they see the state as a heterogeneous, complex result of a compromise settlement at independence, which has become an arena for a partially submerged and on-going tension between international capital and the more popular demands that the nationalist movement embodied (for it was not just petty bourgeois). These conflicts are mediated by, and for the moment smoothed over by, the petty-bourgeois ruling faction. The Mandaza group's approach differs from Astrow's in that it claims to be rooted in analysis of the specific Zimbabwean realities rather than by reference to some ideal scenario for revolution, and concludes therefrom that the future path of development is not predetermined. He and his other radical Zimbabwe contributors still see a real prospect for the eventual emergence of a transition to socialism, coming about through the initiative of a progressive element of the petty bourgeoisie, and involving a transformation of the national movement into a party capable of leading such a transition, thereby effectively mobilizing the working classes.

A very similar approach is followed by some of the contributors to *Zimbabwe's Prospects* (Stoneman, 1988), who agree substantially with Mandaza's analysis but are less optimistic about the prospects. Phimister emphasizes the ambiguous nature of the inheritance, concluding that far from being 'radicalized' (see below) during the war, ZANU and ZAPU increasingly reflected the interests of rich peasants and the educated petty bourgeoisie rather than workers and peasants (despite the fact that many guerrillas could be placed in the latter categories). After inspecting experience from independent Zimbabwe in five areas, Davies concludes that 'we find it difficult to explain why Zimbabwe should be regarded as transitional rather than just capitalist; it is not at all clear even whether the base for transition is being strengthened or not'. He admits that a fuller analysis, including an investigation of the process of class formation, might offer greater grounds for hope. Sibanda sees Zimbabwe's social formation as essentially neo-colonial, with many apparent transitional elements better interpreted as constituting the struggle of the petty bourgeoisie to establish an economic base, so as to become a bourgeoisie proper. As this would-be dominant class has anti-imperialist interests, at least until it reaches an accommodation with capital (as in Kenya), there remains the possibility of sections of it allying with workers and peasants, although again he is not very optimistic.

The approaches in both these books see the 'socialist' and 'Marxist' rhetoric as part of the ambiguity in the present compromise situation, as part of the mediation, and as a prospective future blueprint rather than the basis for present policies. In practice, the armed struggle had no 'socialist thrust' and had 'serious ideological deficiencies' in Mandaza's eyes (1986, pp. 29–30). In asserting this he, like Phimister, criticizes the alternative approach of those analysts of southern African liberation struggles who argue a 'radicalization' thesis: that a prolonged armed struggle can transform an anti-colonial nationalist movement into one that seeks to revolutionize the inherited social and economic structures. This transformation is seen as being generated by two mutually reinforcing processes: the (necessary) conscientizing and mobilizing of peasants and peasant-workers so that they are more aware of, and thus ultimately better able to defend, their interests as exploited classes; and the sensitizing of those nationalist cadres from other class backgrounds to the interests of the ordinary people they have had to rely upon. Given this perspective, some post-independence transformation towards socialism would not be ruled out, as it would for Astrow, but whether it would occur in any particular case would depend on the emerging character of the nationalist movement, the form of its struggle and the particular dialectic in the relationship between political leaders and activists, on the one hand, and the masses on the other.

This mode of analysis has been most commonly applied to neighbouring Mozambique whose nationalist movement did formally change itself from a front into an officially 'Marxist-Leninist' party after independence, but in addition (unlike ZANU) it metamorphosed into a vanguard party (Saul, 1985). It may also be applied to an analysis of Zimbabwe's struggle, and to the extent that it is, Mandaza is correct to point out that as a prediction of post-independence developments it does little to explain actual events, and may thus be used instead as a judgemental device to point to a betrayal of this radical tradition. However, few of the writers criticized by Mandaza do in fact apply the general thesis in this way to the Zimbabwean case. Ranger (1983) perhaps comes the nearest, but his is a variant of the 'radicalising effect of prolonged armed struggle' argument: he views the dialectic of the struggle as one in which the peasant consciousness was strong enough to impose a different radicalizing emphasis on nationalist ideology. He may in fact have overstated the strength of the peasant impact and its ability to survive — a somewhat different kind of romanticism. However the radicalization thesis could be (and is more likely to be) applied in a quite different way to that criticized by Mandaza: by accepting the *propensity* to some radicalization in such situations, it could be argued that the internal transformation did not get off the ground in the particular case of Zimbabwe (or it did so at most only incompletely). This would offer a logical explanation, and one that is not reductionist and overdetermined, of the extent to which social transformation along Marxian lines has remained at the level of rhetoric.

There are still some problems with this radicalization approach, even if it is used to explain Zimbabwe as a case where the transition did *not* occur. And here Mandaza has a point in stressing that other factors, apart from the outcome of internal contradictions within the nationalist struggle can have a decisive influence. The circumstances of the 'deal' under which independence was attained, the character of the inherited 'settler colonial state', and how far it was inherited, the influential impact of the international political forces and multinational capital including the stance of the sub-imperialist neighbour, South Africa, are all rightly stressed as significant, both by Mandaza and Sibanda; indeed such factors provide this work with something of an agenda in assessing Zimbabwe's system and its prospects. Weitzer (1984) similarly argues that Zimbabwe 'does *not* fit this scenario'; although he also questions the whole radicalization thesis, he does still see something distinctive in the Zimbabwean case, that is the re-emergence of a repressive state apparatus, not solely a retention from settler colonial rule, but also a product of the same emerging social and political forces around the new state. But insofar as much criticism of the general radicalization thesis rejects the possible differences between different types of struggles — not only between armed and peaceful, but amongst varying strategies of mobilization in a guerrilla war — it throws out the baby with the bathwater. The dialectic within the struggle may not be decisive on its own, but rhetorically to dismiss all differences is to lose one aspect of the specificity of an African context that may be significant.

The more historical of these issues were in fact first explored in a Marxist (albeit undogmatic) way in the path-breaking work of Giovanni Arrighi (1967, 1970). But rather than just conceptualizing an unchanging 'settler colonial state', he attempted to periodize the colonial state in terms of fluctuating dominance of differing fractions of capital (settler versus imperial; agricultural versus industrial) with differing implications for patterns of economic change and the interests not only of themselves but of the other, black classes in society. The final stage, with the election of the Rhodesian Front in 1962 and the 1965 unilateral declaration of independence (UDI) by Ian Smith's government, represented the victory of a settler, *agrarian capital*, bent on pursuing its own narrow interest and reversing the 'reformist' trends that had been set in motion in the interests of metropolitan, industrial capital. This latter had sought to co-opt a settled, better-off part of the black petty bourgeoisie and working class and to allow some peasants to prosper; its policies would thus have allowed an expanded growth of black agriculture and the expansion of the internal market for manufactures, but would have meant competition for white farmers, skilled workers and professionals.

Arrighi's approach sees a degree of contradiction between metropolitan/ industrial and settler/agricultural capitalist interests — differences that were essentially about how to deal with capital accumulation and with the under-classes (in a political context partly defined by the resistance of those classes) — but also an 'essential commonality of interest between multinational, industrial capital and the African petty bourgeoisie'. It is an approach not completely at odds with Mandaza's, but offering a different perspective on the ambiguities and potentialities in a situation. In particular Mandaza sees little contradiction 'between the white settler factor and international capitalism' (Mandaza, 1986, p. 47); however both agree on the new opportunities for sections of the African petty bourgeoisie with independence. It has been suggested, too (Cliffe, 1984), that Arrighi's approach can be extrapolated to offer a perspective on the post-independence situation and to prompt other questions that can also usefully inform the agenda of this book. Thus: to what extent has international capital reasserted its dominance in a capitalist Zimbabwe since 1980, and has it been at the expense of the settlers, or national industrial capital, and with the unambiguous collaboration of the African petty bourgeoisie? How far have property relations changed, and how much have peasants, skilled workers and/or the middle classes prospered? And how far have the political patterns taken forms compatible with the interests of international capital and an aspiring petty bourgeoisie — are they simply based on seeking political spoils, on factionalism and personality — or do they allow some voicing of more popular needs and interests and some ideological dimension, offering the prospect of the party capable of overseeing a transition to socialism that Mandaza envisages? What does the new constellation of ruling interests imply for the prospects for peasant agricultural growth, land reform and industrialization?

The issues raised in the Mandaza and Stoneman books, the 'radicaliza-tion' theorists with their emphasis on looking at the social dynamics of nationalism, and an Arrighi-type analysis of international, regional and national class forces, are all worth addressing, and they, rather than Astrow's deterministic pre-judging of many of the issues, will inform our analysis. What they all accept, however, is the essentially rhetorical character of Zimbabwe's 'Marxism' thus far, but also the possibility that it is *not* a complete sham. But such insights offer only a point of departure for an analysis of such questions as those raised in the previous paragraph. For, even if the present phase is characterized as 'neo-colonial', and programmes of social transformation that are normally thought of as 'socialist' have not been prominent, that does not signify that there has been no change in the structure of the Zimbabwe political economy, in the balance between the various classes and fractions of classes and in their prospects and their reproduction, nor in the pattern of politics. This work will in fact attempt to spell out such changes since 1980, and in so doing what will be more important than simply charting how far they fall short of some ideal socialist bench mark, supposing there is such a thing, will be to consider how far such actual changes make more or less difficult or complicated some more fundamental transformation of society along socialist lines in the future. But however chary one (rightly) is of 'Marxism' offering some ideal or blueprint, this issue does require some conception of a transitional stage, or at least a process. It therefore raises a particular strand of debate within the Marxian tradition — as to whether there are *stages* en route to the transition from capitalism to socialism, and in particular whether there is some anti-colonial, anti-imperialist pattern possible in Third World countries that involves an economic development that reduces rather than polarizes social and economic inequity — whether this be called a 'national democratic revolution' (a term which has occasionally been used by Zimbabweans, including Robert Mugabe), a 'non-capitalist', or 'socialist-oriented' path (the normal Soviet terminology), or whatever. Uncovering what form such a transitional development could take, structurally, is to fashion the necessary yardstick for evaluating actual developments — a task that we will have to attempt, however partially, because the approaches that we have considered, useful as they may be, do not explore such options. Thus Mandaza and Davies conclude that the content and direction of transition in Zimbabwe have been left largely undefined, hence Mandaza's content-less terminology of 'the post-white settler colonial phase'; this is an accurate description, but it provides no excuse for the failure to tackle the task that he recognizes of 'identifying the *possibilities* for the development of a progressive development policy' (emphasis added). In fact Mandaza does not even define what he means by a 'progressive development policy'. We therefore need to question both the possibility of such a policy this side of the socialist transition, and the nature of its Zimbabwean contours.

2 Geographical and Historical Setting

Any discussion of the political, economic or social prospects of a country must be located in a framework recognizing the physical context: Zimbabwe is a small, landlocked, mostly subtropical country with relatively low overall population density. Its total area is about 391,000 square kilometres, about the size of California, or 60 per cent greater than the United Kingdom. Its per caput income is about US$600, only 7 per cent of the United Kingdom's or 5 per cent of that of the United States, but in the higher range in African terms, above Kenya and about three to four times that of Tanzania and Zaïre, whose total GDPs it therefore exceeds despite a population only a third or a quarter the size. The nearest seaport is Beira in Mozambique, about 300 km from the eastern border, and the whole country is north of the Tropic of Capricorn, between latitudes 15°33′ and 22°24′ S, but about 65 per cent of it is between 900 and 1,500 metres above sea-level and so not subject to extremely high temperatures. The total population was almost 9 million in 1988, giving a population density of about 23 per square kilometre, about 10 per cent of the United Kingdom's. Under 2 per cent of the people are white and less than 0.5 per cent are of Asian origin or 'coloured'.

Equally important as constraints are the burdens of history. Disruption in the nineteenth century of what were once powerful centralized states was followed by complete military defeat and ninety years of incorporation into a pervasive European settler culture and economy. To a greater extent than in non-settler colonies this destroyed most of the basis for re-establishing a distinctively indigenous tradition. Even many so-called 'traditional' customs or institutions turn out on inspection to be heavily influenced by the perceptions and convenience of the settlers (the institutionalization of 'chiefs' being an example). Modern Zimbabwean culture is thus as much a product of European as indigenous influences, but that influence has usually been absorbed and modified or has generated powerful counter-cultures that are modern but still Zimbabwean. Thus Christianity has been widely adopted but is often married with indigenous religion to give rise to 'independent' churches. Liberal democracy and Marxism are part of the array of political discourse.

Finally, Zimbabwe is a part of the wider Southern African region, in which white-dominated South Africa continues to play a dominant role economically and militarily (although its cultural and political influence have declined).

Geography and Climate

The centre of the country is a plateau which divides the Zambezi river basin to the north and west from the Sabi–Limpopo river basin to the south and east. At its north-eastern end, this plateau joins the Eastern Highlands, a narrow belt of mountains extending north and south along the Mozambique border. Only here are there altitudes above 1,800 metres; but as the central plateau declines only gradually, about a quarter of the country is above 1,200 metres. This region of relatively high altitude, the highveld, includes the most fertile and best-watered land in the country.

The agricultural potential of the soil varies considerably: soils with good fertility and moisture retention characteristics are found in all regions, but high proportions of the better quality soils lie on the highveld. Most of the rainfall is convective in origin and virtually all occurs within the summer months, November–March, (excepting the Eastern Highlands, which enjoy an extended period of rain). There is a strong correlation between precipitation quantity and elevation, although the northern and eastern sections of the highveld receive more rain than regions of comparable elevation in the south and west. Rainfall declines sharply on both sides of the central plateau.

The rainfall exhibits a very high degree of local spatial and temporal variation, with variability most marked in the regions where annual precipitation is relatively low. Since the lower elevations also experience higher average temperatures and evapotranspiration, the risks associated with dryland cropping increase rapidly in the middle and lowveld. Despite significant local variations in the quality of soils, rainfall is the primary limiting factor for agricultural production and the principal basis for agro-ecological zoning in the country.

Zimbabwe is customarily divided into five agro-ecological zones ('Natural Regions'), distinguished primarily by quantity and variability of average rainfall. NR I, confined to the Eastern Highlands, enjoys annual rainfall in quantities greater than 900 mm, with some locales receiving over 1,500 mm per year. High elevations and low temperatures allow this rainfall to be highly effective for agriculture, suiting the area to tea, coffee, fruit and forest crops, and to intensive livestock production. Only

2 per cent of total land area is classified in this category. NR II is the primary intensive-farming area in Zimbabwe and accounts for 15 per cent of total land area. Situated in the highveld around Harare, its summer rainfall tends to be reliably in the range of 750–1,000 mm. Maize, the country's staple crop, grows well in this region, as do tobacco, cotton and other grains, and it is also well suited to intensive livestock production. Wheat is also grown as a winter crop under irrigation.

NR III which accounts for 19 per cent of the total land area is best suited for semi-intensive crop and livestock production. Average rainfall is only 650–800 mm, and intensity and variability are significantly greater. NR IV receives 450–650 mm average annual rainfall. Cropping should be restricted to drought-resistant varieties accompanying semi-extensive livestock production, though frequent mid-season dry spells make any form of dryland cropping risky. NR V consists principally of the hot and dry lowveld of the Zambezi and Sabi–Limpopo river basins. In absence of irrigation the slight and erratic rainfall makes this region suitable only for extensive livestock production. The last two regions together account for 65 per cent of the total national land area. For further detail see Weiner (1988, pp. 64–6.)

Only 17 per cent of the land area of Zimbabwe lies within zones capable of supporting intensive rainfed crop and livestock production, and most of this is in the northeastern Mashonaland provinces. Conditions in well over half of the country are inadequate for rainfed crop production and best suited to livestock rearing only.

Communications

Until 1975 over 75 per cent of Zimbabwe's trade passed through Mozambican ports; with the closure of the border by the newly independent Marxist government in Mozambique, the traffic had to be diverted through South Africa. Since independence in 1980 efforts to redirect it have been thwarted by sabotage of the railway lines and ports by the MNR (or 'Renamo', South African instigated 'contras'); it is estimated that in 1985 over 92 per cent of Zimbabwe's trade by rail passed through South Africa. Since then, however, Zimbabwean troops have guaranteed the safety of the Beira Corridor, resulting in about a quarter of the trade taking this route in 1987.

Early History

The area now known as Zimbabwe was settled by Bantu iron-working agriculturalists over a period beginning about 200 BC. By AD 1000 a Shona-speaking culture had established an empire, probably centred on what is now Great Zimbabwe which extended to the coast, and, through Arab intermediaries, traded gold for commodities from as far afield as China. New dynasties, separate states and alternative empires including the Mutapa, Torwa and Rozvi, followed, but by the nineteenth century these had declined under pressure from the Portuguese, slave-trading, and finally the Nguni incursions from the Zulu state to the south. By the time that Rhodes's 'Pioneer Column' invaded in 1890, the Ndebele, who were an off-shoot of the Nguni and primarily pastoralists, had moved in and been established in the south and west for over forty years, with remnants of the Rozvi and some minor states in the north and east continuing a way of life based primarily on crop cultivation subject to occasional raids from the Ndebele.

The first Chimurenga (war of liberation) began in 1896 in Matabeleland, spread to Shona-speaking parts of the country, and was only finally put down in 1897 after much bloodshed (Ranger, 1967). The British South Africa Company ruled the country until 1923 when the whites (then numbering 35,000) opted for the status of 'self-governing colony' rather than union with South Africa. Following the break-up of the federation of the Rhodesias and Nyasaland (1954–63, see below), Southern Rhodesian whites unilaterally declared full independence (UDI) from Britain after refusing to accept a new constitution which would have allowed some black political advancement. Under the impact of sanctions and a guerrilla war which cost between 20,000 and 30,000 lives, the whites were finally forced to settle at the Lancaster House Conference in 1979, and after the election victory of the ZANU-PF party under Robert Mugabe, the country became independent as the Republic of Zimbabwe on 18 April 1980.

The Political Economy of Settlerdom

The initial *raison d'être* for the colonization of Zimbabwe was the expectation of finding a 'Second Rand', it then being thought to be the legendary biblical land of Ophir, from which King Solomon obtained over 13 tons of gold (Minter, 1986, p. 3). Gold was however present in smaller quantities than expected, and although modern techniques revitalized mines that had been abandoned as worked out centuries earlier, agriculture soon took over as the backbone of the settler economy.

This however required the wresting of land and labour from the indigenous people and the eventual destruction of their competition. They had in fact already proved efficient at supplying the food needs of the miners, with the result that white farmers had not been viable before 1908. Furthermore, as the farms, towns and infant industry expanded alongside the mines, they increasingly needed cheap labour which was not forthcoming whilst black agriculture still provided a cash income. Three factors were involved in the whites' 'solution' to these two problems: first, alienation of much of the best land on the high veld, relegating most black farmers to the middle or even low veld, regions not previously regarded as suitable for cultivation; second, the provision of extension services, cheap credit, etc. to whites only; and finally, later on, discriminatory marketing policies guaranteeing white farmers higher prices than black farmers (Palmer and Parsons, 1977, pp. 277–80; Stoneman, 1981b, pp. 129–30). All these measures required the intervention of a colonial state geared to white interests: the key acts were the Land Apportionment Act of 1930, which confirmed the white 'reserves', and the Maize Control Amendment Act of 1934.

Black farmers were thus converted from successful enterprising people growing a surplus of food, and preserving their independence from the demeaning status of working for whites (particularly white farmers), into impoverished subsistence farmers in overcrowded reserves, practising supposedly traditional (but in fact imposed) techniques that were often inappropriate to the unfamiliar harsh environment. Conversely the white farmers developed from being subsistence producers into a highly successful rural bourgeoisie with a claim to being essential to the capacity of the country to feed itself — a claim justified only through their successful destruction of the competition.

One important result in the inter-war period was that, as Arrighi has shown, class formation accelerated amongst the whites but probably regressed amongst the blacks. For the whites after they achieved self-governing status an alliance developed between all the main domestic classes against international capital, for the white bourgeoisie, rural and urban, had different investment priorities from foreign capital and white workers still largely worked for the latter. On the other hand blacks were increasingly disadvantaged, and polarization amongst them was limited (Arrighi, 1967, p. 40; Arrighi, 1970). Destruction of the viability of peasant agriculture both removed competition from the white farmers and provided them and industry with cheap labour; at the same time the inadequate wages denied the incipient black proletariat the means to sustain their families or save for their old age, so that wage remittances to families left in the country were necessary to supplement subsistence food production and provide the wage earner with his only form of old-age insurance. Thus unviable peasant production and below poverty-level wages interacted to inhibit class formation, keeping most blacks as semi-proletarianized peasants.

Not until World War II did a more fully urbanized black proletariat capable of supporting families in townships begin to emerge, and this became significant only in the relatively liberal early federal period. This development occurred because international capital, which required a more stable work-force for the higher level of technology employed, had regained the ascendancy. At the same time a small black middle class of teachers and medical workers began to develop, mainly in the missions; however white fear of competition ensured that restrictions almost completely prevented the growth of a black bourgeoisie, whether rural or urban; as late as the 1970s the only openings for enterprise were in rural bus transport and stores, plus the middle-size commercial farm holdings in the 'African Purchase Areas' that a few of them had been allowed to obtain. On the other hand another strand of white strategy involved attempts to find or create allies in the black population; this strategy was pursued only intermittently and sometimes reversed when it seemed to risk creating competition that would harm white interests. The safest and therefore most enduring efforts went into the cultivation of the supposedly traditional authority of the chiefs beyond anything they enjoyed in pre-colonial times. Their right to allocate land both gave them a privileged position and put their hands on important levers of social control. Increasingly, the chiefs, who were paid and supported by government, were represented as the most reliable voice of black people. The latter as individuals were represented as not knowing their own minds, not understanding democracy, easily led astray by nationalist agitation but, contradictorily, having no real sympathy with the small minority of nationalists, and preferring to live in security under their chiefs. Not until the Pearce Commission of 1972 did this structure of myth come to be seriously questioned by many whites (see Ranger, 1985b; Day, 1975).

During the period of the Central African Federation (1954–63), which linked Southern Rhodesia with the colonies of Northern Rhodesia and Nyasaland (now Zambia and Malawi), the whites, mainly in Southern

Rhodesia, developed a rhetoric of 'partnership' between black and white, unwisely characterized on one famous occasion as being like the partnership 'between rider and horse'. But the partnership between the three territories was also unequal, with Southern Rhodesia extracting much of the surplus from Northern Rhodesia's booming copper mines, and thereby expanding investment in its industry to exploit the captive federal market. Opposition to the federation, widely seen by blacks in the northern territories as a device to prolong rule by whites, who were relatively much more numerous in Southern Rhodesia, brought about its collapse and the independence of Zambia and Malawi.

The Southern African Context

Zimbabwe has been profoundly influenced by forces emanating from South Africa since at least the 1820s, when, following white attacks on the Zulu kingdom of Shaka, the resulting pressures led to the first Nguni incursions. Two decades later the related Ndebele under Mzilikazi moved north and established a kingdom based on Bulawayo and further undermined the crumbling Rozvi states, only to be destroyed in its turn by the white incursion, also from South Africa, in 1890. South African economic and cultural influence dominated for the next ninety years, and independent Zimbabwe can certainly not ignore South Africa's economic weight.

This influence has been felt through investment, trade, transport and labour flows: much of Zimbabwe's productive capital (probably still about a quarter) is owned by South African parent companies, and South Africa and the United Kingdom have always been the key trading partners. Although the Mozambican ports carried the bulk of Zimbabwe's overseas trade until 1975, a substantial minority at least also went through South Africa; after 1975 nearly all was redirected south, giving South Africa the ability to force the Smith/Muzorewa regime to the conference table in 1979, and more crucially to constrain Zimbabwe's militancy by pressure on Mozambique and Zambia, pressure it continues to exert. A number of Zimbabweans have also worked in South Africa, although this source of employment has been much less important than to other countries of the region as the Rhodesian state sought to limit competition for labour. However recruitment for the South African mines was initiated in 1972 when Rhodesia was most dependent on South Africa, with numbers rising to 16,000 in 1978, but they have declined to insignificant levels since independence.

However, the relationship of economic dependence has never been either total or entirely one-way, as South Africa has benefited significantly from the Zimbabwean market. The Central African Federation in which Southern Rhodesia was involved from 1954 to 63 with Malawi and Zambia (then Nyasaland and Northern Rhodesia) was in some measure an alternative centre of industrialization and capital accumulation to South Africa. To what extent modern Zimbabwe possesses such a potential, perhaps within the framework of SADCC, will be explored in Chapter 12 below.

The establishment of 'socialism in one country' has always been a problematic programme, in both theoretical and practical terms. The practical problems are compounded in a country as small as Zimbabwe, and further compounded, as the experiences of Angola and Mozambique have shown, by the proximity of a belligerent reactionary power like South Africa.

It is reported that President Samora Machel of Mozambique had recognized this sufficiently by 1980 to warn the newly independent Zimbabwe not to copy Mozambique's mistakes. This meant preventing a propaganda campaign which would drive out the country's commercial farmers, skilled workers and middle class (mainly white) before blacks had acquired the necessary skills. It also meant denying South Africa pretexts for direct intervention (as in Angola, with its Cuban support) or opportunities for indirect destabilization (as in Mozambique through support for dissident groups). The result was Mugabe's policy of reconciliation, which reassured the whites, and, at any rate for a time, ZAPU supporters.

But in concrete economic terms it prevented an assault on inequality in incomes and wealth. Such an attack would have involved confiscation of white-owned farmland, in conflict with the Lancaster House Agreement (and with adverse psychological consequences throughout the white population, and probably an initial reduction in food production, export earnings and employment), and expropriation of South African capital investment (about a quarter of total productive investment). Socialist rhetoric did not prevent Western support for Zimbabwe (the real constraints were perhaps recognized); a socialist programme would not only have removed most of this support, but would also probably have prevented effective opposition to direct South African intervention.

The Settler State and its Legacy

Rhodesia was in fact run by and as a commercial entity, Cecil Rhodes' British South Africa Company, until 1923. At that stage the white settler population were given the opportunity to opt for internal self-government, which they chose rather than the alternative of absorption into the (then) Union of South Africa. The state, from the days of the Company, had concentrated on promoting European Settlement and thus it was not surprising that 'it had to be at the service of European settlers who came to look upon it as being responsible for having brought them into the country, expected it to be always accessible, and regarded its intervention on their behalf in every department of life as natural' (Leys, 1959, pp. 57–8).

The *interventionism* of this settler colonial state was evidenced in state infrastructure (railways, electricity, etc.) and industry (iron and steel, agriculture, processing, etc.), but also in providing credit, research and other services, marketing for farmers, and similar if not so widespread services for other business, plus protection and an artificially high standard of living for white workers. More fundamentally the state protected farmers and workers against African competition, and they and other employers had a common interest in maintaining a cheap black labour force. Their privileged position was underwritten by various state provisions, including various apartheid practices — job and residence discrimination, influx control into the white areas, pass laws and by administrative practices in the fields of labour, property and the overall running of the economy. For Rhodesia was very much a *managed* economy. Not only was there significant state ownership (starting from the time when the British South Africa Company *was* the state), but state boards also regulated many economic activities; the agricultural sector for instance had marketing boards for most major crops and a Cold Storage Commission to deal with beef. Later there were boards for regulating foreign exchange, issuing licences for production and all manner of other things. These bodies served several functions: they were channels for passing on resources to the different white constituencies; they regulated the potential competition between firms and sectors, dividing up the market and the available foreign exchange to try to please all; and they were also a channel for *participation* by the white community, arguably a more influential channel than the periodic elections. The state bodies usually included, or at least consulted with, the organized interests of the white population — the Rhodesian Farmers' Union, the Chamber of Mines (for the big mining houses) and the Mining Federation (for the small mine entrepreneurs), the Association of Rhodesian Industries, the Chambers of Commerce and the white trade unions, and their different sub-sectoral units. In many senses, therefore, the settler colonial state was a '*corporatist*' state, providing a structured place for a set of interests of the whites (Murray, 1970).

The corporatist representation and mediation of these interests was made easier by virtue of the small (white) population — as Leys (1959) noted, 'civil servants, politicians and all leaders [of business, unions etc.] knew each other'! If they did not settle things at a meeting of an official board or by a delegation, a call to a friend or a chat at 'the club' would resolve matters.

The form that the post-independence state takes is virtually unaltered — the same bureaucratic, parastatal and 'quango' structures, but the style of conducting matters is altered in some respects: the white farmers, the chamber of commerce now rely more exclusively on formal channels to voice their concerns, which are still very much open, rather than personal networks. Black politicians and civil servants were not used to the old-boy networks and found they could not so easily get white business or banks to go along with their plans.

It would be wrong, however, to portray the settler state as unchanging in form or unaffected by conflicts of interests. In class terms the state reflected and consolidated an alliance of interests — the settler farmers, local mining industrial and commercial capitalist interests, subsidiaries of multinational capital, white middle classes and white workers. At one level these all shared some commonality of interests in keeping the black population basically as a separate pool of cheap labour. However, the longer-run interests of multinational and of industrial capital (even if local) increasingly pointed in another direction. They tended to be the leading element in the coalition and used their positions to promote some process of capital accumulation and industrialization, which required the expansion of the local market for manufactures, and in turn more opportunities for some black farmers and for some black skilled workers and middle-class elements. This project which involved the promotion and co-opting of a black middle class, was increasingly at odds with settler farmers, white workers and middle classes whose privileged position depended on eliminating African competition.

These latter forces, numerically larger, rallied behind the extreme right-wing Rhodesian Front party which was elected to power in 1962 and then reversed some of the earlier trends. They reverted to promoting 'traditional' land holding and social control via the chiefs who were seen as sufficient allies in the black population, and attempted to slow down at least the advancement of blacks into business, professions, skilled jobs and commercial farming. In this last period of settler colonial rule, the form of the state changed in some ways and certainly the dominant interests were partially at odds with international and industrial capital, although the latter prospered from the enforced protection of the Unilateral Declaration of Independence by the government of Ian Smith in 1965 and the sanctions that were invoked by the international community in response. Just how far these dominant interests of the 1960s and 1970s have taken a back seat since 1980, and by whom they have been replaced, is explored below.

The Rise of Nationalism

Although modern organizational forms of African nationalist politics only emerged in the 1920s with the first trade unions and in the late 1940s with the embryo political parties, resistance to the racialist structures of settlerdom go back to the very imposition of white rule in the 1890s. The major rebellions of those years, the Chimurenga wars, involved both Shona and Ndebele people and were eventually put down with great cruelty. It has been argued (Ranger, 1967) that this crushing and total, overall defeat of a broad movement was of a decisive, unambiguous and general character and thus explains why there was a long gap before the emergence of 'modern' nationalist politics — a view put forward to counter the notion of a continuous tradition of resistance from the nineteenth century through to today. If that latter view is a nationalist simplification, it is nevertheless certainly the case that the Chimurenga tradition was very much a symbol in the war of liberation in the 1970s.

Although a precursor was formed in the 1920s, the first significant nationalist political party, called the African National Congress, was formed from a number of existing groups and tendencies in 1957. The initiative came from a small group of black professionals and educated people, including some trade-union officials, rather than as a result of a broad popular ground-swell (although there were local resistances at that time). Among the significant features that can be usefully explored through a potted history of the national movement, and that have left their mark on the contemporary party, we should explore: the repression of party organizations and detention of leaders; the pivotal and controversial leadership of Joshua Nkomo; the split between ZANU and ZAPU; and most crucially the 'dialectic' between the formal party structures and any popularly-based movement.

The original national movement went through several formal existences and labels in the late 1950s and early 1960s as a result of periodic proscription. The Zimbabwe African People's Union (ZAPU), founded in 1962, is the one by which it is remembered. There was a very similar group of leaders of these different bodies, with the central position being occupied by Joshua Nkomo, who had been in trade unions in Bulawayo and who was chosen as President as a third-choice, compromise candidate. However, he came to play an ever more dominant role in the organization. His style within the party was one of a personalized rule whereas outside it was of eloquent popular demagogy. This style and his seeming willingness to accept compromise attracted criticism, and the eventual challenge to his position was perhaps the central issue that lead to the breakaway of several other leaders to form an alternative party, the Zimbabwe African National Union (ZANU) in 1963.

The latter only had a few short months of legal existence before both parties were banned, for twelve years as it turned out, in 1964, and so was never able to build up the network of branch offices and local committees of its rival. Both parties then went into exile, while some structure perhaps remained underground and many leaders were in detention until 1974, and so the parties' and their leaders' popular support, and their differing bases for it, could not be made evident before the elections immediately prior to independence in 1980. By then several years of guerrilla war had intervened and both movements had gone through traumas and changes in leadership and ideology as a result of exile and detentions.

The two parties formed a common 'Patriotic Front' between 1975 and 1979, mainly under pressure from the neighbouring 'Front Line States' (FLS), then went their separate ways in the 1980 elections and have now been reunited in 1988. Various explanations have been offered for the original split and as the basis for their continued separate existence. One frequently cited factor is ethnic. Voting patterns in the 1980s do support the idea that ZAPU's support was principally among the Ndebele, and the linguistically related Kalanga, whilst ZANU's was among the majority

Shona groups. Certainly the government's repression of people in the Matabeleland Provinces in 1983–5, in a search for 'dissidents' who were thought to be former guerrillas of ZAPU's armed wing (ZIPRA), seems to support this identification as it took on some anti-Ndebele dimensions. However, the two parties were not equitable with these ethnic groups at the outset, though increasingly cadres and leaders from one ethnic group came to predominate in each party as splits and defections occurred in the 1970s.

ZAPU at first claimed it had the popular base and ZANU was 'elitist' — and however true as an explanation of the origins of the second party, it has not remained so. ZANU in turn claimed a greater radicalism, which had some basis by the 1970s, if not from their inception, in terms of their commitment to armed struggle — a factor which was not unrelated to Nkomo's emphasis on political manœuvring and compromise. And yet despite that characteristic of his political leadership and his emergence as the main hope of the British during the colonial curtain call, he and his party was the one which had successfully developed close links with the Soviet Union in the 1960s and 1970s. In broader ideological terms there were no marked differences between the parties' platforms: both had distinct radical wings that at different moments attempted, largely unsuccessfully, to assert themselves. Only ZANU espoused the official 'Marxist- Leninist' mantle, although they equally claimed and as quickly shed the further title of 'based on Mao Tse-Tung thought' when this suited their fostering of a Chinese connection in the late 1960s and early to mid-1970s.

The Dynamics of the National Liberation Struggle

The long drift into armed conflict had its origins and *raison d'être* in the refusal of the whites to share political power. African nationalist organizations and their political protests became a feature of all the British-ruled territories of Eastern and Central Africa in the 1950s and by the end of the decade the principle of independence had been conceded in the case of Tanzania and Uganda which had no sizeable settler minorities. As nationalists in Malawi and Zambia, direct colonies which also had relatively few settlers, began to seek independence, their pressure took the form of a demand for independence separate from the Central African Federation — partly on the grounds of white domination and the inferior legal position of blacks in Southern Rhodesia. As the British Government began to manœuvre to prevent the break-up of the Federation, it negotiated a modified constitution with the Rhodesian regime. Limited representation of blacks (still leaving them in a small minority in parliament) was stomached by the whites as the price for a promised, later independence. This very limited concession was at first accepted by Nkomo and Sithole, then repudiated by their party and the mass of its supporters.

The ground-swell that provided some popular basis for this stance and that had fuelled political protests and actions in the late 1950s was rooted in urban protests against bad social conditions and segregation but even more by rural discontent. The widespread unrest in rural areas fed off the underlying impoverishment as increasing land pressure bit into the limited and increasingly eroded 'Reserves' and simultaneously denied opportunities of access to the market or improved means of production. But it was brought to a head by the efforts intended by Government in the 1950s to provide agricultural opportunities for Africans, chiefly by the Land Husbandry Act. This sought to individualize land ownership by giving titles, but it thereby offered prospects only for those with more substantial holdings, the 'master farmers' who were the targets of the limited injection of credit and agricultural inputs, the kulaks. At the same time the impoverishment of those with tiny holdings or no access to land at that moment was confirmed and institutionalized for all time — under the new land tenure arrangements they would stand no chance of being allocated land in future. At the other end of the scale the resulting abrogation of their rights to allocate land also upset chiefs and headmen. Further fuelling the discontent of different sections of the rural class structure was the fact that the Act's 'improvement' measures were submerged by its enforced conservation provisions, such as the culling of livestock, forced and unpaid labour on terracing, etc.

It was this underlying ground-swell that provided a broader mass support for the nationalist movement and simultaneously helped propel it beyond negotiated compromises that, in the Rhodesia case would have been well short of majority rule. The political intransigence of the whites was underscored with the change of regime after the 1962 electoral victory of the new Rhodesian Front party, with its explicit platform of protection of white privilege. By then some leaders of the nationalist parties were beginning to consider the need for armed rather than constitutional struggle — although until the 1970s many of them 'saw violence as merely the means to pressure Britain into an intervention ... into convening a conference that would bring about an African government in Zimbabwe', in Mandaza's well-informed insiders' view (Mandaza, 1986, p. 29), rather than as a means of general popular mobilization in a people's war with its implications for economic and social as well as political transformation. Arguably this limited perspective as to means and ends remained characteristic of one strand of nationalist leadership, and was how they saw the eventual decolonization, presided over by the British in 1980 — part of the ambiguous ideological legacy of the national liberation war.

Some efforts at armed intervention were initiated by those leaders who managed to escape the widespread detentions of 1963 and 1964 and went into exile. The first episodes that are recognized as the beginning of the 'liberation war', the second Chimurenga as it came to be called, involved a battle in which ZANU guerrillas were eventually killed or caught around the settler town of Chinhoyi (then called Sinoia) in Mashonaland West. ZAPU also launched several infiltrations of armed columns across the Zambezi and Lake Kariba from Zambia in the next two years, some of them joint operations with guerrillas of the African National Congress (ANC) of South Africa, which provided the excuse for South African armed police to back Rhodesian counter-insurgency for the next ten years.

The tactics of these early guerrilla incursions were to infiltrate sizeable armed columns in some vague hope that they would find a place for a base and arms cache and from which they would somehow make contact with local people. Until the end, the approach of ZAPU did not change much: they seemed to believe it was possible to mobilize what remained of ZAPU branch structures from the early 1960s. These methods played into the hands of the Rhodesian security forces who were usually quickly able to spot and eliminate the columns and indeed by the early 1970s the guerrilla threat seemed to have been held in check. However, in 1972 ZANU began to put into effect a new and ultimately decisive strategy based far more on prior politicization of people in a rural area thus making it safe for small groups of guerrillas to dig roots and slowly begin operations of hit- and-run ambushes and mining roads designed to exclude the government from the TTLs.

This approach was made possible by the support of FRELIMO, the liberation movement in neighbouring Mozambique, that in 1972 had already liberated much of the Tete province that bordered north-east Zimbabwe. After the collapse of the Portuguese fascist state and eventual independence of Mozambique in 1975 the whole eastern and south-eastern border was opened up to these incursions from Mozambique. Unable to stem this tide of guerrilla incursions, or the flow of recruits from the countryside for training in Mozambique and despite armed invasions into the neighbouring countries, the Rhodesian security forces, and the white population as a whole which was trying to man an army and an economy, found themselves over-extended. Before considering the process of negotiation of a settlement that took place at Lancaster House in London in 1979, some critical trends within the nationalist movement in this period, each of which had implications for post-independence developments, must be noted. First is the disintegrating effect of the detention of many leaders of both ZANU and ZAPU, the politically debilitating effect of exile on the remaining leadership groups, and the successful containment of the first phase of the war. The exiles who had to take over direction were politicians rather than guerrillas, and their predictable lack of success was used as weaponry in internal personality clashes, rather than a learning experience, while these in turn tended to lead to a factionalism in both parties often based on ethnic appeals to loyalty. The net result was that after clashes within ZAPU in Zambia in 1970 and 1971 many of the majority Shona-speakers departed to join ZANU, so that the two parties, which had originally had mixed ethnic compositions, became now to a greater extent identified with one or other of the main language groups. It was in part the increased identification of ZAPU with the Ndebele minority that meant that they passed up the offer of FRELIMO to begin operations in the north-east in 1972.

ZANU was more poised to take this opportunity by then because another process, of learning from earlier mistakes, had gone further within their ranks. But both parties were subject to pressure from the guerrillas in the early 1970s in favour of a more politicized, popular base for armed struggle and more emphasis on addressing the social and economic demands of the people. A group within ZAPU, the March 11 Movement, did in fact in 1971 attempt to force a degree of unity and ideological coherence on the sparring leaders but the Zambian government threw them in jail or deported them back to Rhodesia to be hanged for their sins. A somewhat parallel radicalization within ZANU did get further and was partly embodied in the new guerrilla methods of 1972. But conflicts that had features of the old, personality-ethnic type and the new, ideological variety broke out in late 1974 and in the events that led to the assassination in 1975 of the party's chairman, leader-in-exile and instigator of the new strategy, Herbert Chitepo. This was the excuse for all exiled ZANU cadres to be detained by Zambia and the later emergence to prominence of a more radical but politically immature group of guerrilla commanders that became identified as the Zimbabwe People's Army (ZIPA), until their moment in the spotlight was terminated by conflicts in

1977 that led to their detention in Mozambique. This complex series of conflicts and changes in the effective leadership did represent a learning experience by fits and starts — but one from which most of the old-guard politicians, especially those detained inside Rhodesia since 1963, were excluded from active involvement at least until 1974, and thus from learning and being subject to pressures from the popular-rooted, guerrilla movement. It was partly the distinctiveness of Robert Mugabe that he had the wit and luck to be embraced into these movements earlier than other leaders, a process that ultimately confirmed him as the pre-eminent national leader.

This pre-eminence was eventually confirmed by a popular election victory over not only Joshua Nkomo but Bishop Abel Muzorewa. The latter had emerged as a political figure as a result of yet another dimension of the convoluted story of Zimbabwe's African nationalism. In 1970 another of a series of attempts was made by the British Government to negotiate some deal to end the illegality of the Rhodesian government's unilateral declaration of independence (UDI) from the British Crown in 1964. The formula this time involved a judicial (Pearce) commission 'testing out' African opinion about a modified constitution that would give them a limited but slowly growing elected voice. So as not to be outflanked, the two banned and exiled nationalist movements both gave their backing to an above-ground political umbrella organization, the African National Council, that campaigned openly and successfully against the Pearce Commission's proposals. Muzorewa was the neutral initially apolitical figurehead but, when African political bodies were once again allowed in Rhodesia after 1974, he and the Council became contenders for power. His party and a rump of ZANU that stayed loyal to its first and deposed President, Ndabaningi Sithole, plus some groups around some traditional chiefs, became the 'internal' parties after 1975, dissociating themselves from ZAPU and ZANU, that remained in exile and from the armed struggle.

The war was not only a prolonged clash with the power of the white, settler state but also set in train a set of forces that determined the eventual fate of these various leaders and parties. One such decisive force was the structures that were forged below the leadership level in the course of the struggle. The pattern was uneven being severely interrupted between late 1974 and early 1976 in the case of ZANU. As ZANU had only had a few months of existence before it was banned in 1963, there was only a scattering of ZANU cells in various parts of the country in the 1960s. However, the guerrilla presence, slowly spreading from the north-east of the country after 1972 really established the party organizationally, and eventually ensured its electoral victory in 1980. There were a number of levels of organization; first the guerrillas themselves. The ZANLA forces were organized on the basis of provincial commands. The new, post-1972 classic guerrilla tactics of 'people's war' required the establishment first of a basis of support among local people so as to effectively hide among them. In the process, the guerrillas set up other levels of organization among the people themselves.

This pattern of organization has to be seen as one set in a particular context, not of totally liberated regions, but of a patchwork of semi-liberated pockets in a majority of the TTLs. In the neighbouring ex-Portuguese colonies, the war developed in the main in areas without a significant settler presence and whole vast regions became fully 'liberated areas' — but only at one end of the country. This was not the case in Zimbabwe. The Land Apportionment Act specifying racially distinct areas and subsequent legislation had led to a massive occupation of land by settler farmers and at the same time created many, discrete pockets of African reserves, the TTLs. So there was little prospect of whole regions generating and maintaining their own infrastructure and of surviving in isolation from any contact with the colonial regime. Ingenuity and a somewhat different approach was required on the part of ZANU, faced as it was with this fragmented pattern of African reserves, interspaced with white areas through which passed the major arteries of communication.

The party in fact set up different tiers of people's councils. At the grass roots level, there was the village unit covering usually an area equivalent to the *kraal* under the existing administrative system. On average, between eight or ten of these units would make up a base committee which was the old ward or *zsadu*. Above these were the district committees, covering usually one TTL, and a provincial committee. The committees at each level of the hierarchy would hold political education and business meetings at fairly regular intervals. In some areas, such as the liberated zones of certain TTLs, there was no white police presence whatsoever and meetings could be held openly, whilst in other areas far greater caution was required.

Within the committees, there would be a chairperson, treasurer, secretary and people with responsibility for such tasks as agriculture, health, women's organization, youth, political mobilization and transport. Each would have a deputy. The functions of the committees at the various levels differed considerably. Grass-roots village committees dealt with day-to-day problems of feeding and clothing the guerrillas and basic services to the community. But issues concerning the outlay of large sums of money, for example, would be passed on to a higher committee. A certain division in areas of responsibility was worked out between the village committees and the *kraal* head (who was the lowest level functionary within the Administration's local government structure). Some 'traditional' aspects of organizing village life, especially control of land, continued to be carried out by the *kraal* head, alone or with the committee where he supported the aims of the struggle, but the committees dealt with everything concerning the war. The committees also settled disputes and provided a judicial system.

The other activities undertaken probably varied depending on how effectively the Rhodesian state apparatuses had been excluded; in cases where this was complete the committee structure was on the way to becoming an alternative administration. While there was no widespread restructuring of production, the committees did provide the impetus for some self-help. In the field of health, for example, instruction in hygiene was given, the necessity of building latrines and pits to store the rubbish was stressed and in the last few months of the war, local clinics were set up in some areas.

When the guerrillas first arrived in Masvingo (then Victoria) Province in 1976, it was they who chose the people to sit on the committee. But this was not very effective because the local people did not necessarily feel that these committee members had their trust. A decision was handed down rather than emerging from the local community. It sometimes happened that ne'er-do-wells were chosen, elements who put themselves forward for opportunistic reasons. But this was to change, and with experience, it was the people gathered in *pungwes* (public meetings) who were to choose their own representatives. Teachers, nurses, catechists, peasant farmers, traders and those who generally commanded respect within the community were often elected to be the committee representatives.

Outside of the immediate border areas with Mozambique, where the peasants had either been forced into strategic hamlets under the permanent and close scrutiny of armed guards, a form of 'dual power' took shape. Behind the ostensibly quiescent normal peasant daily existence of the TTLs, there grew up activities and structures of a system of dual power challenging the settler state. This was metaphorically — and frequently also literally — a difference of night and day. When darkness fell and the curfew laws came into operation, entitling anyone leaving their homes to be shot by the security forces, villagers would sneak off to the agreed rendezvous for a meeting with local guerrilla units. These meetings were virtually a nightly occurrence in many places. In these meetings politicization occurred and problems not treated by the committee structures were heard and dealt with. Some TTLs became virtual no-go areas to most normal administration but could never become totally proof against occasional incursions in strength, perhaps by air, by the Rhodesian security.

One significant factor in the peculiar situation of dual power that emerged in some of the TTLs was the role of the *mujibas*, youths who formed a quite distinct level of organization between the guerrillas and the people's committees. *Mujibas* knew people living in the area and could automatically detect strangers who might then be observed, questioned or even killed if suspicions were raised. They were intelligence as well as counter-intelligence agents, gathering information about the movements of security forces and discovering the presence of informers amongst the local population. The *mujibas* were also the link between the guerrillas and the colonial economy. They collected contributions from the people for the guerrillas. These contributions took the form of money, food, medicines, drink and clothing. Given that the reputation of the guerrilla was at stake, a strict watch had to be kept on these youngsters who might be tempted to take power into their own hands. Paralleling the *mujibas* were the *chimbwidos* (women and girls), who fulfilled many of the same roles, as well as the tasks of washing and cooking for the guerrillas.

Just how integrated the people were with the guerrillas and the whole movement probably varied between parts of the country and is a matter of dispute. Ranger (1985a) argues it was a close symbiosis but one in which the peasants themselves were able to implant their own implicit ideology of more land and a better deal for peasant producers in a context where the official ideology of ZANU was not spelt out in adequate detail. Kriger (1988) and others have pointed to tensions as well as collaboration between peasants and guerrillas, a relationship, they argue, characterized by force as well as benevolence on the part of the latter, and by support on the part of the former that was often only passive.

Phimister (1988) has rightly stressed another ambiguity in the struggle that had a significant legacy. He shows how inequalities were growing in the TTLs in the 1960s as the RF government tried to compensate for the white farmers' loss of tobacco markets by aiding them in displacing black producers of such products as cotton, maize and cattle, and the impoverishment of poor peasants increased as TTLs were more polarized. And yet both rich and poor peasants were disadvantaged by settler policies and were both mobilized behind the struggle. Thus he argues in contrast to

Ranger that the rural base of the struggle did not resolve which group's interests would be taken account of later, and this in turn meant that apart from some generalized nationalist demand for the return of the land from the whites there was no coherent ideology of social change coming out of the struggle.

But international as well as internal forces had their influences on the trajectory of the struggle and on the eventual settlement. The role of the so-called Front-Line States, Zambia, Tanzania, Mozambique and even Botswana, in supporting (and sometimes impeding) the struggle, and the interventions of South Africa, of Britain haltingly and, eventually, of the United States are part of the story that led up to the Lancaster House deal that will be discussed below.

The Lancaster House Constitution

It is now clear that the British government, which had never been responsible for internal administration, was content to remain largely passive about Rhodesia's status in the decade after UDI. The British pressure for sanctions 'was regarded as a matter of form rather than substance' as the official 'Bingham' report put it (see Cliffe, 1979). A similar indifference to Rhodesia and the region also characterized US perspective, which had been set out in a National Security Memorandum by Kissinger in 1971 as one restricted to rhetorical condemnation of apartheid and colonial rule while conducting 'business as usual' with the white states that were seen as entrenched for the foreseeable future. This relative unconcern shifted rapidly from 1974 with the coup in Portugal and the resulting independence of Mozambique and Angola, coupled with the stepping up of the intensity of the struggle in Zimbabwe itself. These events brought southern Africa to the head of agendas of Western powers, who from then on began to involve themselves in a process of attempting to 'stabilize' the region. The objectives of this 'stabilization' were to promote majority rule in Zimbabwe and Namibia and at least some reform in South Africa, and to seek to avoid an escalation of the fighting in the latter countries — a process that had led to radical regimes in Mozambique and Angola and even the involvement of the Soviet Union and Cuba in Angola.

However, it is not the Soviet menace that most exercised Kissinger: 'we have a stake ... in not having the whole continent become radical and move in a direction that is incompatible with Western interests. That is the issue.' Similarly, Crosland was even more forthright to NATO Ministers in December 1977: '... if the [Zimbabwe] issue were settled on the battlefield, it would seriously lessen the chances of bringing about a moderate regime in Rhodesia and would open the way for more radical solutions and external intervention on the part of others'. Andrew Young when he became involved as US negotiator in Southern Africa in 1976, spelled it out in these terms: 'the USA has but one option, and that is neo-colonialism', explaining that 'as bad as that has been made to sound, neo-colonialism means that the multinational corporations will continue to have a major influence in the development of the productive capacity of the Third World. And they are, whether we like it or not.' The West was bent on avoiding a liberation struggle that could mobilize the workers and peasants behind a programme for an alternative, radical transformation of society (see Cliffe, 1980).

The first steps in pursuing some 'peaceful solution' were in fact initiated very quickly after the coup in Portugal in 1974 and most directly involved two other actors that played, and continue to play, a key role in Zimbabwe — South Africa and the Front Line States, in this instance Zambia. South Africa was by that time already feeling a little over-extended militarily in the region and put some pressure on the Rhodesian government to release detained political leaders as part of a *détente* process. Zambia undertook for its part to promote a cease-fire in the guerrilla war as a prelude to talks about a solution. It was only ZANU, in the form of its exiled wing under Chitepo (not the recently-released Sithole) that realized that a *prior* cease-fire would mean giving away their one and only bargaining counter. The only way that Zambia could deliver on its part of the deal, therefore, was to demobilize the guerrilla movement, which it did from 1974, until the Front Line States reversed their strategy in the wake of the US and South African intervention in Angola in 1975–6.

Shuttle diplomacy by the United States and United Kingdom in fact led to the Geneva talks over the future of Zimbabwe in late 1976. But these were inconclusive; the Smith regime had not yet reached the untenable military situation that had arisen by 1979 to make it ready to offer the kind of concessions that the nationalist movement would accept. They also thought it possible to divide the, by then, four strands of nationalist leadership — ZANU and ZAPU, plus the 'internal' parties of Muzorewa and Sithole. But although it was not possible to get the agreement of the Rhodesians to a package that would have been acceptable to the external parties, the FLS and the OAU, and thus 'internationally acceptable', the kind of terms that were to underpin the eventual Lancaster House agreement emerged at Geneva. They embraced a constitution plus social and economic structures that would preserve some status and/or compensation for white settler interests, but more especially for foreign capital and property, and would in fact thus preserve capitalist property relations even if the racial exclusivity of capital was eliminated. Such a 'neo-colonial' formula would also change the 'cheap, migrant labour type of capitalist economy'. The specific terms that would guarantee that outcome would involve some entrenched political voice for the white minority but, more crucially, constitutional protection of property rights. Moreover, a formula that would offer some economic gains for some classes among the black population while simultaneously compensating whites would ideally require some injection of funds. The United States became the ultimate guarantor of this formula as early as 1976, offering at that time a Development Fund of US$1.5 billion.

In the event, it took another two and a half years of escalating and bitter war, and an attempt by Smith to make an 'internal solution', a form of black rule that excluded ZANU and ZAPU, by then in coalition as the Patriotic Front (PF). But this settlement was not accepted internationally nor by most of the people and the war continued. The RF's final hope of avoiding a settlement with the PF disappeared when Mrs Thatcher's newly elected Conservative government in 1979 did a U-turn and reneged on election promises of ending sanctions and recognizing the internal settlement. Another view, from the foreign office in Britain, and similar ones from some US circles, had calculated that the internal settlement was not viable but felt that a neo-colonial formula that would embrace the PF could still be worked out.

To create the conditions whereby the strong position of the PF inside Zimbabwe militarily was not translated into political clout at the Conference table, the Rhodesian air force and special forces and South African military and economic pressure put a stranglehold on the PF's two main backers, Zambia and Mozambique. Attacks on all their transport arteries rendered these two countries so exposed and economically vulnerable, at the time of a major food shortage, with their link to Salisbury and South Africa their only life-line, one that was alternately squeezed and opened during the Lancaster House Conference, that they in turn gave the PF an ultimatum that they *had* to agree to some negotiated settlement or have their sanctuaries withdrawn. It was this weakening of the PF's bargaining strength that meant that they lost at the negotiating table some of what they had gained initially on the ground in Zimbabwe.

The Conference was convened to settle three issues: provision for cease-fire; elections and other arrangements for the transition to independence; and a new constitution. It brought together the PF plus a Salisbury delegation chaired by Muzorewa which included internal party leaders and Smith and other white politicians and officials under the very active, interventionist chairing of the British government. As well as the pressure for settlement from the FLS, the British also used the prospect of doing a 'second best' deal just with the internal parties as a further lever to extract the PF's agreement to their drafts. The PF agreed to a ceasefire whereby their guerrillas 'came in' to some sixteen reception centres, gave up their arms and stayed there under the supervision of Commonwealth troops for the duration of the election — a potential risk, especially as the Rhodesian security forces were merely to be 'confined to barracks', and then in practice used by the British governor who took over this interim administration. The British role was another concession, for the PF had argued for a dual authority in which they would have an equal say — the only conditions in which they thought they could be guaranteed a fair crack of the electoral whip.

The actual electoral arrangements also involved concessions by the PF and their taking the risk that the election would be fair enough for them to translate their popular support into seats. In the event, the odds were stacked against them throughout the campaign, but the voting itself was relatively free from administrative manipulation — perhaps a reflection of the role of the many Commonwealth and other observers and the army of foreign media covering the elections. The actual electoral system also involved a risk for the PF: twenty white MPs elected by white voters on a constituency basis virtually guaranteed twenty RF seats. And although the Constitution prohibited these twenty forming a governing coalition with a minority black party, a three party coalition was not ruled out, and, according to some suggestions, was the preferred outcome that the British promoted. Once the PF alliance split and the two parties decided to stand separately the hope presumably was that Nkomo could head an alliance. This could have meant ZANU being in opposition even if they were the biggest single party. In the event, ZANU confounded many outside observers and won an overall majority and thus could form a government on its own.

But the nature of the Constitution still imposed profound constraints on what a ZANU government could do. Although white interests and concerns were not as entrenched as in the 1979 'internal settlement' constitution, they were guaranteed for seven years twenty MPs to be elected by the white electorate; the position of white civil servants was bolstered if they wanted to stay and the pensions of those leaving were guaranteed, payable abroad; a degree of independence was guaranteed for the judiciary, the civil service and the military. There was also a 'Bill of Rights', that could not be changed for ten years except by a 100 per cent majority, that vaguely guaranteed the usual freedoms. But its crucial provisions concerned property rights. Government was restricted from any non-voluntary acquisition of property with only a partial exception of 'underutilized' land required for resettlement or other public purposes — and that had to be paid for with full, market-level compensation payable at once. By a late amendment to an earlier draft at Lancaster House, it was stipulated that this compensation had to be remittable in foreign exchange. The net effect of these provisions was that land transfers on the basis of justice or need were precluded, all acquired land had to be paid for in cash with no prospect of the government bonds or other payment by instalment common in many land reforms. Moreover, the scale of transfer of land from whites to blacks would be restricted to what land was offered willingly for sale, or to the readiness of foreign donors to provide foreign exchange for land purchases. In the event virtually no aid was forthcoming save for a relatively small British grant (£50 million) that was their redemption of the promise made at Lancaster House of a massive grant for land transfer; a 'development fund' had been the only price the PF had been able to extract for agreeing to this formula, but it did not materialise.

The ZANU Government

The social and political dynamic of the national liberation movement, especially as it played itself out both at the leadership level and in mobilizing the people during the war, created the underlying conditions for the coming to power of a ZANU government. The Lancaster House Conference offered a formal opening that would allow ZANU to take power not at the barrel of a gun. However, before that prospect could be realized, another hurdle had to be confronted in the pre-independence elections on 28 and 29 February and 1 March 1980.

ZANU decided to split the Patriotic Front once it had completed its joint negotiating role at Lancaster House — a decision which was apparently contested by some of the leadership, seemingly including the military leader Josiah Tongogara who was killed in a car accident in Mozambique days after the conference. Going it alone in fact lessened the chances of a victory by the 'external' nationalists. Given the twenty white seats, ZANU alone could win a majority of black seats and still find itself in opposition. In the actual campaign, they faced tremendous obstacles. The party was fighting the election from scratch in the sense that its very brief legal existence seventeen years before had left no legacy of branches and offices and a party machine at national and provincial had to be set up apace. At the grass roots level in the four eastern and northern provinces of Mashonaland East and Central, Victoria (now Masvingo) and Manicaland, where their guerrilla movement had had a significant presence, they were able to hook into the people's councils set up clandestinely to support the war effort. In the two Matabeleland provinces (with the exception of a few southern districts where the ZANU army had some presence) ZAPU was the 'liberating army', while Mashonaland West and Midlands were the site of less fighting and thus of less party infrastructures.

The biggest obstacles were in actually delivering the vote against the tremendous odds of the administrative harassment they faced from a British governor who chose to let loose the Rhodesian security forces to 'maintain law and order' and to 'police cease-fire violations' as well as run the election. ZANU, and to some extent ZAPU (which fought the election as the PF party), had meetings banned, had their party HQ raided, had to do without any sympathetic media coverage, had their literature, vehicles and equipment held up at the Mozambique border. Candidates, national and local officials, suspected guerrillas and messengers, as well as ordinary supporters were arrested as a matter of course — 20,000 during the campaign, according to Mugabe. There was massive financial and logistical support for Muzorewa's UANC party — four helicopters, a budget reportedly of Z$6 million (from South Africa and other sources), and all kinds of official bias — and yet they won only three seats despite having won 67 per cent of the votes in the 'internal' elections of 1979.

But the overall context was also one of intimidation. The country was like an armed camp with men in uniform patrolling widely. Army personnel, special forces, paramilitary police, the 'guard force' employed by white farmers, and the 36,000 'auxiliaries' reunited under the internal government were all free to move about among villagers especially, for the most part unchallenged now by the guerrillas who remained in the assembly points; despite frequent claims by the regime's supporters, independent observers did not identify intimidation by ZANU (or ZAPU) as a significant factor. (See for instance Commonwealth Secretariat, 1980; Cliffe and Munslow, 1980a.) There were also three attempts, now acknowledged as the work of Rhodesian special forces (see for example Cole, 1984; Flower, 1987, p. 257), on Mugabe's life. On the actual election days, rigging was limited to some instances of the 'helping' of illiterates and the like, and the ballot was more or less secret (due in no small part to Commonwealth and other independent observers) — which fact made much of the Rhodesian pressure counter-productive.

In the event ZANU got 63 per cent of the black vote and won fifty-seven of the eighty black seats — which was very close to what the party officials had predicted. The electoral system was one of proportional representation based on the eight provinces. In the four where there had been a strong ZANU guerrilla presence, the party got more the 80 per cent of the votes and won all but two of the forty-two seats. They got a large majority of the votes and seats in Midlands and Mashonaland West, but won only one seat of the sixteen in the two Matabeleland provinces.

How far these results are to be 'explained' by people voting to reflect ethnic identification, i.e. whether they already identified ZANU with Shona and ZAPU with Ndebele, or by loyalty to the army that had been fighting for liberation in the area is a matter of controversy which will be further discussed in Chapter 6. What the results meant was that ZANU had the basis for forming a government on its own, but that it could not claim mass support in the two western provinces. In the event, Robert Mugabe, as the leader of ZANU, formed a government that included Joshua Nkomo as minister for internal affairs, and some other ZAPU ministers.

Otherwise the cabinet consisted of a mixture of ZANU activists of differing pedigrees. As a result of the several major turnovers, at leadership levels, the party consisted of various 'generations' that had been through quite distinct political experiences. The predominant element in the new cabinet were members of the 'old guard', politicians who had been in the nationalist movement since the 1950s or early 1960s, many of whom had been in detention from then until the mid-1970s, or in the case of one senior minister, Maurice Nyagumbo, until 1979, and had not been exposed to the potentially radicalizing influence of involvement with the popular-guerrilla struggle — at least until its last couple of years, nor were they exposed to any serious study of Marxism in this period. Ranger (1980) has challenged the view (see Cliffe, 1980) that this 'old guard' were less committed to social and economic transformation than those involved in the struggle launched from exile, and certainly the ideological bent of any one individual cannot be automatically read off from their biography. And as a group they have not been more noticeably conservative than another category of ministers, those who had been professionals and academics in the West in more distant exile and only involved in the party's international support work rather than the popular struggle. Most notable among this group was Bernard Chidzero, an ex-UN official and something of a political neutral who has played a crucial role in economic policy making, and Zvobgo, an academic lawyer. Others of the old guard had had the luck to be in exile in the 1960s and early 1970s, and while some had been products of and contributors to the worst of exile factionalism, others had indeed gone through a learning experience, assuming a somewhat more participatory political style, some familiarity with Marxist and liberationist ideologies, and becoming somewhat concerned with social and economic issues. However, the most prominent of those who could be said to have gone through some of these experiences — Herbert Chitepo, the leader of ZANU in exile, Tongogara and J.Z. Moyo of ZAPU (all of them favouring unity) — had all been killed. There were some younger ministers, among them intellectuals who had become involved practically in the struggle in its later stages, like Dzingai Mutumbuka (minister of education, who was to become the party's secretary for economic affairs) and Herbert Ushewokunze, who had several portfolios and gained a reputation as a radical — see, for instance, his published speeches (1984). These were more numerous than those members of the government who in any sense could be said to have been fighters. Several guerrilla activists who had been in leadership had either been killed or, like most of the ZIPA group and another group around Hamadzaripi and Gumbo who had been members of the Dare, the committee that launched the new phase of armed struggle in 1972, had fallen foul of the Tongogara–Mugabe leadership in 1977 and 1978 in Mozambique. But perhaps as crucial as the sidelining of those engaged in some way in the struggle in favour of old guard politicians and professionals who emerged with the Lancaster settlement, was the fact that few elements in the leadership had any coherent and specific plans for a programme of social and economic change when they took power. They were thus more likely to be victims initially of the conservative advice of the senior white civil servants, of the economic orthodoxy brought in by Chidzero and his planners, and of the advice and priorities of aid agencies, in a context where they operated with very severe constraints.

Some of these constraints derived, as we have seen, from the Lancaster House constitution. But the actual political situation of the government, despite its healthy majority, was precarious. In the first few weeks, they were at the mercy of the Rhodesian army; and a coup on behalf of the whites was feared as a possibility — and, indeed (Cole, 1984), it is now revealed that there was a detailed plan for killing off the ZANU military leadership, attaching and sealing off the Assembly Points and taking over the government. There were also very real fears of an invasion from South Africa — which was explicitly threatened in the event of a ZANU victory leading to property take overs and/or a white exodus. Another and related constraint that was to limit options for much longer stemmed from ZANU's own undertaking, strongly urged on them by the advice and their observation of the experience of Mozambique, to avoid a sudden white exodus with all the destruction of services, of property, of institutions and capabilities that that would have entailed. And if further persuasion was needed, the short- run problems of feeding a million people displaced by the war during the year or longer it took them to plant and harvest a crop meant reliance on food surpluses produced by white farmers. More generally, if the transition was to be in any sense 'orderly', and the alternative might well have meant invasion, destabilization, economic collapse and the non-survival not only of the government but of a liberated Zimbabwe, then the what came to be termed 'reconciliation policy', which was a policy of continued concessions to whites and limited structural change and not just a set of attitudes, had to be followed.

The Origins and Extent of Marxist Influences

There was virtually no Marxist influence in the formation of the Zimbabwe national movement. Like most movements in English-speaking Africa it was set in the African nationalist mould. Even in the 1960s, when ZAPU was one of a set of movements in southern Africa that was receiving approval and support from Moscow, the party was in no sense Marxist in its prevailing ideology or leadership attitudes. The same was true of ZANU and its leadership in the 1960s, although unlike the other 'alternative' movements in southern African not backed by the Soviets (UNITA in Angola, SWANU in Namibia, and even the Pan African Congress of South Africa), ZANU did not develop any significant links with Western governments or security agencies nor any tendency to collaborate with the colonial regime. Instead, it preserved its radical nationalism while looking for international support, by getting recognition from the Organization of African Unity's (OAU) Liberation Committee and by turning towards China for military training and other assistance, at a period when Soviet–Chinese conflicts were at their height. It was that link that in the 1970s, led to ZANU adopting the formula that its ideology was 'Marxist-Leninist', and for a period in the mid-1970s even, 'based on Marxism–Leninism–Mao Tse Tung thought', rather than any significant internalization of Marxist-based thought. Indeed there was always a contradiction inherent in a Zimbabwean movement adopting the latter formula, as the essence of 'Mao Tse Tung thought' was not the addition of some further general principle but the need to extend Marxist-Leninist analysis to the specifics of the Chinese (not the Zimbabwean!) context. As we shall see, as ZANU political educators in the mid-1970s sought to give expression to this formula, they only partially succeeded in offering any Marxian analysis of Zimbabwe society and in integrating it with more abstract formulations about class, revolution and national liberation against imperialism.

Some, minority, current of thinking inspired by Marxism, began to emerge in the late 1960s and early 1970s among guerrilla activists in both parties and some intellectuals who were closely involved with them. These influences are only in part traceable to the political instruction which inevitably had to accompany military training for guerrilla war and was provided by Chinese (for ZANU) or Soviet and East European (ZAPU) instructors — although the political dimension was, from the outset and throughout the 1970s, apparently given a much greater emphasis in ZANU's programme.

The first overt result of this emergence of ideas that sought social transformation based on an attempt at systematic analysis of Zimbabwe and its liberation struggle, came from within ZAPU. In the aftermath of a particularly debilitating, open conflict between exiled leaders in 1970, a group of cadres in camps in Zambia that called themselves the March 11th Movement put forward an analysis that characterized both sides as elitist, isolated from the cadres in training, bankrupt ideologically and (insofar as they were pursuing the armed struggle at all) were following the wrong tactics of commando raids without contact with the people. They 'detained' the leaders of both leadership factions in 1971 and tried to arrange a party congress insisting on the need to work out a coherent ideology, but instead they fell foul of a Zambian government that they had supposed might be sympathetic but which was much more worried by their overt socialist rhetoric than it had been by the cleavages within ZANU that it had condemned earlier. The March 11th cadres were themselves detained officially by Zambia for three years (or sent back to Rhodesia) and then dispersed into wider exile, so their direct influence on the movement ended then. But the ideas they articulated, which were probably shared by a larger group of guerrilla cadres than took part in the movement, may have sown a seed then which may have been further nurtured as some of the group eventually returned to independent Zimbabwe.

Certainly similar currents of thought were beginning to emerge among ZANU cadres in exile by the early 1970s, and in the potentially more fertile terrain of a switch by ZANLA to the tactics of 'people's war', in which as noted earlier, politicization of the people and thus the articulation of some social demands became a necessary element. There was a definite but not easily discernible ideological dimension (as well as personality clashes, and lack of contact between cadres and leaders) to the splits that occurred in

1974–5 within the Dare, the committee which supervised the struggle from Zambia. These divisions culminated in the assassination of the chairman, Herbert Chitepo. Political–education documents and practices from this period were clearly influenced by Marxian approaches, including ideas about 'a just war', 'national liberation', 'the role of cadres', culled in part from Chinese formulations. But rather abstract discussions of this sort were supplemented, though not thoroughly integrated, with some Zimbabwean historiography that pointed to racial oppression and social injustice, but not in terms that were analytically different from nationalist perspectives based on essentially liberal and ethical critiques of settler colonialism. Thus there was only a partial working out of the implications of a Marxist approach for the strategy of struggle in the specific context of Zimbabwe, in terms of which class forces could be mobilized for which demands and for what kind of post-independence transformation — even in the thinking of those (by no means a majority) influenced by such thinking. The process did go a little further, at least in the sense of an organized group which debated and articulated such notions if not their further elaboration, with the creation of ZIPA. These were a group of young ZANU commanders who took over for a year or more *de facto* command of ZANLA when Dare members were detained in Zambia in the aftermath of Chitepo's death, and who made a temporary military alliance with ZIPRA military leaders in this period. They lost out in the struggle for power within a ZANU into which the Dare leaders and also Mugabe and other 'old guard' and imprisoned leaders were reintroduced when the party moved its base to Mozambique at the end of 1976, the better to accelerate the struggle that had been partly demobilized by Zambian intervention in 1975. They, and some of the former Dare members were ousted by the Mugabe–Tongogara leadership and spent the final couple of years of the struggle under Mozambique protective custody. But like the March 11th Movement, the ideas they espoused perhaps contributed to the multifarious mainstream of ZANU thinking, and also, via their input into political education of guerrillas and hence peasants, to popular consciousness. This latter influence may have been significant in bringing out even more explicitly the demand for land as the core issue in nationalist demands, an issue that was an instinctive expression of what Ranger (1983) has termed a 'peasant consciousness' — although he may well overestimate this spontaneous contribution.

The two recognizable tendencies that were overtly articulating views that clearly owed something to Marxism, although of different brands, thus became peripheral voices in the mainstreams of their respective parties, and no such groupings have any coherent existence today. However, there are ex-cadres of both former parties, some now in government or still influential in the now united party, who have been exposed to these ideas and who seek, unlike the majority of bureaucrats, to ensure that the official ideology of 'Marxism– Leninism' is interpreted in more than a nationalistic way and is more than rhetoric. However, these tendencies, never thoroughly worked out, let alone officially adopted, demonstrated what a programme for a social transformation towards socialism, worked out on Marxist lines, might look like (a partial but interesting exception is contained in an analysis by 'Yates', 1980). Moreover, many of the left intellectuals inside and outside the government are wedded to increasingly out-dated 'statist' models of socialism. Such a stance can give them common cause with the interests of bureaucrats on certain issues; in a context of inherited strong centralization these may include the furthering of 'control' and the expansion of the bureaucracy itself, but they have little if anything to do with socialism.

State Structures in the Transfer of Power

A further set of constraints on any programme of rapid change was represented by the institutional framework that was inherited from the settler colonial state — although the large size of the public sector and the legacy of a publicly controlled economy were seen as offering some opportunities for 'managing' a development initiative which charted a new direction. The sheer size can be gauged by the fact that government and local government's budget and capital loan accounts, plus the public enterprises, were responsible for some 40 per cent of total expenditures in the overall economy — proportionately larger than for most developed countries and perhaps twice the average for developing countries. It employed over 100,000 employees — some 12 per cent of wage earners, and a higher number of whites than agriculture and almost as many as industry. Part of the size of the public service and public expenditures were a result of sharp rises related to the war, especially in the field of military and general administration. These extra expenditures were only partially curtailed with the end of the war, because any demobilization was compensated for by the absorption of many ZANU and ZAPU guerrillas into the new national army; and although there was a slight drop in general administrative cadres, very quickly after independence there was an increase in the public employees in health and a massive one in education (Bratton, 1980, has proved useful as a source for much in this section).

Apart from its scale, state structures were marked by other features — a high degree of effectiveness in a purely instrumental sense compared to most other African bureaucracies; very marked centralization of decision making; and a high proportion of whites in the higher levels — in 1978 only about 10 per cent of senior rank (tenured posts) were African. In this latter fact lies another reason why a sudden and vast exodus of whites would lead to much of the machinery of life being undermined. However, unlike neighbouring Mozambique and Angola, there were thousands of Zimbabweans who had received higher education in exile and other qualified and experienced blacks at home who had been denied preferment. Fairly rapid Africanization of the civil service was thus possible as well as a policy goal. This process was slowed down in the early period after 1980 because the constitution provided for an 'independent' Public Service Commission, comprising former civil servants with at least five years of experience (initially, therefore with a white majority), required to make appointments on grounds of capability only partly modified by the policy of Africanization. The racial composition of the body has now changed but there may well have been a continuity in the norms followed by the Commission. It is now, however, headed by a former official who had earlier been denied senior posts on the grounds of being 'too young and too radical', although the major flood of appointments of Africans to senior posts is over and the relative positions in the hierarchy of most civil servants has now been settled for perhaps a generation.

Structural shape as well as personnel have affected the nature of state structures. The inherited pattern was of a strong state with effective capability to run certain economic enterprises and to service the wider, private part of the 'modern' economy (e.g. white farming), and to regulate the economy but in a fiscally conservative and economically orthodox way rather to manage change. Moreover, these tasks were accomplished in part through a corporatist network incorporating and reconciling special business interests.

The state was also involved in some social welfare facilities but here its capabilities were not so great and were mainly to the urban areas, and to the white farming areas which were administered separately from the TTLs. The two systems of rural local government were in fact kept separate for some years after independence. The administration of the TTLs and provision of services to them were further and greatly affected by the war. In some areas, most services came to a halt and chiefs, tax collectors and other administrative apparatus disappeared. A new structure of local authorities for the former TTLs, the District Councils, immediately came into being after independence. But these new authorities trying to increase local services were only partly decentralized; they still relied almost entirely on central funding for their budgets. In a few places, these bodies did build upon and link to the informal grass-roots people's councils of the war period, but all too often these were left to erode. It was only from 1985 that village and ward development committees (Vidcos and Wadcos) were set up at an equivalent level, and plans for their integration into a more decentralized provincial and national planning machinery are still awaited.

The Economy at Independence

The UDI period exhibited three main economic phases: a sharp drop in trade and a small drop in national income in 1966–7; a period of rapid import-substitution-led growth (about 7 per cent per annum) from 1968 to 1974, with partial recovery in exports; and economic decline (at about 3 per cent per annum) from 1975 to 1979 caused by the escalation of the war and a rapid deterioration in the terms of trade (Davies, 1981, pp. 207–11). Although GDP was about two-thirds higher in 1979 than in 1965, per caput GDP was barely 6 per cent higher. However there is evidence that income disparities between white and black income earners and between the black employed and peasants had both widened (see Davies and Stoneman, 1981, pp. 99–103; also Stoneman, 1981c, pp. 185–6).

What is clear is that independence found one of the most unequal economies in the world. The 3 per cent of the population who were white earned about 60 per cent of total wages and salaries, representing about 36 per cent of gross domestic income; a further 28 per cent of GDI was gross operating profits of incorporated enterprises (all white-owned). Thus 3 per cent commanded nearly two-thirds of national income, whilst the remaining 97 per cent had *at most* the remaining third (24 per cent wages, 4 per cent subsistence income, 5 per cent profits of unincorporated enterprises — the latter in fact partly white-owned as well). In terms of ownership of wealth, whites had exclusive ownership of almost half the land (two-thirds of the best land), and (together with foreign interests) owned nearly all of the capital in industry and mining.

This is not solely an argument concerning race: the maldistribution would have had many of the same economic consequences had all been black, namely a bias in production towards luxury goods, produced by relatively capital-intensive technology with relatively high-import content. Despite some frustrated attempts to broaden it in the 1950s, the effective market was thus restricted to less than a million people out of a population of 7 million, so benefits from economies of scale were lacking, as were the signals which could lead to investment to meet the basic needs of the large majority.

Such arguments were recognized by the incoming government, having been set out in *Zimbabwe: Towards a New Order* (UNCTAD, 1980). However, either the magnitude of the task was not perceived, or the imposed constraints dictated gradual change, for action did not match the Marxist rhetoric. In fact, as we see below, redistributive measures were inadequate and, eight years after independence, the above picture of inequality needs only partial modification.

On the other hand the economy at independence displayed some strong features that were the envy of many other poor countries: foreign debt was low and the balance of payments was in surplus (albeit through an intensity of import restriction which had harmed growth, as Green and Kadhani, 1986, have shown); the economy was not overdependent on either agriculture or mining, with manufacturing industry contributing over a quarter of GDP. This industry had benefited from forced growth under sanctions and had become well-diversified, including black Africa's only integrated iron and steel plant and the nucleus of a capital-goods sector, thus making it relatively the most substantial in black-ruled Africa. Consequently exports were fairly well balanced: about 40 per cent each from mining and agriculture, with the more sanctions-affected manufactured goods at 20 per cent. There were also much improved terms of trade with the end of sanctions, and the hope of large aid inflows.

Development Strategy

Before independence very little detailed or concrete work was done on development strategy. On the one hand, ZANU published (mainly in *Zimbabwe News*) rather general and abstract statements calling for far-reaching nationalization, land redistribution, workers' control and so forth. On the other, *Towards a New Order* (UNCTAD, 1980) was very cautious, analysing existing inequities and arguing for their reduction, but almost entirely in a spirit of reform rather than structural transformation. The most radical recommendation (which was not followed) was for the nationalization of all banks and financial institutions.

After independence events initially moved fast, and there was the immediate establishment of a ministry of economic planning and development under the prestigious leadership of Dr Bernard Chidzero (for many years a senior official at the UNDP and then UNCTAD, the United Nations Conference on Trade and Development), but as expected the guidelines of the new ministry derived from Chidzero and UNCTAD rather than the revolutionary ZANU tradition. In the face of the high expectations and widespread strikes an interim (rather low) minimum wage was announced followed by the establishment of an independent commission of inquiry into incomes, prices and conditions of service, which began work in September 1980. Despite its very mixed membership, this commission reported unanimously in June 1981 (Riddell, 1981). It reflected to a degree the policy of reconciliation, embodied in its membership of five whites and four blacks under the chairmanship of British economist Roger Riddell. Its recommendations were varied, but focused on raising minimum wages to 90 per cent of the Poverty Datum Line (which needed to be recalculated regularly for different regions), more resettlement and improvement of rural structures, an ending of the split families caused by migrant labour, and introduction of a social security system. Socialism was not mentioned in the terms of reference or the report; the basic assumption was that there was enough wealth (or that with growth there would be) for redistribution to lead to an end to poverty and insecurity without serious cuts in the living standards of the rich.

Expectations were overfulfilled at first: an 11 per cent improvement in the terms of trade plus the sudden availability of credit (much of it labelled 'aid') produced real growth in GDP of about 12 per cent in both 1980 and 1981. It thus seemed fairly modest in 1981 to project 8 per cent growth on the basis of continuing foreign exchange inflows. So it was reliance on these aid inflows in an essentially unchanged capitalist environment that formed the nucleus of the initial development strategy, rather than the promised nationalizations and planning of investment, or indeed planning of any sort.

However, the new ministry and a high-level team of planners from the United Nations Development Programme (UNDP) expected to produce a five-year plan during the year following independence. Political pressures, deriving ultimately from the private (largely foreign) ownership of most of the economy, delayed and emasculated the exercise. Thus not until November 1982 was the first volume of the Transitional National Development Plan, 1982/83–1984/85 (TNDP, 1983), published, with the First Five-Year National Development Plan, 1986–1990 (FFYNDP, 1986) following only in April 1986 on the sixth anniversary of independence. These documents were widely seen as performing political rather than economic functions, as general statements of intent coupled with some public sector projects, rather than as plans as understood in other countries with Marxist regimes; in fact they lacked even the planning instruments found, for example, in France's indicative plans. (See Chapter 8 below for a fuller discussion both of planning and of its ideological context.)

Probably therefore it had been realized by key politicians that serious attempts to mobilize locally generated economic surplus, and to invest it so as to change the structure of the economy in the direction of greater equality, would have raised strong opposition, with consequences both internationally and on the commitment of the still-needed whites. So the solution adopted was to look to foreign aid to promote rapid growth, particularly in infrastructure in the investment-starved communal areas, in some vague hope that a 'levelling up' of the incomes of the poorest might occur without any serious impact on those of the richest. Clearly this strategy (if it can be so considered) underestimated both the extent of income inequality and the prospects for growth, and furthermore contained no adequate mechanism for redressing wealth inequality beyond the small official resettlement programme.

The Consolidation of the ZANU Government

After the confirmation of their position in power after the 1980 elections, the ZANU leadership sought to accomplish three political objectives. First, they wanted to bed the country down into some degree of stability after the years of war — in part this was sought through the policy of 'reconciliation'. Second, they wanted to consolidate their own power, which meant specifically the establishment of their authority as a government and in the process a redefinition of the structure and role of the party. These two aims were seen as being affected by and equated with a third objective — for the achievement of stability and national integration were equated by them with a one-party state. The problem was how to achieve this — and how to do so in the context of a commitment to 'reconciliation' with their political opponents? In the process of pursuing these three objectives, the regime defined its own character and the nature of its relationship with the people.

The policy of 'reconciliation' came into play immediately Mugabe was elected to office, when a very conciliatory speech of acceptance of the premiership persuaded many whites, who had, in some cases literally, already packed, to stay. The reassurances were given a more concrete form with the key appointment of Dennis Norman, a prominent white businessman and farmer, as minister for agriculture, and also of David Smith as minister for trade and commerce. Neither were any longer members of the former Rhodesia Front but were clearly part of the white 'establishment' and their appointments guaranteed that politics in these two key sectors would not be radically different from before. In the next years, the ruling party continued to pursue similar tactics of making concessions to white interests and susceptibilities while trying at the same time to attack the newly renamed Republican Front of Ian Smith as a party, to isolate it from the white population as a whole, and to erode its political position especially in Parliament. They were partially successful in this last endeavour as several white MPs and interest groups like the Commercial Farmers' Union increasingly sought to distance themselves from the confrontational tactics of Ian Smith, seeing their interests best served by a political tone of compromise but with hard bargaining over specific economic issues. Several MPs switched to an independent white political group prepared to ally with government, and this group was able to win some by-elections, so that the RF had less than half the twenty white seats by the time of the first post-independence elections in 1985. However, ZANU's expectations of making further in-roads into the representation of the RF (now called the Conservative Alliance of Zimbabwe — CAZ), and moving to that extent towards a one-party parliament, took a blow when the RF were able to win fifteen of the white seats in 1985. Mugabe spoke bitterly at the time 'that the trust we placed in whites and our belief they were getting reconciled to the new political order was a trust and belief that was not deserved'. However, the reconciliation policy continued to be evident in the treatment of whites, even beyond the 1987 date at which the constitutional provision for white-only seats elected by a white electorate could be repealed. At that time, under the amended system that provided for the twenty white MPs and ten senators to be elected by the other elected MPs, nine whites, some of them former RF members were nominated by ZANU, and of course elected. This was a shrewd move which placated white and international public opinion. There are, therefore, still several white MPs, many of them not even 'liberals' but representatives of the most entrenched white interests, but they no longer 'represent' a distinct white electorate, and are there at the pleasure of the ZANU leadership.

The same spirit of reconciliation has not always been evident in relations with ZAPU and other black political groupings. It was, however, in evidence at first. Nkomo was, reportedly, offered the position of President but turned it down on the grounds that it was largely ceremonial and had no political weight. Canaan Banana, a methodist minister active in internal politics until he joined ZANU in 1976 and himself from Matabeleland, became president. Nkomo was made minister in the prime minister's office with responsibility for the public service, and three other ZAPU members were in the Cabinet. But this honeymoon did not last. In 1982 Nkomo and two other ZAPU ministers were dismissed after a large arms cache was found buried on a farm belonging to the party — although two other ZAPU members remained in government and eventually left the party, later to join ZANU.

Earlier, in November 1980 and again in 1981, fighting had broken out in army barracks at Embeshemi in Matabeleland between ex-ZANLA and ex-ZIPRA guerrillas. From that time some ex-ZIPRA fighters drifted back into the bush in Matabeleland and some deserted the army. After the dismissal of Nkomo from the cabinet, more open acts of terrorism were undertaken by these 'dissidents' in rural Matabeleland. These consisted mostly of the same kinds of ambushes and attacks on white-owned farms and on central government officials that had characterized the war of liberation, especially in the Shona areas, in the 1970s. Unfortunately, the ZANU authorities reacted in much the same way as the Rhodesians. From 1983 the security forces, consisting mainly and notoriously of the special, North Korean-trained, exclusively-Shona-speaking Fifth Brigade, were sent into rural areas of Matabeleland and used strong-arm methods to pacify the local population, making little impact on the actual 'dissidents'.

These ordinary villagers probably had little sympathy with the 'dissidents', even those disaffected ex-ZIPRA who claimed that the revolution was betrayed, let alone the ordinary bandits and South-African-trained malcontents that also were found amongst them. The people no doubt did not inform on the bandits more because of the terror tactics used by the dissidents than through any identification with local Ndebele 'boys'.

After protests by church and aid agencies, Mugabe appointed a commission of inquiry into allegations of brutality and the Fifth Brigade was reined in somewhat after 1984. The dissident unrest was controlled but not eliminated; large columns that had been a feature up to 1984 could no longer operate by 1987. This activity erupted again in some horrific incidents in late 1987 just prior to the party unity talks, and thereafter largely disappeared for six months.

ZANU had never made a secret of its desire to create a one-party state. After its sweeping victory in the 1980 elections, there persisted a belief among some party leaders that it could win over the remaining one third of voters — a proportion of which they thought had been bought by

Muzorewa. However, they were unable to dislodge ZAPU from Matabeleland and even parts of the ethnically-mixed Midland Province in local government elections, and in the 1985 general election ZAPU won all fifteen seats in the two Matabeleland provinces. Elsewhere, ZANU did in fact consolidate its electoral support, winning all the seats in Midlands and Mashonaland West and East Provinces where ZAPU and Muzorewa's UANC had previously held a handful. In these six provinces ZANU lost only one seat to a supporter of Sithole's alternative 'ZANU' in the eastern border constituency of Chipinga.

To say as many authors do (Sithole, 1986, is but one) that what was an ethnic pattern of voting and political loyalty was due to some inherent identity called 'ethnicity' is to explain nothing. We shall delve into some of the specific forms of ethnic groupings and identities in the next chapter, but here it needs to be pointed out that there was nothing inevitable about the regional support for the parties. We have seen how the leadership level of each party was not in the past exclusively of one ethnic group. It was also the case that ZANU had not had the benefit of any significant period of legal existence to be able to build up local membership support. Thus when ZANU guerrillas began to pursue the tactic of establishing themselves among the local people from 1972 on, they were not automatically assured of popular backing. That had to be won, and there are accounts of how communities initially stated 'they had only known ZAPU', but that they were open-minded enough to give this new group a hearing. This opportunity even presented itself in some southern parts of Matabeleland South Province, where ZANLA operated for several months in 1978 and 1979. But they were able to win over many people in these areas only at a rhetorical level; they alienated them by their insistence on using Shona rather than Ndebele as the language of political education and by simply denouncing Nkomo prematurely before explaining their cause and their differences with Nkomo. They thus gave the appearance of being simply opposed to a respected nationalist leader, who was thus given, if anything, greater legitimacy as 'their' leader. This represented a missed opportunity for ZANU to establish a foothold in Matabeleland, an opportunity that receded with the pattern of 1980 electoral support, but disappeared for good with the repression visited upon ordinary Ndebele people (not just dissidents) after the open split with ZAPU in 1982, and the detention and harassment of many ZAPU leaders and officials (see Mpofu, 1980; and Cliffe, Mpofu and Munslow, 1980). Far from any attempt at weaning popular support away from ZAPU and Nkomo, services and projects were held back by government (even food relief at one part of the famine period in 1984) or were disrupted by the dissidents. ZANU thus came to have very little support in Matabeleland, very little of any functioning party apparatus (despite the enforced selling of party cards), and thus no channel for political dialogue with the Ndebele people. Not only were some of the pressures counterproductive in that they alienated the ordinary people rather than won them over, but the Ndebele politicians in ZANU, like Enos Nkala, having wielded the stick themselves, placed themselves in a position where they could not be spokespersons for the concerns and interests of Ndebele people. Thus when the ZANU government let up on their pressures on the people, and it should be stated that they never used repressive means exclusively, the only channel for such representation was Nkomo and his party structure. In the unity talks that recurred periodically from 1985 to 1987 until they were finally successful, Nkomo's position was thus not as weak as it seemed given his limited electoral base and ZANU's use of the coercive and media apparatuses of the state. In the last analysis, only he could politically 'deliver' the Ndebele people, given the lost opportunities for leverage that had gone before. When unity of the two parties finally came at the end of 1987, it was in fact in large part a matter of bargaining about Nkomo's status. This analysis also prompts a question about the future working of the united party: whether it will work like some of the single parties in Africa, such as UNIP in Zambia, as a kind of federation of regional-ethnic coalitions and factions, rather than as a culturally integrated party like the CCM in (culturally and linguistically united) Tanzania.

With ZAPU's survival as a political force at all levels in the two provinces, the pattern of governance took on a different form in Matabeleland. In most parts of the other provinces a network of local authorities, provincial planning and advisory boards, ward and village development committees was set up with the representatives on them almost entirely made up of ZANU nominees. There was thus a virtual one-party system in operation in much of the country. These structures, which will be discussed in detail in Chapter 6 below, did not operate in this way in Matabeleland. There was thus a limit to how far a 'party–state' could be put into being and to the mode of operation of the party itself.

Regional Relations

The Lancaster House agreement restored Zimbabwe to the international community, but cooled its relations with South Africa. The new country spurned closer economic links through the proposed 'Constellation of States of Southern Africa', although it continued to renew the trade agreement which gave preferential access into the South African market to some Zimbabwean exports. Instead Zimbabwe joined the 'Front Line States' (FLS) in opposition to apartheid and minority rule in South Africa and Namibia, and became a founding member of both the Southern African Development Coordination Conference (SADCC) and the Preferential Trade Area for Eastern and Southern Africa (PTA) (see Chapter 16).

There are no formal diplomatic links with South Africa, but relations are handled through the South African Trade Mission in Harare, and there is also an active South African Tourism Board. Ministers refuse to meet their South African opposite numbers (although South Africa may have exerted leverage to achieve at least some secret meetings on occasion), with business being conducted at the level of ministry officials. Perhaps the most significant economic impact made on Zimbabwe by South Africa has been produced indirectly through the so-called Mozambican National Resistance. The MNR (or Renamo) was set up by the Rhodesian secret services in the late 1970s to harry FRELIMO and ZANU. After 1980 South Africa took over its tutelage and relaunched it. Although operating almost entirely in Mozambique, where it has successfully destabilized the FRELIMO government, it has also had serious effects on Zimbabwe through closing the Beira and later the Limpopo lines to the Mozambican ports, so forcing over 90 per cent of Zimbabwe's transit trade through South African ports in the mid-1980s. Zimbabwe moved to protect the pipeline from Beira to Mutare, later extending operations to a permanent guard on the whole 'Beira Corridor' consisting of road, railway line and pipeline, and joint operations with FRELIMO to capture MNR bases in central Mozambique; as many as 10,000 Zimbabwean troops were reported as being in Mozambique at any one time. This provoked a 'declaration of war' by the MNR on Zimbabwe in late 1986, followed by sporadic incursions into eastern Zimbabwe during the following year in which sabotage, abductions and murders occurred; there was some consequent disruption of work on tea estates, primarily because of the difficulty of obtaining seasonal labour. The main worry for Zimbabwe is that some of the MNR rebels are ethnic Ndaus (a Shona sub-group) related to Zimbabweans around Chipinge, who in 1985 still supported the original ZANU–Sithole enough to elect one MP.

Part II
Social Structures

5   Class and Race

Different Approaches to Analysing Zimbabwe's Social Formation

In Chapter 3 we argued that the essential feature of the settler colonial state was a form of capital accumulation that depended on the 'super-exploitation' of black labour, made inordinately cheap because it was not fully 'free', remaining semi-proletarianized with the costs of its reproduction in the next generation being borne by a declining but still surviving 'sub-subsistence' peasant agriculture. The main characteristics of these two related components of the working class, plus the women who upheld the 'household' matrix which provided the link between the 'reserves' and employment in the settler capitalist economy, will be explored in later sections of this chapter. But to get a picture of the social structure, as it shifts, it is first important to see how the different elements relate to the whole. That 'whole' was of course the set of social forces that interacted in the settler political economy and its distinctive pattern of capital accumulation, its contradictions and its dynamic.

One issue that has immediately to be faced in seeking to outline the principal social forces at work is to settle the relative salience of 'class' and 'race' as the embodiment of the main dimensions. Clearly both are important; the key to analysis is to see how they interrelate. At first glance, a state and dominant political culture both marked by overt racist principles would seem to imply that racial identity would be the factor that should be given primacy in analysis. There is some validity in this insofar as whites of all classes formed a politically dominant and economically privileged bloc, that they were united across class and shared a common loyalty and ideology — and that, specifically, white workers were strong supporters of the settler capitalist system and were brought into the fold. But analysis in terms of these racial identities should not be taken to mean that such loyalties were strong enough to transcend differing economic interests. Here was no mindless commitment to a racist ideology, for the broad alliance of whites was within a socio-economic arrangement in which their differing class interests all stood to gain — in general. However, attention to these different class interests also reveals not a complete identity of interest but simply a degree of commonality that made possible a compromise in which conflicts and contradictions could for a time be held in check, in a certain specific historical context.

Clearly the achievement of independence under black majority represented a change in the historical context in which the racial divide was the basis for political division. Thus to understand the nature of that change, the possible re-alignments and re-alliances of class forces, to analyse not the past but the present Zimbabwe social formation, the category of 'race' is not sufficient. However, if we are to carry out such an analysis, it will first be necessary to clarify one issue of the settler colonial past, and its specific interactions of race and class. This is the question of the specific conflicts and contradictions inherent in that dispensation, however much they may have temporarily been held in check, rather than on the obvious racially differentiated structure of compromise.

Several analysts have offered answers — and here we return to flesh out the class dimensions of debates referred to in Chapter 1. Mandaza's view in *The Political Economy Transition* is that the chief contradiction in the settler colonial system was that it excluded and generated opposition among all the classes in the black population and specifically did not allow much room for the black petty bourgeoisie which was emerging despite the constraints on it — the class that could form the leadership of a potential alternative class alliance behind the banner of African nationalism. This argument is supported by other analysts, including both Astrow and Arrighi, and is undeniable as far as it goes. But it offers only a partial perspective on what alternative possibilities await independent Zimbabwe under a 'Marxist' ruling party. Whereas for Astrow the black petty bourgeoisie's leadership automatically rules out any prospect other than capitalism and neo-colonialism, Mandaza feels that in circumstances which he sees in precisely the same terms there are nevertheless prospects for a progressive wing of the black petty bourgeoisie to influence development policy — that is by fostering a de-linking of the economy from world capitalism and reducing 'dependence'. In his view, the new structures are broadly fostering 'imperialist interests', and they are given internal sustenance by the considerable rearguard actions of the whites and by much of the black petty bourgeoisie. While the basic contradiction between the Zimbabwean people as a whole and international finance capital remains, imperialism does not 'impose a permanent solution in its favour'. The struggles that determine what emerges during transition are those *within* the black petty bourgeoisie, as it seeks to run a state that balances 'the contradictions between imperatives of imperialist hegemony and the popular demands of the masses'. Eventually with the sharpening of a second stage of class struggle which is 'both anti-capitalist and anti-imperialist' the progressive petty bourgeoisie can provide the leadership for emerging working-class power and consciousness.

This perspective is useful, and indeed provides this chapter with something of an agenda: to examine the remnants of white settler influence, the role of international capital, the different elements in the black petty bourgeoisie and the size, shape and political consciousness of the working people, peasantry, workers and women in their role between these two classes. However, it does not offer adequate insights as to how to assess the strengths of these classes, other than in terms of their level of consciousness, let alone their interests and interactions one with another, and how these are likely to change during this period of transition. Moreover, even if one accepts that the struggle within the petty bourgeoisie, as they attempt to mediate the broader struggles between working people in Zimbabwe and imperialism, will together be decisive in this transitional period, no purchase is offered on the issue of what structural change is indeed possible during transition. If, as Astrow maintains, in this instance correctly, no immediate transition to socialism is possible, and none is actually envisaged at this stage, what structural alternatives are open? What in fact is at issue in the struggle between classes and fractions in the transition envisaged by Mandaza? What objective possibilities are available? It is here that an understanding of the settler political economy and in particular its contradictions may offer some clues.

One provocative view (Biermann and Kössler, 1980) sees the key to understanding the Rhodesian social formation and its contradictions as lying in its distinctive pattern of capital accumulation. They conceptualize the pattern that we have discussed above as a 'settler mode of production', a distinct variant of capitalism, whereby the labour that is exploited is ultra-cheap by virtue of its being only semi-proletarianized, reproducing itself outside the sphere of capitalist production and the market. This model — a set of 'logical distinct structures' — further requires that the labour be unfree, which required in turn a repressive state mechanism. One basic contradiction of this settler mode — and it is this which makes it distinct from capitalism — is that it is stagnant. There is no imperative within it, given the possibilities of extracting large surpluses from this type of labour, for accumulation of capital through transforming the means of production. The surpluses can be largely consumed in a luxurious lifestyle; little is required for reinvestment. Moreover, the conflicts to which the mode is subject are in fact between metropolitan capital and settler agricultural capital — but they are conflicts not only about markets and the locus of profits, but fundamentally about the pattern of capital accumulation and in turn political and economic mechanisms for exploiting and reproducing the black working people and other classes.

This approach suffers from being too formalistic and its prediction of an inevitable stasis can be questioned in practice — even in relation to the agricultural sector, let alone the industrial that they exclude from this type of analysis. Yet it is useful in indicating some options for post-independence development. If the repressive mechanism was so central a feature, its replacement, at least in its settler form, should allow the emergence of a new pattern of capital accumulation. A key element here, although they do not discuss it explicitly, should be the erosion of measures controlling influx in towns which could lead to very rapid urbanization and a transformation of the semi-proletariat either into a proletariat proper, or (more likely) a lumpen proletariat. There could be a transition merely towards a more 'normal' form of capitalism, where, presumably, labour would be reproduced in a different way.

The prospects for a change in the pattern of capital accumulation and hence in the mode of exploitation and reproduction of labour are clearly crucial if we are to evaluate the prospects facing the regime in Zimbabwe and analyse what are the possible outcomes of class struggle. Is one option what Biermann and Kössler term the 'neo-colonial' of normal capitalism? Can one be more precise about its forms and practices? And is there also a transition that, while not an immediate transition to socialism, changes the logic of accumulation, the reproduction of labour, etc., in what will still be basically a capitalist economy? This approach offers a more useful starting point for considering outcomes rather than mere formulae for reducing dependence in that it also suggests the ways in which internal class relationships may be part of what is at issue.

These 'development' prospects will be explored in later chapters; the class relations in this one. What is not so useful, in this particular task, is Biermann and Kössler's conclusion that it is the settler remnants and their legacy that will be the main forces pushing for a neo-colonial path. This neglects the role of the black petty bourgeoisie, in contrast with one element in another useful set of insights, those of Arrighi (1970). He saw the contradictions in the accumulation process of agrarian capital — it was for instance interested in 'national' development, in contrast to imperialist interests, but was not prepared to allow the expansion of the internal market because it was fearful of the competition from black workers and peasants that would have generated that expansion. But for him these were contradictory tendencies rather than an in-built stasis, tendencies that shaped and reshaped the pattern of capital accumulation over time as different alliances of fractions and classes assumed pre-eminence in the jockeying for power. What was at stake in these shifts in what we have termed the 'pattern of capitalist accumulation' were the issues of how far local industrialization was pushed, in what products, related to the expansion of what kind of market, at what rate, with what opportunities and changes in the size and position of black wage earners and peasants. Arrighi concluded his nuanced analysis of these shifting balances in class forces with speculation about the prospects of a 'neo-colonial solution' to the Rhodesian problem. But he scarcely explored what the content of this might be in terms of economic strategy beyond the statement that it was the strategy of large-scale international capital for retaining its interests, and it involved creating conditions for the development of a black middle class. It is this latter group that he saw as the chief local beneficiaries and allies of international capital in promoting this pattern. In contrast to Biermann and Kössler, who put weight on the settler remnants as the prime local agents of neo-colonialism, Arrighi presumed the emigration of many of the white workers and middle class, who faced the most direct competition, and even of many white capitalist farmers, seeing these classes as having stood in the way of foreign capital's long-run interests. What he also seems to imply, is that such a neo- colonial path would put an end to any 'national' element in the development trajectory — although this may be merely what one reads into his specification of a clear-cut identity of interest and 'possible political alliance of large-scale foreign capitalism and of the black middle class and petty bourgeoisie. In this contemplation of possibilities, he (like most other analysts) downplays the alternative influence of other white classes — manufacturing capitalists, professional groups. He sees them as not in general vulnerable to black competition, but incapable (at least in the conditions of UDI), of espousing any political alternative to RF policies, and also just as wedded to the products and services that meet the composition of demand determined by the pre-existing distribution of income and class structure.

What this analysis hints at, but does not fully explore, is a prospect that contrasts with this unambiguously neo-colonial path — of a 'post-settler' development path that is oriented to 'national' industrial growth promoted by an alliance of locally-based, (almost entirely) white *industrial* capital, sections of the black petty bourgeoisie and middle classes, and based on mass consumption for the black working population rather than luxury consumption of a limited, but highly paid, white market. Such a pattern would imply the expansion of opportunities and incomes for either white wage earners or surplus crop producers or both, which would in any case alter the terms of reproduction of labour, but how these would alter with what effects on the social structure would depend on whether the redistribution of income was primarily at the wage earning or peasant producer end of the continuum of black households. Just what are the possibilities of such a national, transitional development, with such different implications to those of a more completely neo-colonial capitalism, will be discussed later in this work. In this chapter we will attempt to explore the different elements of the class–race social structure to try to identify their changing position with independence and where their 'interests' might lie. But in turning first to the bourgeoisie and petty bourgeoisie, Arrighi's approach (also reflected in Baylies, 1980) of distinguishing a number of differing interests (on the basis of race, internal versus international, by economic sector and by type of product) should be well borne in mind if one is to avoid over-simplification.

The Bourgeoisie

Other chapters document the relative economic significance of the white commercial farms, the mines and the manufacturing industries and of the specific, organized interest groups that represent them. What we aim to do here is to review how the personnel involved in owning and running these enterprises act as a class — to what extent are they a single coherent group or do they act as factions? What are their 'interests', especially in the sense of having any coherent project for Zimbabwe's development? And what are their relations with and relative strengths compared with other social groups?

The large commercial farms are largely run by owner-managers, though there are absentee owners and there are some corporately-owned large ranches and estates. Although only a small proportion of the white population, they were able to remain the dominant political core of the ruling white alliance until 1980. Their present position is influential rather than in any way dominant, and is often used to mount (usually effective) rearguard actions — for example against an expanded resettlement programme and reduction of compensation, or against the increases in the minimum wage of 'agro-industrial' workers proposed by government in 1985. So, it is doubtful if they have any longer any coherent strategy for the long term — other than their obvious present aim to stay in the country for the foreseeable future. They are not yet affected by a crisis of confidence that might generate an exodus, and that is only likely to change with the hotting up of the conflict in and with South Africa, or some sudden radical land reform rather than a continuation of the present limited one or its gradual acceleration. In fact, they did modify their stance over black peasant farming in 1980, which they had kept in a debilitated state for decades, now welcoming some commercialization and growth in production. This was a reflection of their more enlightened self-interest in changed political circumstances, which also gave rise to a rationalization strategy. They have rationalized geographically, withdrawing and actually encouraging settlement in the more peripheral (and lower potential) areas away from the settler heartland; and economically they have reduced labour and introduced more equipment; and they have been seemingly content to allow peasants to take much greater shares of the maize and cotton markets, whilst themselves resorting more to tobacco and diversifying into other crops. During the UDI period with their enforced dependence more on internal than external markets they certainly were committed to national development, but this may now have changed back to an indifference to industry and to the widening of the internal market caused by the changed nature of their produce and their less secure position.

These statements may have to be modified to the extent that there has been an Africanization of this fraction of the class. Because it is officially somewhat frowned upon, especially for officials, the exact extent of this is a matter of speculation. That it has occurred is beyond doubt, however, and the Commercial Farmers' Union are prepared to speak of the 'political weight of their "new members"' — but it has probably not been on the same scale as in Kenya. Insofar as it is happening there may be a slightly longer-term calculation, but not necessarily any greater commitment to national development. There could be some benefit to them in a coalition between commercial and kulak farmers that might urge private land tenure in the communal areas, but this would in fact strengthen resistance to any meaningful land reform.

If the farmers are at best only passively concerned about interested in overall national development, perhaps only as it generates internal market growth, is it in fact possible to talk of a 'national bourgeoisie', in the sense that Marxist regimes elsewhere have identified such a class as a possible ally in a transitional stage of development, a class that would be interested in building up local production rather than acting as 'compradors'? Manufacturing industry has in fact developed to a significant extent in Zimbabwe, even if as a result of fortuitous and exceptional stimuli — World War II, the Central African Federation, UDI. Indeed it was already contributing more than agriculture to GDP by the 1950s, although it was never able to translate that into comparable political clout. Some of the industrial interests represent state capital — iron and steel, power, etc., — and this is likely to be a significant force, although not so far an expanding one, as there has only been some purchasing of shares in a few companies, no outright nationalization and little new state enterprise. Private manufacturers are of course either small family or company businesses, overwhelmingly white, but also some international corporations. They do take common action through the ZNCC and CZI and their sectoral and regional committees and through their representation on parastatal bodies, and the dividing line between 'local' and 'foreign' capital is in practice blurred. As Arrighi (1967) and Baylies (1980) both maintain, a more differential analysis and actual linkages would have to be made by any government interested in a more nationally or regionally-oriented development — making distinctions between those producing for internal or external markets, those just concerned with assemblage or last-stage processing rather than the local production of capital goods, and even between different corporations. Thus Arrighi singles out the Anglo-American Corporation, as it is a major owner but also far and away the largest economic actor in the whole southern African region, and thus has exceptional leverage. It is also a transnational that is local as well and thus in some sense may have more of a long-term commitment to the region than other international companies, but how far to Zimbabwe as opposed to the region or even just to South Africa is unclear. Whether as an ally of 'national development' or a foe, its special position and weight mean that it deserves separate treatment in working out any strategy.

The mining sector of the bourgeoisie is also divided, but again not sharply, between small, local enterprise and large transnationals but, because of its massive dependence on overseas markets, there is only a limited sense in which any part of this fraction is committed to broader-based development. And because of this same dependence, nationalization is not to be seriously contemplated: if done without full compensation it would alienate the purchasing TNCs and cut the industry off from access to the markets they provide, and if compensation were paid, given low world prices in some cases, it would only relieve the present owners of a loss at considerable public expense.

The Black Petty Bourgeoisie

The white middle classes, consisting of officials, shopkeepers, managers and technical personnel, were sizeable but, typical of the classical petty bourgeoisie, were not an independent political voice with a perspective or project of their own, other than a reactive support for white dominance to protect their privileged access to many of these positions from black entry. Many of the analysts we considered at the outset of this chapter have in fact suggested that settlerdom inhibited the formation of a black petty bourgeoisie, whereas it would be more accurate to say that black entrants were cut off from certain middle-class positions — in the bureaucracy, in managerial, technical and supervisory roles, especially in large and medium size enterprises, and in trade in major (white) urban centres. In fact, there were other slots, most not as remunerative, of a petty bourgeois nature that were open to blacks. These were in petty trade in black townships and TTLs, in teaching and other professions in those areas, but most significantly among the black farmers in the so-called Purchase Areas.

Although numerically small and operating on a fraction of the scale of whites, this latter group of 10,000 farmers were responsible for a third of the marketed produce from black farmers at independence. They had been able to achieve a certain amount of accumulation, often using traditional means, like polygyny to build up a labour force, and moreover they had used this advantage as a basis for moving into business opportunities locally and in the towns, and to get privileged educational access for their children. Cheater (1984) convincingly argues from a case study of Purchase Area farmers that they represented an important exception to the correlation of class with race and that as their class awareness undoubtedly grew in the last two decades, subjectively and objectively 'their class alignments came to lie with white commercial farmers and with the urban bourgeoisie'. The better-off of this group are perhaps best considered part of the capitalist class, and it is they that have provided the leadership of a relatively effectively organized interest group, the Zimbabwe National Farmers' Union (ZNFU). This group has consistently put forward the case for a policy of their being assisted to purchase white farms as an alternative to their resettlement by the poor and landless. Of course, they were not the only group of better-off black farmers, as there was significant differentiation in the CAs, as we shall see below, and 'master farmers' from among them have also been able to accumulate in other spheres. They do articulate similar interests (for instance, they were able to get resettlement criteria modified to include what was projected as a 'leaven' of experienced farmers rather than just the landless), but their different social context means that they are not so isolated from the currents emanating from the broader cultural forms of peasant life in the CAs as the freehold farmers are — set off in discrete areas, forming a different community and forging a differing culture.

In trying to understand the significance of the various elements that make up what is often a residual category, the 'petty bourgeoisie', some of the most influential writing in the African context has come from Kenya, which because of the similarities of settler colonialism could have some relevance to Zimbabwe. There, it is argued (Cowan, 1981; Leys, 1978), a class of traders and larger peasants had managed some preliminary accumulation of capital — in the decades before independence, despite settler restrictions, and were poised to use their new dominance of the state that they inherited at independence to give free reign to, and indeed to be a vehicle for, their further rapid accumulation and their conversion from a *petty* into a full-fledged bourgeoisie. In a second and more contested part of the argument, it is asserted that this indigenous bourgeoisie is not 'auxiliary' to international capital but 'national' in the sense of promoting its own interests and processes of accumulation and using the state, on occasion, against the interests of foreign capital. In other words Kenya is claimed to have transcended the simple 'neo-colonial' situation, or gone beyond Mandaza's view in the Zimbabwean context of a ruling *petty* bourgeoisie wedded to international capital.

In comparing these theses with Zimbabwean realities, it can first be acknowledged that the black petty bourgeoisie occupies a different political space from the white. Unlike the latter, it has indisputably provided the leadership to an African nationalism that mobilized a broad swathe of other classes; it provides most of the personnel of the new regime and sections of it, like the ZNFU and the similar organization of businessmen, the Zimbabwean National Chambers of Commerce, are organized to promote their interests. It is also clearly the case that some of these groups as well as some political and civil service figures do have some conception of the new state bending things their way to allow them to replace the whites in the bourgeoisie, in much the same way in fact that the whites did for its constituency.

In tracing the actual path of class formation in Zimbabwe and the particular character of this strategically placed class, what is striking is that its growth and form owe as much to the socio-economic structures inherited from settlerdom as any prior accumulation in farming or trade and their access to state power. That is to say the nationalist victory did little to undermine the structure of the colonial political economy but did displace a lot of whites, during the war or after, who enjoyed economic positions and the accompanying life style. So the process was not just the emergence of a black petty and real bourgeoisie but an Africanization of existing ones; the slots were there, vacant. The farms, businesses, bureaucratic and managerial posts were there to be occupied, but so too were the vast suburbs of large, gardened bungalows, the sports clubs and watering holes, only sustainable with the private transport, household and other servants, and the incomes and class differences that go along with them. Those blacks that are now part of the petty bourgeoisie have entered a class with considerable economic power and social status.

In fact, however, the state has not yet been so unambiguous a vehicle for the personal aggrandizement of its own personnel, or this class as a whole, as in Kenya. There have not been subsidized loans for farms and businesses, nor the open sale of state-acquired enterprises. There has indeed been an attempt to check this process of the embourgeoisement of the bureaucracy and of politics, through the imposition of leadership conditions by ZANU on its own personnel in 1984 (see next chapter). Of course, there is no way of documenting how effective such curbs have been in insulating ruling circles and the party from accumulation by this class. It is part of the everyday coinage of political talk that many members of the government and parliament have acquired farms and /or other businesses — but also that this process has not so far gone very far within the bureaucracy — civil servants talk of keeping ministers honest and committed to social change. Insofar as this charge is true it raises the question of why a party leadership that is busy following its acquisitive instincts should even bother to make life difficult for itself in the first place. For structural determinists like Astrow, the answer would have to be that it is a cynical piece of deception. Other answers must draw attention to the extent to which there might be different tendencies within this broad class.

When we pursue this question, the first doubt is as to whether the petty bourgeoisie is indeed a class, in the sense that substantial elements of it, and not just sub-sections like the ZNFU, share a clear consciousness and are all bent on using state power to transform themselves into a bourgeoisie. Rather they may be best described still as a class in formation with as yet unclarified interests and goals. In addition, there are cleavages among this set of strata. In part they are ideological. There are some people, especially in government and party, and among intellectuals, who while sharing this same background see themselves as a progressive element among the petty bourgeoisie that is not only more genuinely committed to the socialist rhetoric but which attempts to contest the terrain of ideology, and also of policy formulation and implementation concerning such matters as land reform, planning and industrial relations. On some issues the 'Marxist' formulae might win support from other sections of the bureaucracy whose interests, rather than their ideological commitment, makes them pursue statist solutions to issues and generally to wish to expand the role of the state, and thus the opportunities within it — a phenomenon not unknown in other states where the internalization of 'Marxism' is more extensive. Thus in Zimbabwe, among bureaucrats there is little support for privatizing land in the Communal Areas along the lines attempted in Kenya, and by the 1951 Land Husbandry Act in Rhodesia, rather there is a preference for some leasehold use of land by families that is conditional upon state-imposed rules of 'proper husbandry'. Whether there is a consciously worked out alternative programme for implementing some programme of social transformation that would operationalize the official 'Marxism– Leninism' is doubtful however — partly because this progressive element consists of a vague intellectual tendency rather than any organized group. But certainly the contestation between these various ideological tendencies will be significant in determining how far in the next few years those among the petty bourgeoisie who are close to the state strike out to join a national bourgeoisie — although it will be the involvement of other class forces that ultimately will be decisive in shaping the actual direction.

The petty bourgeoisie is also fragmented along lines other than those of ideology. If there is doubt over how far there is any kind of left strategy emanating from progressive intellectuals of this class, there must also be considerable doubt as to how far the self-interest of the class as a whole is given any coherent, broader perspective in terms of some outline of a rightist development strategy. All too often members of this class, especially those with influence, are caught up in more limited ambitions to acquire wealth, but also more political influence — both for its own sake but, crucially, also because it can be the avenue for accumulation. And this pursuit of personal status in these recent years of vast, new openings leads to competition and conflict — Mandaza is correct in seeing the prevalence of factional infighting in this recent period — played out through a form of clientelist politics where alliances are formed between operators, each seeking to build up a particularist base of support. The political ambitions of these 'barons' becomes equated with job and business and land opportunities for key followers, and with services and projects for their localities. This has lead to divisions in the political realm not only between the majority Shona and Ndebele–Kalanga, the fault line that fuelled the ZANU– ZAPU cleavage, but also between the factions within ZANU based on the Shona- speaking 'tribes' — the Karanga, Manyika, Zezuru, Korekore, etc. — divisions which Ranger (1985b) correctly points out have been 'created': initially as part of the missionaries' and colonial state's 'divide-and-rule' policies, but more recently by typical petty-bourgeois politicking.

The Working Class

The settler-colonial experience of Rhodesia shaped the structure and character of the working class in Zimbabwe in a number of distinctive ways. The white regime, like others in Africa, fostered racial barriers to various avenues for social mobility of blacks and generated an essentially migrant class of worker-peasants. The specifically Rhodesian pattern differed from that in neighbouring South Africa only in that white immigration was later and more limited, so there were no white 'peasants' nor 'poor whites', but it also differed from that in Kenya, which had so few settlers that there were virtually no white workers. In Rhodesia, white workers were recruited for the mines initially, and then for other enterprises and to run the infrastructure. They occupied the skilled, the white-collar and the professional slots, although they increasingly protected their privileged status as compared with black workers by an often artificial definition of the jobs they performed as 'skilled' — a pattern that was formalized by 'job reservation'.

Several consequences stemmed from this 'two-tier' structure of the labour force. First, the white train-drivers, mine foremen, foundry workers and chief clerks organized themselves to retain an economic and social status of privilege, to match their political weight. They occupied spacious bungalows in the vast white suburbs, employed black servants and belonged to clubs which were similar if not the same as those for white businessmen and senior officials. Their social and political attitudes were if anything more racist than those of other whites cushioned by property from direct black competition. Many of these have left Zimbabwe, and their political influence is now negligible, but a legacy remains in the style of some of the older trade unions that were originally white, and even in the actual hierarchy of some unions. Yet more intractable problems survive in the job and pay structures and the substantial houses, with the standard of living they demand for their up-keep and into which the black inheritors of white-collar and skilled jobs have moved. The pattern of income distribution even among wage and salary earners is still remarkably skewed — the lowest paid 40 per cent of the labour force receives only 15 per cent of total incomes. Included in this lower-paid segment are domestic servants, a group whose large size (still about 100,000) is a further consequence of the sharing of white workers in the privileged settler life.

A second consequence of a white, upper stratum of the working class (and of the middle classes), and one that was recruited in part through immigration, was that technical training of all forms was provided at a level far less than the relatively developed economy required, and such training as was later provided was heavily oriented towards young whites. There were, as a result, relatively few trained black skilled workers and technicians but, paradoxically, because of 'job reservation', an underutilization of the capacity of those blacks who had received education and training or the many who had acquired practical skills on the job. These latter were able to replace those whites who left in a relatively smooth manner. But although formal education has expanded rapidly, it is still too academically-orientated and weak in technical training.

The actual structure of the labour force that resulted from the specific characteristics of settler society and the shape of its economy was one where the number in wage employment, about a million, was in fact a higher proportion of the total population (15 per cent at its peak in 1975), than in most African countries. The effect of the exodus of some whites, especially from agriculture, combined with the uneven and modest growth of the economy since 1980 has meant that the overall figure has remained almost static — although the composition has changed, with permanent agricultural labourers declining from 350,000 in 1975 to 260,000 in 1985 (there has been a partly compensating increase in low-paid casual work, mainly by women). Of the other three-quarters of the labour force, domestic servants still make up a substantial number, about 100,000. They and the agricultural workers have the lowest level of minimum wages allowed for under the post-independence legislation and they are poorly unionized. A good proportion of these poorly paid workers in fact originate from Mozambique and Malawi, and although many have been absorbed as Zimbabweans and few could be considered migrant workers, their less secure status further curbs any tendency towards militancy. But 'industrial workers' in the broadest sense (including mining, power and transport) make up a significant segment, some 300,000. Many of these latter have been unionized, however. There are also about another quarter of a million workers employed by government, including the education and health sectors. Only the teachers' union has been significant as an organized entity among the public service unions.

The first trade-union activity began in the 1920s and had a significant impact on worker and nationalist consciousness, but that was curbed by repression and by the legislative provisions of the Industrial Conciliation Act of 1934, which (although amended in 1959) was not superseded until 1985. It controlled all black trade unionism, explicitly making it apolitical. However, struggles from the 1950s to the 1970s did build up some union membership, which, even if it was only tenuously linked to the growing nationalist political movement, did win some formal recognition for an economic role in the institutionalized framework for wage negotiation. So by independence, there was some union representation, mainly for semi-skilled and skilled industrial workers, with some formal status for itself and some welfare and wage benefits for its members (Sachikonye, 1986).

It is clear that the nationalist movement was organized among professionals, teachers and the emerging black middle class and only to a limited extent had roots in the urban working class — or, even less among labourers in white commercial agriculture. Its radicalism was, however, fed by rural resentments in the 1950s and the people's war of the 1970s was certainly based in the countryside; the rural people were relied upon for support in many areas and in return were given political education and mobilized. In contrast, apart from a dramatic attack on the oil refinery in Harare in the latter days of the war, there was almost no overt guerrilla or other action in the towns. This apparent quiescence of the black urban population has been put down to the limited strength of the organized unions and the partial, trade-union consciousness that it bred. It it used by other analysts, who are Marxist purists like Astrow (1983), as a measure of how far the nationalist movement was 'petty bourgeois' in character and 'populist' in orientation. In fact, the quiescence was in part only apparent. Some workers did participate or give support to the nationalist struggle, but often clandestinely. Many also shared in the political education — but at weekends when they were at home in the rural areas, for it must not be forgotten that the category of 'workers' is not exclusive in Zimbabwe; they are members of the same families as the dwellers in the CAs. Their consciousness is ambiguous (Cheater, 1988), that of worker-peasants, complex, but not by definition any the less radical. The ease with which the

Rhodesian security could impose repression in the towns, and in the isolated and encircled dormitory 'townships' where the workers lived, was in fact so much greater than in the countryside — and this further accounts for the lack of explicit actions or even demonstrations.

In fact, there was a great upsurge of worker militancy in the months immediately after independence. Beginning within days of the election of the new government in March 1980 and continuing to June, a 'contagious rash of strikes', in Sachikonye's phrase, broke out in enterprise after enterprise — mines, farms, factories, hotels; in private concerns, multi-nationally-owned firms, local companies. One explanation of these outbreaks was precisely that it was a pre-emptive set of not very clearly articulated demands for a new deal, demands that attempted to short-circuit the slow and cumbersome machinery of disputes and claims under the old, repressive settler-state mechanisms. The demands were for an immediate betterment in wage levels that were pitifully low — if they were supposed to maintain a family. Partly because of the low wages many workers' families supplemented their incomes on a family holding, or lived with relatives in the rural areas — a structure that in turn maintained the low wages. A careful study of the almost 200 strikes that occurred in 1980 and 1981, shows that they were mainly concerned with immediate economic issues such as pay and working conditions but many also involved demands for dismissal of abusive and racist managers and reinstatement of dismissed militant workers (Sachikonye, 1986). They thus to that extent challenged the basic character of the type of capital–labour relationship and the wage-negotiating machinery that characterized colonial Rhodesia. They represented a challenge by workers in however an incoherent and unorganized form – to capital if not to capitalism.

The character of the working class, the forms and level of its consciousness, and the extent of its links with and differences from the rural population are all related to the particular patterns of urbanization. The racist policies of white Rhodesia were centred around restrictions on the black urban population. The towns were in fact designated as white areas, which meant that blacks could not own property there or live there without some kind of permission. Segregated black townships were allowed and later required by law, but it was not until 1960 that these were no longer classified as 'European', allowing blacks to own land in them for the first time — and even that measure was reversed, like so many other matters, by the RF government in 1969.

The efforts of the Rhodesian state had been not only to restrict the black urban population geographically but to restrict the numbers to those who were employed and whose presence was 'required'. Thus 'pass laws' were in operation until 1960, restricting the influx of families in particular; most urban housing was for single males — at least until the policies of the Garfield Todd government began to envisage a 'housed and settled' black urban population after the 1951 Land Husbandry Act had generated landlessness and pressure of movement to the towns. Despite these moves, however, restrictions on movement were such that the relative proportion of the black population that was urbanized actually fell slightly in the 1960s — a pattern that was totally at odds with patterns everywhere else, even South Africa.

By 1970 only some 20 per cent of the black population was living in urban areas, and they were overwhelmingly in 'townships' — vast areas of basically adequate housing though barrack-like in character and quite separate from the commercial centres and the extensive, luxurious white suburbs. Despite that, the urban population was becoming more settled — a third were born in town, and more were with wives and families than as single adult males — and thus, for a proportion, ties with the rural communities were becoming less close. The size of the urban population and consequent overcrowding grew very rapidly during the later stages of the war that so affected the countryside. But how far anticipated return to the village has in fact occurred must be open to doubt, for independence not only meant the return of peace to the countryside but also an end to those various administrative restrictions that restricted urban housing and the black urban dwellers to those authorized to be there. What persists, however, are that as well as a genuinely urbanized element of the working class, many workers and would-be workers retain rural ties — they have their family there or at least some of the school-age children, retain a plot of land or some livestock, and aim to retire there. What also persists is an urban spatial pattern that owes much to apartheid-style town planning and which reinforces divisions and consciousness, even if the purely racial character of those segregated suburbs has been modified and is now more a matter of class.

In a contemporary context of greater urbanization, of few restrictions on people staying in towns but also of increased land pressures only slightly relieved by resettlement and slow growth of employment, the problems of unemployment (as opposed to its disguised form of rural underemployment) is becoming more manifest. The 1982 Census recorded some 268,000 'unemployed', all apparently in urban areas, representing 10.8 per cent of the total labour force; the actual number, especially if rural areas are added in, was likely to be much greater. Since then the massive expansion of education, especially at a secondary level, has begun to produce numbers of school-leavers far greater than can be absorbed into wage employment — to the extent that it has become a grave concern of government. In his budget speech in July 1988, the finance minister, Bernard Chidzero, estimated that there were some 900,000 unemployed, or 30 per cent of the total labour force.

The Peasantry

There is nothing 'traditional' any longer about the peasant population and most of it could not be classed as 'subsistence producers', which is how the outside world thinks of African rural dwellers; many of them do not grow enough for their own subsistence; a few are market-oriented, and almost all have sources of income outside farming. In fact, African peasants began to produce for the market in the first decades of colonial rule, when the whites were still looking for gold and regularly bought grain and meat. The heyday for the peasants was also realized very early, in the first years of this century. As noted in the history of settlerdom, thereafter they were moved off the best land, gradually excluded from the market, by discriminatory price and transport arrangements, and then starved of most of the technical improvements and credit that became available after 1945. Riddell (1978) argues that real incomes from farming in the TTLs in fact went down from 1948 to 1970 by a total of 40 per cent. This was the result of the combined effect of land pressures in land areas that remained finite during this period, overcultivation and overgrazing of land and thus its degradation.

Since 1980 this pattern of impoverishment has, as we shall see, dramatically shifted in aggregate terms. The more widespread provision of credit, extension services and inputs, fairer prices and market services have led to great increases in the proportion of grain and cotton crops purchased by the marketing boards from the Communal Areas (the new name for TTLs). But absolute levels of income from farming are still not high and large pockets of poverty and inequality persist. In order to see the present condition of this peasantry a sketch of farming patterns found in different parts of the country is first required. African farming is a smallholder system based on the family. Following the introduction of the plough, almost all CAs, except some of the lowlands along the north and south borders, cultivate with oxen. The main crops are maize and imported crop for which there is a ready market, but which does not survive the drier years in the poorer ecological regions as well as indigenous sorghum and millet. Livestock are a crucial stand for farmers in drier areas like much of Matabeleland and the south of Mashonaland, and they provide the power for agriculture — but also they require extensive areas of grazing land, which usually consist of designated 'commons'.

The differentiation in landholding has partly been held in check by the partial institutionalization of traditions of allocating land to those who need it, especially new families — but often only at the expense of the common grazing. But there are significant and growing proportions of landless rural households — averaging from 6 to 11 per cent in the different provinces according to a 1983 Government survey (ZNHSCP, 1984). But probably half of all households have below 5 hectares — what is regarded in the resettlement schemes as the amount of arable land needed to give a family income approaching the minimum agricultural wage. But the distribution of livestock is even more skewed. Over 40 per cent of rural households have no cattle of their own — and thus not only do they have no other source of income or food, but also they are reliant on borrowing or hiring from others to get their ploughing done. Surveys show that farm income of those with draught animals is often twice that of other farmers who may have higher costs if they hire and also cannot ensure timely planting.

Another source of inequality is, paradoxically in circumstances of land shortage, a shortage of labour (especially in crucial seasons of planting and harvesting) on the part of households with most of their labour force absent working for wages elsewhere. Those migrants who are earning reasonable wages can repair this gap by hiring labourers, but for the poorest families with low earnings this is not possible — and indeed they may be faced with the hard choice between making themselves available as seasonal labour and working their own plots at the critical seasons. Those households referred to as 'women-headed' are among those most likely to face this kind of predicament and their situation will be discussed in the following section.

In fact the most significant indicator in distinguishing rich and poor in the rural areas is neither land nor cattle but the size of existing and past remittances of members of the household in paid employment. A large proportion of households will have one or more members working for wages, usually away from home — some commuting, some returning at weekends from nearby towns or mines, others staying for longer periods farther afield. Over a third of all households reported receiving remittances in the Household Survey (ZNHSCP, 1984) — but this may well be a case of *under-reporting*. Over a period most males will have been involved in migrant labour at some point in their lives.

The reliance on off-farm incomes is sometimes taken as simply evidence of, and a solution to, the inadequacy of the farm system and land holdings to yield sufficient income. But over the years of institutionalized migration, of 'split families' with dependents staying in the rural areas, interconnections between employment and farming are manifold and complex. The holding represents a means for supporting, however partially, the other household members; it offers the security of social insurance against unemployment, sickness, old age. But also over the years, the remittances, other earnings and savings have in turn had an effect on rural society. They have been the main source of such equipment and improvements as have been introduced — ploughs, scotch-carts, fencing. Even today when credit is now more readily available, it is still quite usual for fertilizer, seed and other inputs to be purchased by wage earners and be brought back to the district. Given the fact that off-farm incomes not only help people survive but contribute positively to accumulation in agriculture, and given that minimum wages and social welfare facilities do not yet guarantee survival of whole families, plans (like the Riddell Commission) for inducing an end to what is called 'part-time' farming and forcing people to opt for either job or land are premature, unnecessary, unrealistic and also unworkable. (On this issue, see Bush and Cliffe, 1984.) The fact of regular receipt of remittances from migrant labour or other earnings from jobs or trade, or their absence, and their size, tend to be correlated with the availability of livestock, of equipment, availability of inputs and even size of holding — but with the off-farm income being the better determinant of both living standards and farming opportunities.

Rural communities can in fact be categorized on the basis of their life-chances and the survival strategies available to them in terms of various 'clusters': those with relatively secure, well-paid, often white-collar jobs (e.g. teachers), who tend to have the most farm assets. They are quite distinct from other families who receive much more modest remittances, and from full-time farmers. Then there is another group, largely made up of women heads of household and their dependants, who have no access to outside earnings and very few farm resources (small plots, no livestock, no inputs) and for whom labour is also a scarce commodity.

Perhaps we can synthesize these and other investigations by saying that rural society may consist of five categories and sub-categories, distinguishable on grounds of both farming capabilities and external incomes, as follows:

— those who live off outside incomes and so do not farm much;
— those with no income and few farm resources or labour;

(both of these may 'own' plots that are not cultivated fully, but the needs of the two are quite different)

— those who have high external incomes and more substantial farms;
— those less well-off peasants   — with some family members
                                                        doing low paid-jobs;
                                             — without jobs.

Their different circumstances will also dictate certain structural relations of dependence and exploitation between them. Their differing interests and claims will have to be taken into account in shaping policies to meet their needs.

The Special Position of Women

In exploring the basic social structure it is important to look at the gender dimension and see how it interrelates with the class and race dimensions. It is also important to understand the position of women as a backdrop, assessing how far it has been or may be changed as part of any programme of social transformation.

In fact, women were actively involved in the liberation struggle. There were some fighters; there were many others who joined the nationalist movement in exile working as teachers, administrators, etc. In the villages the young girls, *chimbwidos,* played a key role as the eyes and ears of the guerrillas as well as performing more domestic tasks. And the majority of the peasant population that was mobilized for supporting roles were women. There was an expectation therefore that independence would bring women a change in their status.

Certainly there have been significant enactments to improve their legal position. In the realm of 'family law', women have guaranteed rights of maintenance of their children, whether married, divorced or born out of wedlock. They, and not their in-laws, are due a share of conjugal property on divorce or when widowed. Most crucially, and affecting all areas of law, the Legal Age of Majority Act of 1982 means that a woman on reaching 18 is no longer a minor, as she was regarded under the institutionalizing of customary law in the colonial period. In relation to employment and other things affecting women's economic status, equal pay and equal access to all positions are guaranteed by law. Women have also benefited from the minimum wage legislation, especially in areas like domestic service and agriculture, where they have provided a large share of the poorest paid workers.

To understand the significance of these changes, however, it is necessary to look at the conditions governing women's status in the past. The key to understanding is the institution of marriage, as the form it took reflected much in the whole network of kinship relations and practices, and the position of women within the household and the community. Marriage was in fact an exchange between households and kin groups: the young woman from one lineage became a member of another, which now had her labour and her reproductive power available to them. As a seal on this exchange the groom's lineage contributed bridewealth — what was called *roora* in Shona society and *lobola* in southern Africa more generally — usually in the form of cattle. It was the elders of the lineage, who controlled cattle, that negotiated and guaranteed these exchanges, and in turn regulated and controlled the new wife, her labour and her children but in some measure offered some protection — against a husband who was too violent, demanded too much work of his wife, made her pregnant too soon after the last birth, or initiated divorce. There was by the same mechanisms some control over the younger men of a lineage by elders, who controlled land as well as livestock, marriage and behaviour. Women had access to use of land and thus a livelihood for her children and a partially protected position, though as a 'minor' and dependant, within such framework — but not outside it. On divorce she left the lineage, and her children; when widowed the land and her husband's property reverted to the lineage — as she did often, to be looked after by a husband's brother.

Some of this structure was eroded under colonial rule. The settler state institutionalized what it wanted and understood of 'customary law', and often intervened in fact to prop up the power of elders and chiefs over women, young men and land. However, despite these efforts to resist change, the onset of capitalist wage and property relations and especially the prevalence of migrant labour altered lineage and household structures. Young men could, and were encouraged to, earn money by going away to work and thus became more independent of lineages and elders; *roora/lobola* came to have a monetary form and rather than disappearing, often became inflated. Men could set up a homestead and a household more on their own — and often a long way from the wife's in-laws because of land scarcity. Wives were thus a degree more independent but for them any benefits were often outweighed by the lessening of protection from the lineage. Their long-term security was more in the balance as husbands' divorce or separation initiatives were less constrained — and also more likely given their long absences. Marriage became more a transaction between a husband and the wife's father, and more of a commercial transaction — but that very access to money that gave the husband independence from his elders gave him power over his wife, as long as and to the degree that she had no other access to cash, the commodity which was becoming increasingly crucial to survival (much of this paragraph derives from Pankhurst, 1988).

The status of women generally showed some tendency to worsen under colonialism, but the actual position of women varied — depending, not surprisingly, on the different households and their economic position, especially their access to some part of cash earnings as well as other resources. Thus even within the rural areas, and within a context where almost all households would have male labour absent for some periods, and where consequently women had a much increased burden within the household division of labour, a household where reasonable earnings were being made and were actually being remitted back home would be able to hire to overcome labour bottlenecks, and, if in turn they had adequate land to make hiring labour worthwhile, there would be adequate food and some relief to the women's burden. Households with less land and meagre remittances would find extra labour was neither available nor profitable and would have difficulty making ends meet. But at the bottom of the scale today can be found those households that are 'women headed'; the bond that secured male labour and remittances is, for one of several reasons, severed. These households have been found to be as much as 20 per cent of all households in some communities. The women in them have an enormous burden of domestic, child-rearing and agricultural work, and often have the smallest holdings, may well not own or have access to oxen for ploughing and have no money to hire them. At the same time their need for cash for necessities, and for food for their families because they have neither enough land nor time to provide their own subsistence, drives them to find time in their overburdened lives to earn cash — by brewing, prostitution, casual labour, etc. For these households, there is no obviously available antidote to their poverty, even through land reform or job-creating rural public works programmes.

Given some of the circumstances facing them, it was not surprising that women were involved in the liberation struggles — although even that may have been beyond the time and resources of these poorest groups mentioned above. Their hopes of dramatic improvements in their conditions were in fact restricted, as were other prospects for social change, by provisions of the Lancaster House constitution. Although the usual fundamental rights to be treated equally under the law were enshrined in the document, specific exception was made to family law and customary law. It is some measure of the commitment of the Mugabe government to gender equality that the various enactments listed earlier in this chapter have in fact been passed in an effort to circumvent the conservative restrictions imposed by the British–drafted constitution.

However, the implementation of many of the measures enacted has been far from automatic. Thus, although widows and other women on their own are entitled to be allocated land in the resettlement exercise, the pressure from male relatives has often inhibited them from applying. Women are supposedly free to make their own marriage contracts, and thus it is up to them whether their father negotiates for *lobola*, but the practice is different. In a survey of marriages in Harare, only 5 per cent were registered without bridewealth payments. Minimum wages theoretically protect women in the poorest-paid jobs, but in practice they have often meant a loss of jobs or the hiring of men in preference, or the acceptance of wages below the legal minimum for fear of dismissal. Nor has the party and government been unambiguous in their efforts to promote improved status for women, even though there are a few women in the Central Committee of ZANU, Parliament and even two in the Cabinet. Male dominance is only ceded with great reluctance. When the Legal Age of Majority Act's implications were underlined by a court of appeal judgment that a young woman had the right to sue for seduction damages (perhaps the most prevalent type of case brought to customary courts), the male response was a 'general uproar' (see Kazembe, 1986 p. 391 for this and other information here). The Act itself has been blamed, using an ideological appeal to puritanism, by fathers faced with losing *lobola*, husbands and would-be seducers, for ushering in loose living, and even for the cases of baby dumping that have been brandished about by the media. The most glaring official outburst of this kind of male attempt to reimpose restrictions on women by puritanical appeals was the round-ups and 'repatriation' in 1983–4 of hundreds of women found in public places in the city on their own who were dubbed 'prostitutes'. Fortunately, the outcry of protests from women's groups was substantial enough for

Mugabe to intervene to call a halt to this action and to apologize, although some women remained in 're-education' camps for some months.

Part III
The Political System

6   Party and State

Organizational Structure of the Party: Its Origins and Present Form

At the central level and in formal terms, the story of the evolution of ZANU's structure is simple. There have only ever been two general party Congresses: the founding one in 1963 which brought together people who had split off from ZAPU and chose the first central committee, and the second in 1984 which consolidated and amended the structures of what was by then a ruling party in an independent country. There has recently followed an important extraordinary Congress of ZANU to approve the unity agreement with ZAPU, but which in formal terms merely expanded the central committee. However, the actual operating structures and personnel have undergone many and varied changes in this period.

The original central committee chosen in 1963 consisted of five officers, with the Reverend Ndabaningi Sithole as president and leader, and including Robert Mugabe as secretary general (as he is officially to this day), Enos Nkala as Treasurer (now secretary for Finance), plus four other committee members (of whom Enos Chikowore and Morton Malianga are still in leadership positions), and six 'under-secretaries' of whom three are still prominent. Most of this central committee were detained (along with Nkomo and most ZAPU leaders) in 1964 and only released in 1974 or later. Two of the key figures are dead — Takawira (the original vice-president) and Herbert Chitepo (the national chairman) both in controversial circumstances but almost certainly killed by the Rhodesian regime. But before his death Chitepo, in exile in Zambia, set up a committee to run the party and prosecute the armed struggle, called the Dare. That body included some central committee members also in Zambia, although there were others like Enos Chikowore, Nathan Shamuyarira and Eddison Zvobgo who were in more distant exile, working for the party but not in the Dare. The membership of the Dare was reconstituted following elections (presumably by guerrillas and cadres) in 1972 to include Josiah Tongogara, who had received military training in China and become the military commander, and two younger militants returned from studies abroad. These changes were seen as giving what was the *de facto* operating leadership a more radical edge, in line with the adoption of more militant, politically-oriented guerrilla tactics of people's war. Although, as we shall see below, the changes in the Dare have been interpreted as more to do with the party's factionalism. There was then a break in leadership continuity in 1975 when the Dare and most active fighters and cadres were detained for eighteen months in Zambia, and after the resulting winding down of the armed struggle the young guerrilla commanders of the ZIPA group picked up the baton. Meanwhile, and unknown to the outside world, the detained central committee members had rejected Sithole's leadership after he had publicly rejected the armed struggle (according to one report by the Rhodesian prison chaplain, as a way of saving his neck after he was charged with plotting Ian Smith's assassination; see Smith and Simpson, 1981). However, when he and the other detained leaders were released in 1974 as part of a *détente*-exercise involving South Africa, the Front Line States (FLS) and Western governments, the FLS would not accept Mugabe or others in his place. So then, for two years, while ZIPA commanders kept something of ZANLA together as a viable fighting force, and formed a military alliance for a time with some like-minded ZIPRA commanders, the formal party machinery went through a period of flux. Sithole was reinstated by the FLS and agreed to a shot-gun marriage with other groups in a new African National Council. This included Nkomo's ZAPU, the short-lived FROLIZI which had tried, with Shamuyarira among others, to supersede the two older liberation movements in exile, and the internal umbrella organization under Muzorewa. This organization broke up after two unhappy years. Apart from Sithole, individual central committee members who were now released but still inside Rhodesia were somewhat free-floating until Mugabe and Edgar Tekere went underground and left the country. With the renewal and rapid build-up of the armed struggle in late 1975 and 1976, political leaders of various former organizations were now scurrying about trying to get themselves accredited by the guerrillas and/or the FLS. Nkomo, whose readiness to talk to Smith had precipitated conflicts and the final break-up between ZANLA and ZIPRA elements in ZIPA, was able to reimpose his dominance over a reconstituted ZAPU, including both ZIPRA and the branches inside the country that had been set up during its longer preexistence in the 1950s and 1960s and maintained some shadowy existence.

ZANU was effectively reconstituted as a movement in 1977, when for the first time different 'generations' of leaders and of structures were all free to take a practical hand in the organization. These consisted of Mugabe and Muzenda representing the old central committee, which also included Nyagumbo who was still detained, and Nkala and others still in Rhodesia. The former were the only two old-guard politicians who had gained acceptance by both the two other key elements, the guerrillas of ZIPA, and the Dare members, once detained in Zambia but by then released. But also involved at that time were other old central committee members and activists who had been in more distant exile, often as practising professionals or students, who now came to Mozambique to associate themselves more actively with a new movement, which was clearly on the road to power. The new operating leadership included an amalgam of some individuals from all these groups — but it was only reconstituted after struggles in which most of the ZIPA and some of the former Dare members were expelled — struggles which, as in the early 1970s, were only resolved in favour of the victors by the intervention of the FLS, most notably in this period, Mozambique and Tanzania. (The legacy of these several struggles will be considered below.)

The new leadership was an alliance of forces pivoted around Mugabe, and those identified with the old central committee, on the one hand, and Tongogara and military commanders like Nhongo and Tungamirai (now heads of the army and air force respectively). This leadership group were able first to command the loyalty and then gradually able to exert command over the guerrillas not identified with ZIPA and the huge flood of new recruits. They were also able to build up in the 1977–9 period an administration that could handle information, the international, diplomatic and public relations tasks, education and health and other services for the fighters, trainees and the vast flood of youngsters who flocked over to Mozambique — bringing in for these tasks old activists like Shamuyarira and Zvobgo (both in exile in academic posts), and younger, professionally trained people who had been active in ZANU's international support activities, like present ministers Ushewokunze, then a doctor in Birmingham, Mutumbuka, Mubako and Fay Chung (academics in Zambia).

It was this new leadership coalition plus the administrative apparatus and the ZANLA top echelons that constituted the central organs of the ZANU party that 'came out of the cold' and back into Zimbabwe to fight the eve of independence elections in 1980. ZAPU also brought back a not dissimilar set-up, but one where the leader, Nkomo, could assert himself without too much worry about acceptance (despite ideological differences within the movement), and where the ZIPRA cadres were far fewer, were less-politicized, but better trained in a conventional military sense.

Commentators at the time rightly spoke of ZIPRA as a 'professional army'. The same, unchallenged leader plus the shadowy persistence of local branch networks, at least where they had been reactivated in Matabeleland during the last stages of the war, perhaps gave ZAPU more continuity on the ground. However ZANU was not starting from scratch in its efforts to build up a national structure. It had besides the central organs, but symbolically identified with them rather than organizationally integrated, the 'people's committees', which operated effectively at the grass roots level during the war throughout the rural areas of Masvingo, Manicaland, Mashonaland East and Central Provinces, and in parts of Midlands, Mashonaland West and even a pocket of Matabeleland South. There was even a hierarchical network linking village people's committees to a branch level and in turn to a 'district' committee, but the observations of one of the authors at the time suggest that this 'district' level referred to a much lower level unit than the districts which formed the few sub-divisions of a province in the country's administrative framework and which were also to become the basis for local government units. So as the parties both set up national headquarters and an electoral machine at the centre and offices at provincial and district level, there was a difficulty, partly geographical, partly of political style, in linking these new structures reaching down from Harare, to the formerly clandestine networks. These of necessity had had to be very local, had not easily developed communications over large areas, and insofar as they had, had done so from the bottom up.

The mere identification with a party label and leadership sufficed in the 1980 elections to give ZANU a walk-over in almost all the areas mentioned above where there had been these grass-roots networks. The task of bridging the gap between that level and the centre as part of a restructuring of the party, got under way, but only slowly, after the formation of a government, the setting up of a local government structure and local government elections, and the consolidation of the independence regime. A framework of provincial, district, and branch organs was spelled out on paper, and each of these organs was to elect officers and, crucially, delegates to the second Congress. The setting up of this structure and the choosing of delegates was under way for almost two years before the ZANU Congress was held in 1984, with some 6,000 delegates chosen from the provinces through the lower level networks.

The Congress approved a new party constitution which provided for much broader-based central organizations — a Central Committee enlarged to ninety from the twenty-six that had come into existence through co-options in Mozambique and after independence, and which was the main decision-making body in between meetings of the Congress, but with a fourteen-person Political Bureau that would deal with all regular party matters. This Political Bureau is appointed by the party's presidential commission — the party president (and secretary general), Robert Mugabe and its deputy president and vice secretary-general, Simon Muzenda — now supplemented, presumably, by the second deputy president and vice secretary-general, Joshua Nkomo — and consists of the Central Committee's officers — the secretaries for finance, administration, information, youth and women plus five other members. Each of the latter is in turn the head of a party commissariat dealing with various policy areas — foreign affairs, national security, production and development, transport and welfare, culture.

Party–State Relations

Apart from these measures to restructure the party at all levels, the 1984 Congress also proclaimed the supremacy of the party over government bodies in outlining the main directions of policy — in this and other respects presaging a one-party state. To this end it appointed five standing committees whose job would be to oversee government policy in particular areas (corresponding roughly to the commissariats) — political and policy, the economy, legal and constitutional, social and welfare, national security. However, the extent to which there has been detailed supervision, or indeed even coincidence between party principles and policies and actions of government, must be open to question. In fact, Mugabe's introductory speech at the 1988 unity Congress admitted that the objective whereby the political bureau would 'superintend, supervise and administer all government ministries in accordance with the policies and programmes of the party ... has not been achieved', although he reasserted his commitment to it and felt that 'we haven't far to go'. Whether effective oversight is in fact close must be open to some doubt, as the mechanisms set up provide little *independent* grasp on the specifics of policy matters. The committees are themselves made up of ministers, and what one observer described as 'old faithfuls' and are thus not likely to promote a line very different from or critical of government departments. Although it must be admitted they have shown themselves capable of at least articulating a more radical position than that of government. The manifesto for the 1985 election offered a relatively detailed set of policy guidelines as well as a review of previous achievements, which, in an area like its call for agrarian reform for instance, was proposing measures in advance of what government ministries before or since have been prepared to contemplate. But this example also illustrates the limited extent of that closeness of oversight and ability to impose sanctions necessary to achieve the compliance of ministries. This limitation may owe as much to the fact that the committees, of ministers and other officials, are busy people with little time to devote to such extra study and monitoring. Nor can they rely, in these party functions, on an alternative source of expertise or of bureaucratic skills, given the very limited capacity of the party's secretariat. Some possibility of change in these regards might be expected following the new composition of the 'unity' government in January 1988 which included two vigorous, but controversial, former cabinet ministers, Herbert Ushewokunze (who also claims radical credentials) and Eddison Zvobgo. They were given positions without portfolio in the president's office, but they are also charged with specific party roles. How far these measures were designed to strengthen the party, or to remove awkward trouble-makers from government, will be proved in the practice.

Another measure of the 1984 Congress had potential for ensuring greater socialist commitment, at least in the negative sense of trying to prevent the drift of those in power towards establishing themselves as part of the bourgeoisie and thus with an interest in maintaining the existing socio-economic order. A 'leadership code' was drawn up which sought to prevent party leaders — ex-members of the central committee, and of provincial, district and branch executives — and government officials — ministers, provincial governors, army officers and senior civil servants — from owning businesses, receiving more than one salary, or income from rented property, or from owning more that fifty acres of agricultural land. These measures were taken in a context of public grumbles and scandals about the personal aggrandizement of politicians: there were demonstrations by women and students in 1983 against 'corruption'; and Mugabe himself criticized unnamed ministers for their 'bourgeois' proclivities in early 1984. Indeed there is a feeling among some Zimbabwe analysts that the code closing these openings came after the horse had already bolted. The 1988 unity Congress was in fact charged by Mugabe with reaffirming the code — perhaps more necessary given the reputed property holdings of Nkomo and his colleagues — and seeing how it could 'operate more effectively', suggesting that even the requirement that leaders make periodic statements of their assets was not enough to ensure compliance.

Leaders and Factions

The effect of these changes at the second party Congress clearly strengthened Mugabe's hand. He had always been general secretary but not officially leader of the party, until his replacement of Sithole in 1974. Even then this change was made by a small inner group of fellow-prisoners, and neither was it known that he had become leader for some time, nor was it recognized by neighbouring states. He came in practice to his eventual position of prominence through gradually winning the approval of guerrilla fighters who were suspicious of most of the prominent position holders, but he had to establish and maintain his position after 1976 with the help of alliances and in the teeth of leadership conflicts between 'generations'. There was a sense, even after independence, in which he was simply the foremost of a group, at the head but not necessarily in total command of a party that contained many elements, and his situation depended on continued approval. Mugabe's situation was for long in marked contrast to the uncontested position and dominating practice that Nkomo had been able to assert in ZAPU. The Congress formalized the greater authority that Mugabe had been slowly acquiring, and in turn rebuffed and constrained some of the challengers of that authority.

The new constitutional arrangements enhanced Mugabe's position first by giving predictably much day-to-day control of party affairs, in the context of a much enlarged and thus unwieldy central committee of ninety members, to the small political bureau that is nominated by the party president, a position that Mugabe holds as well as that of general secretary. A second ploy was that the method of nomination and election of central committee members required each provincial delegation to put forward a panel of forty 'national leaders', ensuring that those who went forward to the run-offs had backing from several provinces. In general this was a way of combating regional factionalism, and specifically it excluded some controversial figures with a single, strong provincial base. One such was former internal affairs minister Zvobgo, who had challenged Mugabe's authority if not his position, not on any identifiable ideological grounds but rather on the basis of personal standing — although he was later on in the Congress found a place on the central committee, probably as a result of some deal.

The nature and content of the leadership contest that has characterized post-independence Zimbabwe has in general not been overtly ideological — with one exception. Herbert Ushewokunze, initially minister of health,

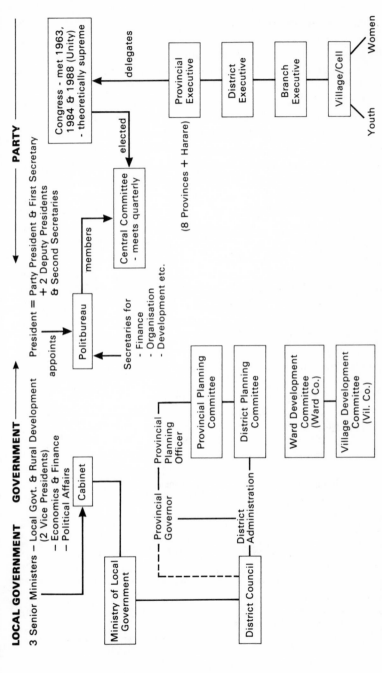

Figure 6.1 Party organisation

later minister of transport, emerged, not on the basis of any overtly Marxist track-record, as something of a radical voice, urging more militant policies, though often of a nationalist as much as a socialist sort and not always well considered. What influence he had was via his public pronouncements (collected, significantly, in a book — Ushewokunze, 1984) for as a ZANU member from Matabeleland, and an MP from that region in 1980, he had little if any local base. In this, his occasionally troublesome outspokenness can be contrasted to the factional politics indulged in by some of the other influential ministers and party leaders. The other key figure excluded from the political bureau at that Congress, and also from the new unity Government of 1988, Zvobgo, epitomized this different pattern. He had built himself a regional basis in Masvingo province in the south, as local party organs and their Congress delegations were chosen in the early 1980s. Among the patterns of patronage he used was that of sanctioning (and not merely turning a blind eye to) squatters occupying land, but only those in his bailiwick. Other figures also made their bids, and competed with each other, for influence in the provincial party networks. Another forceful and controversial figure, Edgar Tekere, who lost his ministerial position as well as his balance, after killing a white farmer, was able to re-emerge to prominence after capturing the chair of ZANU in the province of Manicaland, only to be sacked and to be deprived of party membership in 1988 for his outspoken attacks on the one-party state and corruption in high places.

Table 6.1 The Government of Zimbabwe, January 1988

President	Robert Mugabe
Vice-president	Simon Muzenda
Senior ministers in the president's office:	
without portfolio	Joshua Nkomo
for political affairs	Maurice Nyagumbo
for finance, economic planning and development	Bernard Chidzero
Foreign affairs	Nathan Shamuyarira
Information, posts and telecommunications	Witness Mangwende
Defence	Enos Nkala
Home affairs	Moven Mahachi
Justice, legal and parliamentary affairs	Emmerson Munangagawa
Higher education	Dzingai Mutumbuka

Primary and secondary education	Fay Chung
Industry and technology	Callistus Ndhlovu
Trade and commerce	Oliver Munyaradzi
Transport	Simbarashe Mubengegwi
Mines	Richard Hove
Lands, agriculture and rural resettlement	David Karimanzira
Labour, manpower planning and social welfare	John Nkomo
Public construction and national housing	Joseph Msika
National supplies	Simbi Mubako
Health	Felix Muchemwa
Energy and water resources development	Kumbirai Kangai
Natural resources and tourism	Victoria Chitepo
Youth, sports and culture	David Kwindini
Cooperatives, community development & women's affairs	Teurai Ropa Nhongo
Local government, rural and urban development	Enos Chikowore
Ministers of state in the president's office:	
for national security	Sydney Sekeremayi
for the public service	Chris Anderson
for national scholarships	Joseph Culverwell

Insofar as these influential people offered a challenge to Mugabe it was to his authority rather than through the articulation of an explicitly different programme. However, the tendency for these barons with their local bases to compete with each other at the national level posed several different kinds of difficulties within the party. First, the sustaining of their local base and the furthering of their national standing determined their tactical calculations rather than the furtherance of any coherent strategy. They had to be opportunist and acquisitive to gain the spoils to be able to pass them on, and there were thus in-built tendencies apart from their own personal interests, to corruption and to nepotism. Indeed, in proposing the Leadership Conditions at the Congress, Mugabe was moved to urge delegates 'not to follow the corrupt'. A second effect was that their competition, using, as it did, local support, stirred up a factionalism among leaders and top officials that was supposedly based on the ethnic groups that were identified among the Shona. Zvobgo, and others with whom he competed for support in the south, were seen as representing the Karanga; Shamuyarira and others, the Zezuru; the latter's dialect was also Mugabe's but he seemingly struggled to keep himself above such ethnic factionalism. This in- fighting in turn fed on supposed conflicts that have been seen by some to be behind disruptions in ZANU as far back as 1974–5, leading to the killing of Chitepo. This has been a lasting perception despite a more complex reality in which strategic differences and not ethnic loyalties played the major role, and wherein Chitepo was most probably killed not by the 'other' faction but by a Rhodesian agent (see Martin and Johnson, 1985, and Cliffe, 1976). Nevertheless, the perception of ethnic rivalries has tended to have a defining influence on the whole nature of politics internal to the party, thus necessarily obscuring any strategic, ideological or simply class concerns by a screen of factional fighting for spoils, spoils that could best be generated simply by factional leaders obtaining access to the benefits of the socio-economic status quo. But these tendencies in turn affected the external political stance of the party, particularly in how it handled relations with ZAPU.

There were clearly differences in the ZANU leadership, especially from 1983 until after the 1985 elections, about whether to negotiate a unity or simply to steamroller ZAPU aside by administrative means. There were even some who would have gladly contemplated legislating a one-party state by fiat if it had not been expressly forbidden until 1990 by the constitution. There were certainly those who supported the strong-arm methods of the security forces in Matabeleland with some gusto although clearly others saw these as counterproductive. It may be that unity was finally a result of the combination of alternating this iron fist with a velvet glove of negotiation, although Mugabe did appoint a commission of inquiry into possible excesses in 1984. Even when unity talks got under way after 1986, one reported stumbling block was the fears of some other ZANU leaders of the consequence with respect to their own influence in making way for Nkomo and other ZAPU leaders in cabinet and central committee.

Thus the unity that has been achieved denotes some success in dulling these kinds of factional influences. However, now that it is has occurred it remains to be seen whether the old factions within ZANU and between ZANU and ZAPU continue to be the currency of intra-party politics or whether mobilization behind (and against) some programme now becomes more possible. Certainly, some of the rhetoric for a single party has been couched in the latter terms — and it is this issue we will now examine.

ZANU, ZAPU and One-partyism

The leaders of ZANU have had the creation of a single party in their sights ever since their overwhelming election victory in 1980. What they have disagreed about is *how* to bring it about, and (possibly) what kind of single-party system — whether *de facto* one-party rule, or the enactment of a single-party constitution. They were in fact constrained in the latter regard by the Lancaster House constitution which precluded a one-party system until 1990. Even so, there were probably some in the leadership who would have been prepared to legislate it anyway, find a way round the constitution or at least remove the other parties in practice. There were others, the hot-headed Tekere surprisingly among them, who warned against legislating ZAPU out of existence, but still advocated achieving a one-party state by clean-sweeping the elections. These differences were of course reflected in their shifting and conflicting attitudes towards ZAPU, varying, as we have seen they did, between repression and negotiation. The fact that the unity was finally achieved through agreement rather than over ZAPU resistance will of course be crucial in lessening the authoritarian tendencies inherent in a single-party regime, and will in turn have a defining influence on the working of the party-regime. And ZANU has said it will leave the constitutional provisions to turn their course until 1990.

If there were differences about how a single-party rule was to be obtained, there was near unanimity about that objective. So it is instructive to explore *why* that should be. A useful article by Shaw (1986) does in fact afford a careful scrutiny of the several arguments that have been put forward by party leaders. The list of justifications are, in fact, far more reminiscent of the classical arguments of African nationalism than Marxist discourse. There is an appeal to African 'tradition', which as Shaw points out is a questionable, certainly selective, interpretation of history, and whose relevance as a justification is equally questionable. Other statements that Shaw quotes assert that it is the 'will of the majority', which again, even if empirically provable, is a questionable justification, in democratic theory, for removing personal rights. To which another argument would answer that Western democratic theory is not applicable to Zimbabwean conditions, which is an arguable proposition of course, but one that in the event is couched in terms of the need for an untramelled approach to development (a modernization argument), rather than that it is a bourgeois form. The most common justification, however, is in terms of promoting national unity. So just at the moment when President Nyerere begins to doubt publicly the wisdom of a single-party state, Mugabe cites Tanzania as the example to be followed, where 'one party represents just that concept of unity [that] we really want'. There is no perception here that Tanzania's enviable unity may owe more to its *lingua franca* and to the good fortune of its ethnic multiplicity, wherein no group dominates, rather than to the institutional forms — a significant caution, for elsewhere, as in Zambia or Kenya, a single party has not put an end to ethnic factionalism. Here Shaw questions not only whether a single party is the sole or even the best vehicle to promote integration of a nation, but also wonders 'how the building of nationhood can be part of the proper role of a party which identifies itself as Marxist'? Shaw has a point in so far as he draws attention to the fact that such arguments as are advanced are not those characteristic of a discourse that sanctions the central role of *the* party as a vanguard of the one revolutionary class (or class alliance).

However, there is an answer to his rhetorical question if one goes beyond the logical and ethical precepts that he applies to recognize that the foundations for the institutional form which Zimbabwe politics will take for some time to come are in process of being laid. There is no doubt that as long as the basic divide remained that between ZANU and ZAPU, as they have been constituted historically, the stuff of politics would have revolved around ethnicity and factional clientelism. The danger to any socialist project of the persistence of that kind of politics is hard to exaggerate, offering as it does in much of Africa a mechanism for the (very limited) political incorporation of some members of the underclasses into the existing socio-economic system and blunts a class awareness and organization. As such, clientelism has been correctly seen as the typical form that hegemony takes in underdeveloped countries where real economic concessions are not on offer (Charney, 1987). Certainly, the ethnic factionalism and clientelism that affected politics between, and thus in turn within, the Zimbabwean parties inhibited a contestation in terms of programmes based on ideology and class interests. The unity of the two parties can thus be seen as a necessary step towards an institutional form that would allow a 'Marxist' politics to emerge, specifically among the 'left' that certainly exists inside both ZANU and ZAPU. In the short run, some of the nastier ethnic wounds show some signs of healing. The winding down of the unrest in Matabeleland, marked for instance by most of the 'dissidents' accepting amnesty in 1988, is of great strategic importance, especially given the opportunity that the unrest presented for South Africa to fan it. Whether unity is a *sufficient* condition for class rather than ethnic politics, however, has to be doubted and it remains to be seen what kind of internal party politics emerges within the new, united party. Moreover, while there was a discernible left within ZAPU, such weight as its leaders may now have in the new party is likely to strengthen the right.

It also has to be conceded to Shaw and other commentators concerned about the implications of one-party rule for the Marxist project that even if there is validity in the above argument that unity could mark a shift from factionalism and clientelism, it is not one that has been advanced by party leaders in their search for unity. This realization prompts a need to penetrate further the issue of what is the actual motivation for the push towards one-party rule. That the other justifications rehearsed above may represent merely the rationalizing rhetoric rather than the actual calculations of leaders becomes more likely when one recognizes that they 'rarely deign to argue the case ... its desirability is a given, and its necessity taken for granted' (Shaw, 1986). What then might be the unstated reasoning behind what so often seems a somewhat frenetic determination on the part of some politicians to promote one-partyism?

It is hard to put it down simply and solely to the ambition of a would-be privileged class, as the reductionist argumentation of analysts that we consider in Chapter 1 like Astrow might argue. Or, at least, if there is a petty bourgeois project afoot it has to be explained why it is a different one from that of the leaders of the ruling party in next door Botswana, who undoubtedly represent an accumulating class, but who seem just as determined to maintain all the trappings of a competitive party system as ZANU leaders are to promote one-partyism. Clearly the explanation of the difference lies in the assimilation of an ideology, often subliminal — one that does have echoes of those tenets of 'Marxist-Leninist' doctrine that exalt the party and democratic centralism — but one that often abstracts from those elements of Marxism that are concerned with the transformation of the socio-economic system. This ideological stance is concerned with a project for the transforming of society, and not just immediate accumulation, but in some of its guises it is a project that is statist and aiming at *control*, a central element, even if some of its adherents seek bureaucratic means for essentially benevolent, if paternalistic, reasons. One can thus understand the shared determination for one-party rule as a project that unites those who seek a strong state as a corollary to a pattern of personal accumulation with others who are more concerned to see a state-directed pattern of development.

There is thus in these circumstances a threat on the one hand of the ethnicity–clientelist pattern persisting if some pluralism persists within the one party, while on the other the prospect of a drift into authoritarianism under a single party cannot be dismissed. This could be either of a bureaucratic variety as in the 'people's republics' or of more personalized sort that has emerged in some African single-party states, both of the left (like Guinea) or of the right as in Kenya — if the latter case the authoritarianism would be combined with clientelism. The impediments to such possible trends are in the first instance constitutional, but whether the door will be shut after 1990 on any future parties, or any form of organization other than that sanctioned by the party, is an important question — whether, in other words, the single party aims to maintain itself indefinitely and in changed circumstances and whether it will seek to monopolize all political activity. A second factor for the moment, is the leadership style set by Mugabe, who does seem to be collegial in his approach even when his authority is challenged, and is also prepared to entertain open and rational debate. But ultimately it will depend on what broader popular voices can make themselves heard, through or outside the party. ZANU has in fact been seeking to work out, not entirely satisfactorily as yet, some relationship between itself and the trade unions — the ZCTU were represented at the second and the unity Congresses, but this of course could as likely lead to incorporation as a strong workers' representation. The peasantry, mobilized during the war perhaps to give essentially passive approval to the party rather than to articulate their own demands, has if anything been more marginalized in post-independence developments. But how far it still has a voice will be discussed in more detail in the section on local politics below.

Central Decision–Making Institutions: The Constitutional Patterns

As we have seen, the Lancaster House constitution defined the institutional form of the independent Zimbabwe state, and in some respects that was an unsatisfactory compromise as far as ZANU was concerned. Much of the commentary and much of ZANU's irritation has focused on the concessions that had to be made to white power. The most glaring of these was the twenty white seats in the lower of the two houses of parliament, but crucial here was that these were to be elected by a white-only (in fact including the small coloured and Asian populations) electoral roll and on the basis of single constituency, first-past-the-post elections. This latter provision was an anomaly given that the eighty black seats were to be elected on a provincial, proportional representation system, but it meant predictably, given the nature of the white electorate, that *all* the twenty seats were controlled by Ian Smith's RF. One immediate calculation made by them and the British during Lancaster House was that this would put the RF in the position of kingmakers, but although this was forestalled by ZANU's election success, the RF was not confined merely to a minority voice in legislation. The entrenched provisions of the constitution relating to such key matters as property and other rights, and the provision for multi-partyism, gave them a virtual veto over constitutional change for some years. This period is now coming to an end. The whites–only electoral roll for twenty seats was abolished in 1987; the property rights can be changed in 1990. In retrospect the concessions to give whites a political voice will have only been for a very limited period in historical terms, although the property rights may well have a longer-term significance not just in terms of economic concessions to whites but as a lever to make the country safe for capitalism.

Other provisions of the constitution, though less noteworthy, had significance in that they aimed to shape the structural form of Zimbabwe's politics. In general, what was being patterned was the familiar 'Westminster model' — a system of government in which a prime minister and cabinet had central power, derived from their party's success in elections for the legislature. But even some elements of this system have been reshaped. The most visible has been the switch in 1988 to a presidential form of government in place of the prime minister with a ceremonial presidency. The actual resulting increase in Mugabe's power is probably mainly symbolic. However, in appointing a new cabinet at the time and coinciding with the union of ZANU and ZAPU, a new structure was introduced that grouped the hitherto somewhat uncoordinated ministries under 'senior ministers'. Nkomo was one, in the president's office. Maurice Nyagumbo, a member of the 'old guard' of the original ZANU central committee had control over 'political affairs', while Bernard Chidzero, already minister of finance and planning had oversight of all economic ministries. This kind of centralization was perhaps necessary where ministers had proliferated, as the price of keeping people sweet in various political compromises.

Another, more fundamental, change is on the cards with the creation of a *de facto* single party in 1988, even though it cannot, constitutionally, be made *de jure* until 1990. The essence of the claim of any cabinet system of government to be 'representative' lies in the electorate choosing between contending would-be ruling parties, one of which translates a legislative majority into executive power. This was in fact the route (or at least the final step) that ZANU took to power in 1980, claiming fifty-seven out of the eighty black seats in an election based on the proportional representation election of provincial lists. This system was modified to a single-member constituency, first-past-the-post system in the second general elections after independence in 1985. At that time, ZANU consolidated its position, increasing its share of the 'common roll' vote from 63 per cent to 77 per cent and its seats to sixty-four. But ZAPU lost only five of the twenty seats it had in 1980 — all of them outside Matabeleland, where it showed itself still the majority party. This latter result was bitterly resented by some ZANU supporters, who went on the rampage, attacking people thought to be ZAPU supporters, in several townships. In the longer run, it was perhaps the realization that ZAPU could not be steam-rollered out of existence, nor its Ndebele supporters easily won over, that reconciled leading circles in ZANU to the need to *negotiate* a single party, through a mutually agreed unity — even if they used some strong-arm methods to create circumstances that made it hard to refuse their offer.

With the union, however, the notion of an election to choose a government will have to take a different form in 1990, when the next elections are due. If constitutional forms are left the way they are, then it is conceivable that the electoral process would consist basically of the nomination of official ZANU candidates who are then technically unopposed — a pattern that has characterized many local government elections in the Mashonaland provinces where ZANU has been virtually unchallenged. However, it is possible that some variant of a competitive election, like 'primaries' between candidates of the single party, along the lines of the systems in Zambia, Tanzania and Kenya could be introduced. As yet there is no inkling of what kind of single-party constitution will be introduced; it is in any case not possible until 1990, although the strong presumption is that there will be one. It is also possible that the same constitutional form of single-party elections could operate either as in Tanzania in a fairly open way, with the 'centre' really acting as a neutral as between candidates, and thus one in which the system acts as a useful recruiting device; or on the other hand its operation could be marked by intra-party factionalism with a centre that is partisan and manipulative, as in Zambia and Kenya. With Zimbabwe's history of factionalism it would take much effort of political education and central leadership restraint to avoid the latter.

One other crucial element of government structure and practice that was defined by Lancaster House was the constitutional provision of a politically 'neutral' and professional civil service through the operation of a semi-independent Public Service Commission. Its members are confined to ex-senior civil servants and it has considerable control of recruitment, promotions and appointments of senior personnel; ministers have to put up with the senior officials they are given. This mechanism did initially provide job protection for white officials, but most senior white officials have moved on (many to South Africa whose government deliberately allowed them to cash in their pensions at inflated rates). The effect of the independence promoted by the Public Service Commission does partly control nepotism, but more significantly it has reduced the extent to which the bureaucracy can be responsive to broad political goals of social transformation rather than narrow professional norms — although some individual civil servants come from a background where they do have some commitment to social change.

Inherited State Patterns

The structural form that the new state has taken owes as much to aspects of the inherited settler state as to the provisions of Lancaster House, however. One dimension of the colonial state was its racial dualism. There were various departments of government that ministered to the needs of white society and the white-owned-and-run economy; there were partial, inadequate and mainly quite separate institutions that dealt with the black population. For much of this century the latter were 'dealt with' almost entirely in a regulatory manner — they were designated certain areas and confined to them; the flow of labour and the terms and conditions of that labour were controlled; there were efforts to control how they used land to prevent them 'despoiling' it. In the last two or three decades of colonial rule, there was some, limited, provision of education, health, agricultural advisory and other services in the black townships and reserves. But these were only allowed to develop in separate areas with different systems of local government according to race. And one of the Lancaster House concessions was to preserve this division partially with separate 'rural councils' in the former white-only rural areas, with some limited power of local taxation chiefly to fund roads and schools, and newly created district councils, dependent on central funding in the CAs. Only in the late 1980s are these being integrated, as we shall see in the next section. Until the 1970s agricultural services in the two types of area were provided by two quite distinct departments, and although these are now integrated in one ministry, some legacy of dualism persists in the differences in thoroughness of the services provided for the two sectors and in the definition of an agriculturalist orthodoxy that is still essentially derived from planning large-scale capitalist farms and ranches.

One specific institutional pattern was the centralized nature of the administration of black areas. Everything had once been under the 'Native Affairs Commissioner' with his officers at the district level who in turn selected and controlled the chiefs and headmen. By the 1950s and 1960s the central control was provided by the ministry of internal affairs which ran not only this system of provincial administration but also black agriculture. Most of such services and agriculture have now been hived off and 'internal affairs' is a separate ministry for local government. There are no longer District Commissioners, but their more political replacements are now under the ministry of local government which remains a very powerful ministry; it was, for instance, able to wrest responsibility for resettlement and overall planning of rural development from the more technical ministry of lands and agriculture. The philosophy of control, even though it is benevolent, is also hard to shake.

One legacy of these ministerial responsibilities for agriculture and rural development is that the ministry with the technical know-how tends to take a non-interventionist stance, of being available for consultation on request — a pattern that suited the large white farmers but is inappropriate for the peasant farmer. Meanwhile, responsibility for the overall planning of this sector is in the hands of a strong ministry with an interventionist tradition, but one that tends to conceive of approaches to problems in bureaucratic terms; thus appropriate land use, for instance, is unlikely to be planned in the round and with reference to the environmental interaction with a coherent but differentiated community and implemented through a consultative, participatory dialogue but rather by specifying rules and working out modes of compliance.

The past patterns of the separation of black and white rural areas and administrative responsibility for them and the attitudes of the old internal affairs ministry affect in turn the whole area of decision-making in the realm of economic planning — traditionally a key area in 'Marxist' regimes, to which we shall turn below.

Economic Decision-Making

Conventionally one feature of mainstream Marxist regimes has been an emphasis on a process of central planning of the economy that situates investment and production choices within an overall national plan. Zimbabwe in fact prepared a three-year Transitional National Development Plan (TNDP, 1983) after independence and also a First Five-Year National Development Plan (FFYNDP, 1986) covering the period 1986–90. However, these plans do not correspond to the central planning system — the specifications of output goals are mainly in monetary terms rather than physical quantities of actual production; targets do not carry a status of legal enforceability; the planning directorate has a relatively weak and limited coordinating rather than directive role; most crucially, most enterprises are 'private' and not amenable to state directives — although, as we shall see, the state is not without some instruments for ensuring implementation of plan targets should it choose to use them.

One key instrument for directing the economy is in fact not the planning directorate, but a Treasury, which is in the same ministry (of finance, economic planning and development), but has retained the strong and central role it always had. It thus keeps a very close hold on all public expenditure, but does so in terms of conventional norms of expenditure control, considering returns, if at all, only in the short run and immediate sense, with little concern for knock-on or multiplier effects, and income-generating prospects. It has definitely been the dominant partner in the marriage with the former ministry of economic planning and development. This tendency is reinforced by the status of the incumbent minister, Dr Bernard Chidzero, who has held both responsibilities for some years. In fact in January 1988 he became one of the three 'senior ministers' with coordinating responsibility for all economic ministries. Moreover, he has reached this eminence not by virtue of any political base within the country, rather he has always had the reputation of a technocrat who was something of a political neutral, but from the experience he would claim as a long-standing, senior official of UNCTAD and UNDP (although he earned his doctorate from a thesis on international politics and is not, as is often assumed, an economist). This standing has been much exalted by virtue of the backing he receives from a 'constituency' that consists not of some region or sector of the country but of the international economic institutions. One avenue through which the narrow, monetarist and anti-socialist orthodoxy of the IMF and World Bank is exerted effectively in the management of Zimbabwe's economy is by these agencies' expressions of (and threats of withdrawal of) their confidence in the country's economic management, which is in turn identified with Chidzero and his policies. This is not to say that his policies are indistinguishable from theirs — far from it: he presided over measures that brought about the suspension of the IMF programme in 1984 (see Chapter 13), and he frequently points up his disagreement with these agencies over the question of subsidies.

The possibility of more effective planning, at least of an indicative sort and in relation to the rural and regional economies, has been strengthened by recent moves to set up a more thoroughgoing system of provincial and district planning linked to the central process; a National Planning Agency was in fact set up for this purpose in early 1988. But this still leaves key sectors of industry and mining that are mainly in the hands of private capital outside direct government control. Even in these sectors, the state could, and to a degree does, exert a certain amount of direction over levels of output, investment and growth, through the elaborate structure of import quotas — itself a legacy from the settler state, and particularly the period of UDI and sanctions. This mechanism is under attack from the free-market orthodoxy of the World Bank as an unwarranted interference in trade, but is in fact a potential means to assert priorities of production goods over consumption, and to prioritize essential consumer imports. It could also be a means of prioritizing investments in certain types of industry and of technology. Linked to the Treasury's role of control of the Reserve Bank, there is the potential for being able to control capital outflows and the balance of payments, as the Smith government seemed effectively to do. But in practice this proved more difficult than expected for a time, for reasons partly to do with the influence of informal networks of officials in government, the central and private banks, and importers who, when they were all white and committed to UDI, ensured that controls worked with a smoothness that has not been possible since. (Nevertheless overall control has ensured current-account surpluses for the past three years.) The same kind of informal influences, together with the 'corporatism' that was a characteristic of the Rhodesian state, as we noted in Chapter 1, have also served to limit the extent to which planning, especially in the sense of prioritization of productive capacity in key sectors and other national indicators of need rather than 'demand', has been possible through the regulation of import quotas. The allocative process at the apex, between broad sectors, is not handled by a governmental body that is linked centrally into the planning machinery; and within sectors is done by 'quangos' which include those businesses that are themselves the importers. There is thus more of a bidding system than one of allocation on a rational basis, a tendency to simply vary old-established quotas, and a situation where established enterprises hold centre stage and newer ones are at the back of the queue, which might well exclude the innovative, the black entrepreneur, and even local capital as opposed to foreign subsidiaries.

The import quota machinery is but one example of the institutionalized role of established business in economic decision-making. It certainly implies a compromise with national planning goals let alone socialist objectives — but it is a compromise that is not only a product of the 'neo-colonial deal' but would have to figure in any 'national democratic strategy', where some sectors of capital were seen as allies in the promotion of some national development strategy. But such a strategy requires a much clearer working out of which sectors, and which types of local, foreign or other capital are to be accommodated and which peripheralized. It would then require a more selective screening of the economic decision-making channels to prioritize involvement rather than to accept business representation along established patterns and on its own terms.

Local Government and Local Politics

The greatest institutional innovation since independence has occurred at the local level. A new system of local government for the CAs was set up in 1980, indeed these were the first truly representative local authorities in the black areas; and they have since been modified by unifying their District Councils with the local authorities left over in the white areas. Local political party organizations have been formalized where there had been only the informal people's committees set up to pursue the war (if any bodies at all). These two sets of institutions have in turn dispossessed the former chiefs and headmen of most of their former powers, though not necessarily their prestige and actual influence. Local bodies for organizing and implementing development have also been set up in the 1980s at the village and ward level. In fact, such has been the plethora of new institutions that there is in practice significant confusion at the grassroots level, so that responsibility for actual functions is not clearly prescribed and overlapping and perplexity can result.

The settler-colonial state, as we have seen, developed a centralized and authoritarian mechanism for the administration of the black rural areas — a line staff of centrally-appointed commissioners stretched from the eight provinces to the fifty-three districts and below. Their agents below the district level were the chiefs and headmen, appointed and paid officials whose selection was supposedly based on customary pre-eminence and rules of succession. Their 'traditional' position probably meant more in Matabeleland, for the Ndebele still retained a more centralized, hierarchical system than did the Shona at the time of white conquest, and their status there probably remained more intact even until the eve of independence. However, even in these areas the officials of the settler state went about 'inventing tradition', as Ranger (1983) puts it, and indeed the UDI government intensified this process, reversing some partial attempts that had been made from the 1950s to bring a representative element into local government. The chiefs' grass-roots level powers, especially to allocate land, were restored, and they were given a national political role — the sole black allies of the late settler regime.

Councils were first established in black rural areas in the late 1930s, but only a few, and they consisted of chiefs and headmen plus nominated members. In the 1950s 'African Councils' were broadened to include elected members, but with chiefs dominating and often with DCs presiding. They were given some limited taxation powers but any capability for administering services was undermined by a search for 'tradition' which led to a splitting down of the few sizeable councils that did exist, so each chief had his own council. As it was, only half the black rural areas had councils by the mid-1960s and the process was not completed even by 1979. Similarly in urban areas, township councils were established and while obviously not based on 'traditional' authorities, they had limited powers; most urban services, including housing in black townships, remained in the hands of the white-dominated city and town councils. So an effective and representative system of local government had to await independence.

Even if the African Councils were ineffectual in providing services through local government, the system of local administration was certainly operative. The chiefs and headmen held courts and, until the partial individualization of landholding in the Land Husbandry Act of 1957 (and again when it was abolished), they had a big say in the allocation of land to meet new needs and needs of new families under the so-called 'communal' system of land tenure. And even though these powers were conducted in concert with the 'spirit mediums' who were a central and still powerful element in Shona religion (Lan, 1985), despite the spread of Christianity, in a context of increasing land shortage the chiefs thereby had a crucial lever of social control to ensure compliance with government rules. But it was not their prescribed powers, or their traditional status, that gave this system of local administration its authoritarian character. That stemmed from the extent and kinds of control the settler government sought to exert over the black population. First, it should be realized that in many regions people were living in, and chiefs and headmen were being set up to run, areas into which they had been shifted to make way for white settlement. Such major population movements continued until the 1960s, and then as a counter-insurgency measure during the war. And people were also shifted around within the TTLs ('tribal trust lands'). There were periodic programmes of 'centralization', by which was meant the herding together of the scattered homesteads where people had their land, into neat rows of clustered houses in a *kraal* or village, for reasons more to do with ensuring control than rationalizing land use (a process which was given its logical extension with the rounding-up of people into larger, 'strategic hamlets' during the war). But even in relation to land-use crucial to every family's day-to-day activities and their survival, rules were imposed — for the proper tilling of soil, the forced reduction of cattle herds to fit the (reduced) grazing areas, plus a host of conservation measures. Unfortunately, part of the 'statist' tendency in recent policy-making circles seems to want to harp back to the promotion of both the centralized villagization and the enforcement of land-use rules that characterized settler rule and that were so resented by the peasantry. The pattern was somewhat different in Matabeleland, which had a sparser population and greater dependence on livestock. Chiefs there had greater authority and remained powerful throughout the colonial period, though their authority was based more on their large herds and their command over the labour of others than on control of land. Their position was not effectively challenged during the liberation war, though it may have been during the last few years of dissidence.

The authoritarian character of this colonial administrative system stretching down to the *kraal* level, the grouped residential unit, derived from its interventionist character, an intervention that sought social control rather than 'development' and that was hardly counter-balanced at all by some modicum of representation in an inadequate local government system at a somewhat higher level. The chiefs and village headmen were instruments of varying effectiveness for affecting these tasks, and occasionally the ambiguity of their position between their people and a white government led some of them to take part, even lead, resistance to government plans, such as those for removals.

The authoritarian character was of course further strengthened in the many areas where there were guerrilla operations, as part of the counter-insurgency strategy in the liberation war. Over half a million people in the north-east and along the southern border were moved into 'strategic hamlets' or further displaced from their homes. But even in many other areas, most of the provinces of Mashonaland East and Central, Manica-land and Masvingo and some parts of the other four, there were curfews, restrictions on movement of people, of animals, and of food and other supplies, and collective punishments. There were army personnel, para-military police and reservists, special forces and pseudo-guerrillas, anti-stock theft units, guard forces that protected the white farms and their boundaries in the CAs, and, in the last months of the war, there were the notorious 'auxiliaries' recruited under the banner of Muzorewa when he was prime minister, lumpen youths from the towns who were brought in to terrorize rural communities. And yet paradoxically as these measures became more draconian, and the security personnel denser on the ground, their effectiveness and the ability to implement any policy other than occasional 'punishment' was whittled away, as the guerrillas wrested first clandestine, night-time, control and then increasing degrees of indepen-dence in many CAs. As a result of the space they won, local government or other official personnel, tax-collectors, chiefs, police and even other security forces were forced to withdraw, and the people's committees took over certain tasks of self-administration. Among the several effects of the partial breakdown of settler authority in many CAs was, on the one hand, a disruption of many services, including those provided from above by local authorities and national ministries. But, on the other hand, at the grass roots level some activities, often schools, were promoted by the people's committees — and chiefs' and headmen's powers over land allocation (their chief source of patronage) were curtailed, sometimes leading to an 'alternative' land committee, more often to a free-for-all which involved taking land that was abandoned, used for grazing or, where possible, that belonged to whites.

How far this popular mobilization and self-organization went — whether it was passive or a submission to the new authority of the guerrillas, as opposed to an active backing of the war effort combined with widespread grass-roots democracy — are matters of debate among those beginning to document the history of the liberation war. Ranger (1985a), as we have noted, sees a radical peasant consciousness as having had some defining influence on the overall nature of the nationalist movement and argues that in the restructuring of the fractured administrative and local authority system that was necessitated after the war, the peasants would at least be able to bargain for new, less authoritarian arrangements as one of the key terms for their once again accepting central authority. More specifically he points to the emergence in Makoni district in the north-east during 1980 of a 'network of village ZANU/PF committees ... [as] effective centres of administration' in the CAs, who 'heard cases, allocated land'. Cliffe and Munslow (1980b) had also noted the existence of such people's committees in parts of Masvingo Province prior to independence, seeing them as having some potential for grass-roots democratic expression and self-administration, and indeed embarking on tasks such as distribution of relief supplies and of agricultural input packages in the emergency situation of 1980 (as they did in Makoni too) and even undertaking 'development' tasks such as public health education. Other analysts like Kriger (1988), who reanalyses the Makoni situation, believe that the extent of peasant mobilization and active involvement in the war is overstated, and/or that the mechanisms of a largely unreconstructed state easily reasserted its control (Weitzer, 1984) — explaining thereby the absence, as they see it, of any 'radicalization' tendency in the post-independence period.

However, what is easily refutable, at least about Weitzer's thesis, is that there was not simply a reassertion of the old security mechanisms of control, for there was a clear need for the restructuring of state structures at the local level, and in the process significant institutional changes were in fact made. The authority of the 'Provincial Administration' as it reached down through the Commissioners and District Offices to the chiefs and headmen had been severely blunted; the capacity for central government agencies to affect any measures at the local level had been impaired; such local councils as had existed had been discredited. At the same time there were some spontaneous organizational initiatives at the most grass-roots level. The independence government had thus to redefine the administrative channels it itself would use to exert authority in the rural areas and the terms of the relationships with the people and any local institutions that had emerged, but also to reconstitute some system of local authorities, and later development planning bodies. The place of party institutions in these new arrangements and the extent of central control of local activities through party mechanisms was also at issue. This issue of the form of central control took on special meaning in Matabeleland, where chiefly authority was still marked, and where party mobilization behind ZAPU led to opposition to the centre. Another question that must be asked as we turn to document the new institutions that were set up, concerns their *social* character. In particular, insofar as Ranger (1985b) and other commentators were correct in saying that the popular support for the nationalist movement incorporated the whole swathe of rural class elements, we need to ask: how far was there a shift in the representation of different strata? Whatever differences of opinion there are about the social and political character of the nationalist movement before and during the war, there is more of a consensus here that the post-independence restructuring of local administration, local government and politics represented something of a 'conservative restoration' (Ranger, 1985b), in many if not all respects.

The first steps were, however, progressive; the single chain of command from the ministry of internal affairs to the *kraal* was eroded. The commissioners were replaced by governors who continued to coordinate central ministries, but no longer had control of a line of agents at sub-district levels. They had to 'liaise', setting up development committees, and to 'oversee' as with district councils, but no longer simply to 'command'. Although chiefs were not abolished, no new ones were appointed to fill vacancies and their judicial functions were taken over by local magistrates, trained for this role, and their land allocative powers were taken over by the District Councils set up in 1980 in all of the fifty-three districts — the first ever comprehensive rural local government system in the country. These councils only covered the Communal Areas of the district and were still subject to the control of appointed provincial authorities; separate 'Rural Councils' operated in the white farming areas. Moreover the latter had their own sources of revenue, the former did not — although this latter omission was probably a deliberate concession to the widespread resentment of the earlier 'African Councils', which were seen as an instrument where impoverished rural areas were deprived of all but the most meagre services which they had to pay for themselves and a recognition of the reality that during the war many communities had successfully ended tax collection. In fact considerable revenues, for reconstruction and to some extent development, were made available through the District Development Fund, which even though it was a central provision and potentially an instrument for control did quickly make possible the replacement and building of a local infrastructure and a vast mushrooming of local schools. As representational bodies these councils operated in a different manner in different provinces. In Masvingo, Manicaland and Mashonaland East and Central where ZANU was completely dominant the only contestation was for the party nomination as ward councillor. How such 'primaries' were carried out varied but often involved hundreds of party members. In this first-past-the-post system where members would often line up the candidate of their choice, the manipulative abilities and patronage of some chiefly elements and better-off 'progressive farmers' was sometimes decisive. This tendency for poor and middle peasant interest to take a less prominent place was reinforced by the new formal party officers and committees, and also delegates to higher levels up to the Congress, that were gradually set up in the years leading to the Second Congress in 1984, but set up from the centre down and often involving descending hierarchies of patronage, as noted in an earlier section of this chapter. In Matabeleland, ZANU's efforts to contest local elections were frustratingly disappointing for them and local authorities were ZAPU-dominated, but thereby in some degree of increasing opposition to the centre, and partially starved of funding — unlike the local one-partyism that was a feature of the ZANU-dominated provinces. In some parts of Midlands and Mashonaland West councils were mixed and often divided.

Even in the four Shona provinces neither the new local government and party structures, nor the ward and village development committees (Wadcos and Vidcos), which were set up in 1985, built upon the spontaneous people's committees. These persisted through 1980 and 1981 perhaps, but then began to wither — the district councils were at a much higher and more remote level, and the party and the development committees were instituted from on high and only after a delay when the people's committees had already begun to decline. What this pattern also means however is that even in these four provinces the party hierarchy stops a little short of being an instrument of central control down to the village level — and in the other areas the party competition, locally, or between centre and district, also precluded this.

Further changes occurred from the mid-1980s with the proposed amalgamation of Rural and District Councils into a unified system of local government. It is too early to say how far the working of these combined councils, their politics and their systems of service provision and of financing, will allow for a redistribution of services away from the well-served former white areas to the CAs. The local impact of another proposed innovation — for an integrated development planning structure — also cannot be assessed.

Trade Unions and Industrial Relations

At first sight it might be expected that Zimbabwe would have a highly developed trade-union movement, with significant political influence, as is rapidly becoming the case in South Africa. With the single exception of the latter country, the proportion of the population in employment is higher in Zimbabwe than elsewhere in sub-Saharan Africa. And there have been recent cases of labour militancy: independence in 1980 was followed by two waves of strikes: by the end of 1980 there had been 150, losing over 300,000 production days (Wood, 1988, p. 291), by far the most serious labour unrest since a general strike in 1948. But they were not sustained beyond the immediate post-independence period.

Yet out of over a million people in employment in 1987, only about 190,000 were unionized (p. 284); that is about 18 per cent (or at most 28 per cent if the 370,000 farmworkers and domestic servants are excluded). This is a rise from an estimated 11 per cent overall in 1979 (p. 288), but, as Wood shows, far from evidence of a massive upsurge in trade-union power and influence. Gains in membership over the 1981–5 period were recorded mainly in mining, building and construction, and to a lesser extent in clothing, footwear and posts and telecommunications; on the other hand there were significant decreases in estimated membership in engineering, iron and steel, and food and allied industries, and to a lesser extent in chemicals, banking and finance, and local government.

Their lack of political clout is, however, not just a matter of limited numbers. The context of the historical weakness of trade unionism in Zimbabwe is the structure of racial legislation, and in particular the Industrial Conciliation Act (ICA) of 1934 (amended in 1959), which was designed to emasculate black trade unionism and in particular to prevent it developing links with the nationalist parties; legal strikes were effectively ruled out by a battery of restrictions. This legislation underpinned a structure of corporate paternalism, involving employers, the state, and trade-union officials, which saw unions as instruments for restraining worker excess. In the words of a prominent (white) trade unionist (quoted by Sachikonye in Mandaza, 1986, pp. 255–6) in 1980:

a good, developed union run by professional, educated men… can help rather than hinder the economic development of industries. Unions are a braking mechanism, as opposed to the damaging wildcat strikes that we are seeing now... They can render assistance both to employers and employees.

The fact that the speaker was Howard Bloomfield, the white president of the multiracial mineworkers' union illustrates another dimension of the problem: that unions were not only devices for state or employer control of the work-force, they were also instruments for substantial advance by white workers and for discrimination against and control of black workers. Of fifty-seven unions in 1979, thirty-four were 'non-racial', but mostly very weak, and twenty-three were white dominated, and indeed the main institutional vehicles in the industrial relations sphere for maintaining white worker privilege. In the mining union, for instance, the structure ensured that barely 1,000 (white) skilled workers could outvote over 4,000 (black) semi-skilled workers; indeed there was little reason for blacks to join such unions, and in the mining industry some 3,000 did not (Stoneman, 1981c, p. 183). There was similar white dominance in the powerful railway workers' union.

As independence approached the disincentives to union membership of this corporate-paternalism were reinforced by a situation approaching martial law in many areas, by poverty which reduced the resources to sustain workers in a strike, and by political divisions among the contending 'internal settlement' and liberation movement parties. All these served to further weaken the movement.

A key fact of Zimbabwe's liberation struggle is that the victorious party, ZANU-PF, was at its weakest in the organized labour movement. The small and fragmented pre-independence black unions and congresses, insofar as they were independent of the regime, tended to be run by officials linked to (or be the creations of) ZAPU or the compromised 'internal settlement' parties, ZANU-Sithole and Bishop Muzorewa's UANC, and were thus instruments for political competition and inter-union factionalism. In this context the ZANU-PF election manifesto promised freedom of speech, assembly, association, procession, demonstration and strike action, and the new government initially appeared to favour the strengthening of trade unions and the encouragement of workers' participation, probably because this was seen as helping to extend the party's own political base. In his post-election victory broadcast Robert Mugabe (quoted in Wood, 1988, p. 288) declared:

workers will be established into various committees which have a management role... First we must study the position of the workers. The trade union movement is very weak in this country. It has always been, and it is necessary to promote a unitary movement rather than a multiplicity of national movements.

Perhaps knowledge of the other parties' influence conditioned government's generally hostile reaction to the 1980 strike wave which was interpreted by Sachikonye (in Mandaza, 1986, p. 254) as 'a coordinated response by capital, in conjunction with the state apparatus'. The state apparatus was of course still the apparatus of the previous regime, and in May 1980 did not exactly correspond to the new government's thinking. So when the minister of labour Kumbirai Kangai (quoted in Wood, 1988, p. 289) told the National Trade Union Seminar in May 1980 that —

I firmly believe that the regulated system of labour relations which we have here in Zimbabwe is more beneficial for the community as a whole, rather than the dog-eat-dog philosophy of the so-called free labour movement which operates in some countries held to be more developed than our own

— he may not have known that except for the substitution of 'Rhodesia' by 'Zimbabwe' he was using word for word a speech delivered by the former Rhodesian minister for labour, Ian McLean, in 1970. But it demonstrates the lack of any coherent policy on the part of the new government. (Robert Mugabe himself described a bakery strike as 'nothing short of criminal', and Kangai used the McLean speech again as late as September 1980.) Nevertheless, the government's response to the strike wave was to promise a minimum wage bill (effective from 1 July 1980), and to recognize the workers' committees which had sprung up during the strikes. In mid-1980 it called a meeting of leading trade unionists which was to lead to the formation of the Zimbabwe Congress of Trade Unions the following February, with the aim of eliminating factionalism, reducing the influence of other parties, and generating some links with ZANU. At the same time 'Workers Committees' were set up, with guidelines setting out aims and specimen constitutions. These attempted to reincorporate worker militancy by offering some involvement in shop-floor industrial relations, but denying them any bargaining rights over pay or grading; occupational health and safety issues were however conceded to be their concern. Thus just what the respective functions and the links between workers' committees and trade-union branches were envisaged to be was never clarified, and so worker representation was fragmented. However, the lack of democracy, in either structures or traditions in trade unions and the new ZCTU (ibid., p. 300), meant that few workers joined them, and those who did were inactive. The result was corruption, exposed publicly in the case of the ZCTU in 1984, which was then run by a caretaker administration including senior trade unionists and ministry of labour officials until the second congress in July 198. Lack of democratic involvement still however prevented any real control by the workers, and in November 1986 the new general secretary and several of his staff were dismissed for misappropriating funds.

Matters seem to have improved considerably after the election of the new ZCTU president, Jeffrey Mutandare of the strong Associated Mineworkers Union. However, it is not yet clear whether the clean up of corruption in unions and the ZCTU is merely a result of ministry control, or whether leaderships are becoming more responsive to collective control by members. Mutandare himself has frequently been critical of government policy towards unions, saying that their role had been hijacked (presumably by the ministry of labour). After the first wage freeze in 1982 (there was another in 1987), government has set maximum and minimum wage levels by decree. According to Mutandare many firms treat the minimum as a maximum (in the early days sometimes even *reducing* wages of workers who had previously been paid more), and coupled with the difficulty of striking legally this has greatly reduced the role of collective bargaining with management.

But he has reserved his major criticisms for the long-awaited Labour Relations Act of December 1985. Although this act established a number of formal advances for workers' rights (including the right to organize, the right to strike in defence of the existence of a union or to avoid occupational hazard and the right to automatic dues deductions) its overall effect was to centralize power over the unions onto the minister of labour. Many of the ICA's corporate control measures are retained, including a virtual ban on strikes through the very wide area defined as 'essential services'. In Mutandare's view (quoted in ibid., p. 305) the act

conflicts with certain ILO conventions; the large majority of unions are classified as being in 'essential services', and so are not allowed to strike. There's too much ministerial influence: the minister ... can overrule any constitutional decisions that they've taken ... ministerial agreement is needed for any wage agreement that we reach; the minister can direct that the employers not send dues straight to the union but that these be placed in a trust fund. So all in all, the minister has ... powers to throttle the unions if he wishes.

In general, then, the corporatist labour controls of the pre-independence period have been rationalized and extended although the power of employers has been reduced. There has also been some offering of a union voice in public affairs via the party — the ZCTU was represented at ZANU's second Congress — but hardly at all in state committees and quangos until the formation of the National Advisory Council in 1988. Government itself has sometimes attempted a paternalistic welfare intervention, for example the decree in 1985 that agro- industrial workers were to be treated as industrial rather than agricultural workers for purposes of determining their minimum wage, but in this case employers forced it to reverse the measure through threatening to close down. The Labour Relations Act clearly relates to a continuing capitalist context, to corporatism rather than any form of socialism, even of the statist variety as understood by ZANU. It is, however, a corporatism in which capital and the state are in a sense stalemated rather than symbiotically dependent. If worker identification of statist concepts of socialism with corporatism grows, membership growth will continue to decelerate, and unions may well lose credibility and become narrow economistic vehicles for the few. They will certainly not become vehicles for developing a more participatory concept of socialism.

The Farming and Business Community

Whites still heavily predominate amongst commercial farmers and business people. Although there are no reliable statistics it is generally assumed that the roughly 6,000 white farmers in 1980 have shrunk to below 5,000 through amalgamations and sales for resettlement; a few hundred large commercial farms are now owned by blacks. Particularly in the latter case a proportion are run by salaried managers, but overall the majority are owner operated, although they are increasingly protected legally through becoming limited companies — in fact 70 per cent are now in this category; this makes personal land ceilings as a basis for land reform difficult to apply. The Commercial Farmers' Union (CFU) is a powerful lobby, with significant influence on government both over such issues as prices, but also on more strategic questions. This influence, which is largely due to the importance of agricultural exports, is marshalled with the help of a professionally staffed office. Small-scale commercial farmers, originally the African Purchase Area farmers, number some 8,000 with farms of average size about 200 hectares, one-tenth of the LSCF average. They have only limited political influence, and are organized separately in the Zimbabwe National Farmers' Union (ZNFU), although there are proposals to merge with the CFU and the peasant farmers' NFAZ.

The business community is organized in the Chamber of Mines, the Confederation of Zimbabwe Industries (CZI) and the Zimbabwe National Chambers of Commerce (ZNCC). Numbers are again hard to judge, but although there are some 15,000 registered companies in Zimbabwe there are only somewhat under 1,000 members of the CZI and 3,000 of the ZNCC. The CZI (which in fact groups together the provincial organizations to which members actually belong) seems to be quite representative of manufacturing industry, including parastatals such as the Dairy Marketing Board (DMB) and the Cold Storage Commission (CSC), but is dominated by the views of transnational corporations (TNCs) whose larger resources partly determine the directions of research; as the majority of senior management of the latter are Zimbabwe residents, and as TNC subsidiaries benefit from the same market protection and export incentives as domestic companies, the policies of the two groups do not diverge as much as in many other countries. The majority of business people are white Zimbabweans, followed by whites with British and South African nationality. A growing minority are blacks, who have already held top positions in the two organizations.

Although an upper limit for the size of the business community is about 10,000, like the commercial farmers, it wields considerable influence with government. Although naturally opposed to socialist ideology, it has long experience of working in an environment of strong state control, and avoiding unproductive confrontation. This was not so generally true in the first years of independence, when more of the business community were South African (or worked for subsidiaries of South African companies), but government support in suppressing the strike waves in 1980 and 1981, and denying the workers' committees real power persuaded the more far-sighted that capitalism was not under threat. It is notable that although Ian Smith and his Rhodesian Front (renamed first the Republican Front and then the Conservative Alliance of Zimbabwe) retained majority white support until 1986, business sensibly kept its distance, preferring not to antagonize government; indeed in the 1985 election bodies like the CZI and the CFU publicly dissociated themselves from the CAZ.

Thus the CZI has established a close working relationship with the relevant ministries so as to lobby for extra foreign exchange, facilitate investment approval, handle labour issues, and so forth. In general it seems to recognize that government has problems both with allocation of foreign exchange and with attempting to satisfy the expectations of the poor for social services, health and education. Therefore it understands the causes of the large budget deficit (and spokespeople have explicitly recognized that such expenditure helps dampen wage demands); it also commonly accepts that labour-intensive technology is more appropriate in Zimbabwean conditions, and wastes little time putting forward capital-intensive or foreign-exchange intensive projects to the Investments Committee. In part this is due to a recognition of the realities, but it is also the case that the CZI represents the interests of national capital to a government that is increasingly pragmatic in seeing the merits of favouring such interests (as it has always done with regard to white farmers).

At its congress in 1985 considerable opprobrium came the way of the CZI for opposition to sanctions against South Africa. By 1986 adjustment had occurred, and the 600 delegates passed a statement *in favour* of sanctions by acclamation (no opposing speakers were recorded). Later that year officials stated that relations with government were continuing to improve on the basis of almost daily consultations on how to meet the consequences of sanctions. A new business-oriented organization, the Beira Corridor Group (see Chapter 16), was set up in 1986 to promote the use of non-South African trade routes.

Peasant Organizations

Many analysts have characterized the mobilization during the national liberation war as a peasant struggle. One of the most influential works on the war (Ranger, 1983), as we saw in the Introduction, in fact sees the peasant element not only as providing an active, widespread *base* of support, but as actively contributing a radical, egalitarian ethos to the movement as a whole in favour of a better deal for the peasant. The extent to which the peasants were actively involved, let alone provided the ideological direction, has in fact been questioned (Kriger, 1988; Moore, 1988), but it is certainly the case that the peasants in many areas were effectively mobilized — at least to give passive, vocal, and at times active support to the war, although how far to defend and promote their own interests is less evident. We have in fact seen how people's committees were formed at the grass-roots level, in many areas. And although patterns varied over the country, these committees often threw up an alternative leadership to that of chiefs and local headmen, and possibly including less well-off as well as less influential peasants — though it would be wrong to see these as dominated by poor peasants. Neither ZANLA nor ZIPRA seemed to have concerned themselves with patterns of local differentiation among the peasantry. In some areas there was some continuity following independence which allowed these people's committees to continue to play a role in a different context. They were available as local branches of the party — at least in areas where there were no divided party loyalties. In some areas they provided a network for local development initiatives. However, a number of characteristics reduced this potential for continued involvement from the grass-roots up, and limited the extent to which the potential was realized. First, the strength of the grass-roots organization lay decisively, in the best instances, in the *interaction* of peasants *with* guerrillas. With the withdrawal of the latter, there was a draining away of much of the initiative in charting goals and of the broader raising of consciousness, plus, moreover, of the actual strength to withstand pressures. A second complication in the new post-1979 situation in fact, was that new pressures were coming from outside the local community. The immediate aim of government efforts in the first months was to consolidate peace and start reconstruction — and local committees did play a role in mobilizing self-help labour, distributing food, seeds, implements etc., and in registering people for resettlement. Next on the agenda was the setting up of a new system of local government and then of party branches. The details of this restructuring are given above, but here it is significant to note that they were top-down initiatives which did not in their terms of reference take the pre-existing popular organs into account. One further implication of this was that the lowest level of local government, the district council, and even the wards that were the councillors' constituencies, were at a level and on a scale that was still remote from the grass-roots peasant universe of the *kraal*, and were organized in geographical entities much bigger than (and that thus did not connect up with) the people's committees. This was even true of the party branch structure, which was built down from the centre through province and district, with branches at the sub-district level following different boundaries from the people's committees.

It was not until 1985 that specifically development-oriented sub-district bodies began to be instituted. These were the village and ward development committees (Vidcos and Wadcos) — and although they were in part shaped to build on the people's committees, little of the substance of the latter remained by the time they were instituted, and in any case their boundaries were drawn in an over-formalistic way, which ignored most pre-existing units whether of people's committees, chiefdoms or whatever. In practice some concrete legacy survived in some places. Thus, although the new district councils were given formal power to allocate land in the communal areas, replacing the chiefs (who in many instances had in fact lost that power in the war), they were at too remote a level to make decisions at a village level. In at least one district known to the authors, Chibi, in the south, the *de facto* authority was delegated to the informal people's committees. Elsewhere, confusion often surrounded land decisions, as chiefs and headmen attempted to reassert their role in the vacuum created by the distance of the council, but this did not go unresisted.

Control over the disposal of land, always one of the key issues for the peasantry, tended to be removed further from the hands of the poorer peasants by another trend that was undermining the legacy of popular mobilization. In the contests for office in local government (often decided by limited 'primaries' or other nomination procedures to get the party's candidacy) and in the party, there is evidence (Cliffe, personal observation, Masvingo; Ranger, 1983) that better-off elements — richer farmers, traders, even chiefs and headmen that had been discredited — were able to use their status and ability to manipulate clientelist networks to reassert their local dominance. Such tendencies were further fostered by the patronage politics that began to affect the party in-fighting — as 'national' leaders began to jockey for provincial and district level prominence.

In these and other ways much of the organized basis for peasant mobilization has been dissipated. This does not necessarily deny the persistence of a latent peasant political consciousness that may be remobilized to defend their interests. Indeed there are manifestations of such an attitude, most notably in the continued widespread proclivity of 'squatters' to occupy land which they see as unutilized: abandoned farms, ungrazed pasture, uncultivated pockets of large commercial holdings, state and forest land. There is some evidence for the continuing strength of the peasant movement in government's response. They had assumed that squatting would be a short-run phenomenon, but when it continued in the years after independence, and in the absence of widespread resettlement, they sought to regularize that which had occurred, and proclaimed an intention to 'remove' new squatters after a certain date. This nettle has not been grasped in most cases, even in one instance when a white farmer had a high-court injunction requiring the police to remove squatters from a farm he had bought. So peasants continue to vote with their feet. This counter-pressure on the land also has many, less clear-cut forms than out-and-out squatting. People let their cattle stray, cut down fences on commercial grazing land bordering communal areas; they cultivate plots, rent land, and try to do other deals or to get local authority action to give them more elbow room. But all these pressures, even squatting, are not unambiguous evidence of informal mobilization by the land-hungry, poor peasantry. Some of these initiatives are opportunist moves by would-be entrepreneurs to get more assets, or organized pre-emptive 'illegal' efforts to get politicians to act officially, or even part of the patronage extended by aspiring politicians.

Insofar as there is any effective voice for peasants through such non-formal action, through the legacy of popular committees, through Vidcos, local authorities or party branches, one limitation (and one that lends itself to be absorbed into clientelist politics) is that such a voice is always going to be local, and probably therefore also parochial. The need for some broader mechanism for peasants to speak as a *class* was implied by an unelaborated proposal in the TNDP (1983) which called for the setting up of Peasant Associations. If this proposal had been implemented at a time when the popular legacy was still alive it could have done much to organize rural dwellers as peasant producers and to offer a channel for their interests to be articulated nationally. As it was, any such articulation of the interests of agricultural producers had to come from the farmers' unions or the cooperatives (see below). In addition to the Commercial Farmers' Union (CFU), there was, as we have seen, the ZNFU which represented the purchase area farmers and articulated their special interests, closely identifying with the CFU on many issues. There was in addition the National Farmers' Association of Zimbabwe (NFAZ) which did in fact form a representational body of farmers from the CAs. Its history was as an organization of the few 'master farmers' recognized and given help by the colonial agricultural authorities, but today it plays a broader but still ultimately ambiguous role. On the one hand it presses with some vigour for a fair share of opportunities for CA farmers and for a much greater scale of resettlement, and it is prepared to consider some land reform in the CAs but not one that gives individual titles or is indifferent to the demands of the poor. On the other hand, while it by no means represents only the interests of the 10 per cent or so of substantial CA peasants, the NFAZ does tend to adopt the ideology of the settler agricultural bureaucracy and the other farmers' unions, that CA dwellers can be divided between 'genuine farmers' and those who are not, either because of absence or some purported lack of knowledge or indifference. There is thus no sensitivity either to the fact that many of the poor farm their small plots poorly through a shortage of inputs, labour, oxen, etc., or to the existence of a need for land to return to as a form of 'social security' as long as that cannot be provided by other means. But the potential in the NFAZ to represent ordinary middle peasants, if not particularly the poor, is likely to be undermined by present government proposals to integrate it with the other two unions. Without a good deal of careful structuring and politicization, this could bind the interests of peasant farmers to those of commercial farmers, with the latter in the driving seat, and therefore it could subordinate poor peasant interests even further.

Cooperatives

There are three largely unconnected strands to the cooperative movement in Zimbabwe. The largest in terms of formal organization are the marketing cooperatives that bring together individual farmers under the umbrella of a society that collects, transports and sells their crops. Many of these bodies also provide a channel for buying farm inputs. For many years the white farmers organized their crop marketing and supplies of fertilizer, seed and equipment in this way, so there is nothing intrinsically anti-capitalist about cooperatives as such. Towards the end of the colonial period similar organizations were set up among African smallholders. The local level society to which each farmer-member has the right to elect officers is the 'primary' cooperative — several of these in an area are then federated into a 'union' of cooperative societies. And the unions that exist in Zimbabwe belong to an 'apex' organization, the Central Association of Cooperative Unions (CACU).

There has been significant growth in marketing cooperatives since independence — as much a result of the changed economic context and political self-confidence in which peasants are trying to produce for the market, as of direct government stimulus through the department (now ministry) of cooperatives that was set up. There were over six hundred marketing primary societies registered by the end of 1985. The volume of trading they were involved in had more than doubled between 1980 and 1983 and they now handle a significant proportion, but not the majority, of produce marketed by peasants.

No detailed study has so far been made into the working of these primary societies. A government report (Chitsike, 1985) does imply a tendency towards factionalism and clientelism by its reference to group loyalties of committee members and the role of ethnicity and religion. And although this does not seem to be based on much concrete evidence, it would be surprising if there is not the same tendency toward favouritism and inefficiency in the allocation of jobs and services (thus inflating operating costs and lowering members' returns) that are discernible in most such cooperatives in Africa. However, it is also indicative that the report in question identifies this problem simplistically as one that can be handled by better trained, qualified and supervised managers and other paid staff, proposing in fact a unified service for cooperative employees under government control — a *bureaucratic* solution rather than a *political* one of educating and mobilizing *members* to take greater advantage of the democratic form of the cooperative institutions to defend their interests and in the process combat clientelism. This response may be seen as typical of an anti-cooperative stance which is one tendency at work in both party leadership and civil service but especially of some of the personnel who have had responsibility for cooperatives (Hanlon, 1986), especially marked in relation to producer cooperatives (see below). It is perhaps part of a broader anti-socialist position, but such attitudes may have more complex roots. There is active support for those cooperatives, marketing in particular, that can be integrated into a generally capitalist economy, and these are indeed welcomed and promoted by agri-business capital, as well as by the state, as a way of rationalizing and integrating dealings with a mass of small producers. But these views are coupled with a statist perspective among other officials who seek to promote cooperatives as part of a 'socialist' programme, an attitude that also sees their convenience to a government bent on 'control' of a collectivity of 'managed' peasant producers.

In fact such strength as the marketing cooperatives have is at the union rather than the primary or apex level, which means in more general terms that the prospect of cooperatives becoming effective forums for organizing peasant producers to defend their interests is not great, either at the grass-roots level, where they might be able to take charge of their own affairs and their relations with market and state, or at a national level, where their voice might be heard by government alongside the effective national representation achieved by commercial farmers.

The second level of cooperative organizations are the producer cooperatives, or 'collective cooperatives' as they are termed in Zimbabwe, wherein groups of producers share means of production, and organize their labour collectively in some joint enterprise. There are perhaps eighty of these that operate larger farms, some of them acquired by the group on their own initiative, purchasing existing commercial farms from their pooled resources. Others are the Model B resettlement farms, whereby an existing commercial holding is made over to a cooperative. These latter are intended particularly where the complexity or amount of infrastructure involved in production (e.g., overhead irrigation; tobacco curing barns) is such that it would be a waste to dismantle it and parcel out the holding as on other resettlement schemes. These agricultural producer cooperatives have a mixed record of success. A few are producing at a high level and provide a good living for their members, showing what is possible. Many have low productivity, use only part of their land, and offer returns to members that are less than the minimum wage. There is persuasive evidence that these shortcomings are not inevitable but rather a failure to reach a potential that does exist, a failure that owes more to a lack of supporting resources, and perhaps to the difficulties that stem from the very complexity of the enterprises than to some inherent limitation in cooperative production. Thus half of the Model B cooperatives received no development finance from government, only 16 per cent of funds budgeted in 1981 for such costs were in fact disbursed by 1984, and no new allocations were made thereafter for establishing any new agricultural cooperatives. In addition, there are as many collective cooperatives running industrial firms, commercial businesses and even mines as farms, with again a mixed record of economic success. Estimates (Hanlon, 1986) suggest that counting farming cooperatives, there may be about 800 collective cooperatives active in the country with perhaps 25,000 members. Many of them were started and/or involve ex-combatants and thus their membership, though small, is likely to be more politically aware and vocal than that of the marketing cooperatives. In fact there is an umbrella organization, the Organization of Collective Cooperatives in Zimbabwe (OCCZIM) to which about a half or less are affiliated, which plays a coordinating and servicing, but also a representational, role — often raising general political issues as well as voicing cooperators interests. The government officials dealing with cooperatives seem to have a somewhat uneasy relationship with OCCZIM, perhaps because of its vigour and independence, and have in fact proposed that it be merged with CACU in a single apex organization — for reasons of 'efficiency' and 'coordination', but this would certainly dilute its radicalism. But for all its vocal ability and occasional visibility, OCCZIM has not succeeded in getting much financial backing for production cooperatives. Many of those in farming have not even got the 'development grants' to which they are entitled, and nothing like the credit that government still provides for commercial farms. But, as Hanlon (1986) suggests, this is not just a negative attitude towards cooperatives; within government there are friends as well as enemies, but also ignorance and inexperience of how they work, and not just malice.

As well as these officially registered Cooperative Societies involved in marketing and production, a third strand consists of very widespread cooperative activities of a more informal sort, especially in the countryside. These include everything from women's savings groups (although many have been curtailed as a result of misappropriation of funds by an umbrella organization in 1985, there are still 7,000 in the country), to groups of a handful of neighbouring households who share oxen and ploughs or form a labour team. The government report suggests that 20 per cent of the rural population belong to such 'pre- cooperatives'. Studies have been made in Wedza district, which has been the site of a protracted pilot project to promote all forms of cooperation, not necessarily formalized, and to gear agricultural extension to these groups rather than individuals. They indicate that the larger proportion of the population is now involved in such groups, and the number has been growing and that, on many indicators, the members of the groups get more from their farming than those who are outside the groups. This suggests that cooperation, if not always Cooperative Societies, actually pays. However, their extent in Wedza is by no means typical of most districts where there has not been such a campaign, and government has been surprisingly slow to replicate this success story elsewhere by adopting a group approach to agricultural advisory work or by such measures as providing farm credit on a group basis.

Thus, in summary, cooperatives of differing sorts are quite widespread and are fairly popular initiatives. Yet the official rhetoric favouring this promotion is translated into a practice that is at best ambiguous, and in terms of concrete resources wholly inadequate. But there are those in government and party who do contest for their promotion, and the outcome of their efforts will be a significant element in the struggle for any longer-term transition that could put socialism on the agenda in Zimbabwe. Unfortunately, however, the terms in which these efforts are couched — the need for a single cooperative structure (which would dilute the determined independence of OCCZIM by the more instrumental, passive marketing cooperatives), for greater governmental control and emphasis on professional management rather than self-management — all are bureaucratic tendencies which, however well-intentioned, will tend to inhibit the democratic and representational potential of the cooperative movement.

Part IV
The Economic System

8 Economic Structures and Their Development

In this chapter we shall pursue our theme of the categorization of Zimbabwe's political economy through an analysis of its economic structures. Among the questions we wish to answer are the following: eight years after independence, does Zimbabwe's economy show any of the characteristics of a transition to socialism? And, if so, is it on a course leading to a deepening of these characteristics?

A socialist economy will differ from a capitalist one in several clearly defined ways. In general we would expect that the means of production (as well as infrastructure) would be socially owned, that the role played by the market would be reduced by central planning, that the price structure would reflect planning priorities rather than world prices, and that there would be a high degree of equality. Each of these four characteristics may be modified in particular cases: thus 'socially owned' need not necessarily mean ownership by the state; planning may be restricted to broad priorities, with the market operating within the parameters so described; smaller countries necessarily dependent on trade may find it essential not to depart too far from world prices; and income inequality may become considerable either through market forces (as in Yugoslavia) or through the rise of bureaucratic privilege. But we must not make the mistake of identifying socialism with any of these characteristics in isolation: capitalist (or fascist) states frequently have substantial parts of the economy in public ownership and make extensive use of planning; other capitalist countries in pursuit of nationalist aims may have internal price structures far from world prices, and some capitalist countries have limited skewing of the distribution of incomes, and pay a high 'social wage' (through free or subsidized health and education services, unemployment, old age and other benefits).

We must also not make the mistake of discussing the question in static terms. Even where the capitalist state is destroyed in a socialist revolution, socialism cannot be constructed in a day: there must be a period of transition, at the end of which (on one definition) we reach socialism, when all the means of production are communally owned, and distribution is according to the principle 'from each according to their abilities to each according to their work'; only with communism do we (in theory) achieve 'from each according to their abilities to each according to their needs'. But in either case ownership of property ceases to be a source of income.

Perhaps a key criterion should be the attitude to capital aside from its ownership: does it 'create jobs' and then employ labour? Or does labour, directly or through the worker-controlled state, employ capital? Under capitalism, the productivity of capital is the main criterion (labour productivity being mainly employed in a very narrow context to identify 'overmanning') so that unemployment can be tolerated; under socialism it is labour productivity that becomes the main criterion, but in the context of the state *as a whole*, so that there is no point in solving the low labour productivity in a particular factory by transferring workers to the charge of the state: what the low productivity shows is the need for more capital to allow the labour to meet needs more efficiently.

Eight years after independence Zimbabwe is on most criteria, therefore, still a capitalist economy: most production, whether agricultural, industrial or mineral, is still carried out by private capital — about half of it foreign — in firms in which the management prerogative to manage is largely unquestioned by the work-force. The inherited state holding, largely in infrastructure, has been expanded modestly into productive capital in almost all sectors, including banking; in no sector, and in few sub-sectors apart from copper-, tin- and coal-mining, steel, and possibly pharmaceuticals, however, does the state hold a dominant share in productive capacity.

Zimbabwe's is also a market economy, in which firms' decisions are based on calculations of private profitability. It is not, however, a *free*-market economy, and if the work-force does not question managerial prerogative, then government does. In investing, in importing inputs, in exporting output, in paying or firing workers, in expatriating profits, firms are under tight government control through a network of committees in the ministries of finance, economic planning and development (and the associated Reserve Bank of Zimbabwe — RBZ), industry and technology, trade and commerce, and labour. In exchange for the loss of autonomy, firms benefit from a high degree of protection, and in many cases, of monopoly on the local market. This pattern of government control, but by parastatal committees representing capital in the sector concerned, is a legacy of the 'corporatist' elements of the settler-colonial state (Leys, 1959; Murray, 1970), still identifiable despite being modified by UDI and independence.

The work-force are also effectively constrained from striking, and state provision of social services, including education, healthcare and housing, relieves firms of the costs of ensuring a healthy and reasonably contented work-force. Furthermore, in interviews businessmen have explicitly indicated their acceptance of government spending on health and education and the consequent budget deficits as helping to moderate more radical demands for higher wages, participation, nationalization, etc.

Zimbabwean capitalism is thus alive and well, although in a rather tight state corset; it is also much more 'efficient' in orthodox terms than expected — hence the surprise of World Bank teams, which have been forced to accept that their expectations of discovering serious overall inefficiency have not been borne out in practice. Nevertheless, its 'efficiency' has inevitably suffered compared to a hypothetical free-market situation in which it would not have to pay high minimum wages or purchase costly local inputs; and it is not therefore in a position to launch Zimbabwe on an export-led boom. Even so, overall welfare is probably higher than it would have been in a free market, partly because of the higher local demand that is thereby sustained.

But if government controls have reduced the freedom of isolated capitalist firms, they are not being transformed into a structure of planning instruments designed to create an alternative dynamic, whether of a socialist or of a state-capitalist type. This is because they remain almost wholly negative: controls prevent firms freely importing, exporting, investing, sacking workers and so on; but they cannot require them to buy local (or SADCC) substitutes, to export if the local market is more profitable, to invest for long-term growth rather than short-term profit, to hire more workers or to create more jobs by choosing a more labour-intensive technology. To be sure some of this happens to some extent, both through denial of the alternatives, and through some minor incentives (primarily in exporting), but the situation remains one in which, for example, a government committee has the power to refuse to allow an investment designed to produce fashion shoes for the luxury market, whilst having no power to command investment in the production of much-needed work-boots. One lever that appears to have proved effective (if with some ambiguous consequences) is the World Bank-financed export-revolving fund, which has helped to raise exports of manufactured goods.

There are two main approaches to explaining this structure of contradictory elements. One argues that government lacked the political will to
implement radical policies (partly because of pro-capitalist elements it was
in alliance with, partly because of fears of an escalation into premature
confrontation with imperialism). Another interpretation is that a conscious two-stage process was envisaged: first, create the national democratic revolution; then, when this is consolidated against international
forces, progress to the socialist stage (see Chapter 1).

The outcome in either case is that the economic philosophy proposes
planning and socialism, whilst the practice inhibits or humanizes capitalism, adds a little state enterprise, and provides social services, adding up to a
national capitalism much like European welfare-state capitalism, but
without the scale of productive capacity needed to sustain it. In fact, no
third way has yet been found between the Scylla of a potentially disastrous
head-on confrontation with international capital and the Charybdis of
acceptance of a neo-colonial status with benefits to a corrupted elite and
nationalist rhetoric for the masses (the formula adopted in many poor
countries). In Southern Africa this choice has been made even more
difficult by the very real threat of intervention by the South African state,
and the negative example from Mozambique of the consequences of a
precipitate white exodus. Thus the economy remains heavily dependent
with declining chances of self-reliance.

Planning

The first publications relating to development strategy were *Growth With
Equity: An Economic Policy Statement* (Republic of Zimbabwe, 1981)
published in February 1981 and the documentation relating to the
Zimbabwe Conference on Reconstruction and Development (ZIMCORD
— MEPD, 1981) held the following month. The former, a short
document of nineteen pages, began with a radical analysis of the economy
and lists of objectives on a sectoral basis and with regard to labour, social
policy, finance and investment. The broad objectives started with: '[to]
establish progressively a society founded on socialist, democratic and
egalitarian principles' (paragraph 10 (i)) and '[to] end imperialist exploitation, and achieve greater and more equitable degree [sic] of ownership of
natural resources including land; promote participation in, and ownership
of, a significant proportion of the economy by nationals and the State'
(paragraph 10 (iv)). But they concluded with 'Government recognizes the

vital role which foreign investment can play in the development of industry' (paragraph 114) and listed seven areas in which it would be welcome (paragraph 120).

More significant in concrete terms were the commitments to establish a Zimbabwe Development Bank, a Zimbabwe Development Corporation, a Mining Development Corporation, and a State Trading Organization (pp. 17–18). Although the others were indeed established between 1984 and 1987, the key institution for promoting planned industrialization, the Zimbabwe Development Corporation, was still being discussed in 1988.

The ZIMCORD document (MEPD, 1981) was aimed at potential Western donors, and was therefore lighter on socialist rhetoric. Indeed its preface referred to 'the crucial significance of the experiment in moderation and reconciliation which the Government of Zimbabwe is pursuing, to the whole future of Southern Africa'. Rather than arguing for socialist transformation it emphasized the need for 'post-war recovery programmes' (pp. 2, 25–33), and although the importance of land redistribution was reiterated, it was in the context of winning international financial support to make this possible. It recalled that the Kissinger Plan of 1976 had suggested that US$1.5 billion would be needed to finance land transfer, and that assurances of help in this direction had been made at the Lancaster House conference in 1979. Unfortunately it had never proved possible to tie these assurances down — acquiescence in this vagueness was one of the crucial concessions forced out of the nationalists — and in fact only £50 million had been firmly promised (by the United Kingdom), and other countries did not add to the sum significantly.

The report called for gross investment of Z$3,898 million over a three-year period, Z$1,906 million in the public sector, with total foreign funds needed at Z$2,302 million. Of the latter figure, Z$1,254 million was sought for specific projects at the donor conference, and promises were received to this amount (although much had been promised earlier). Not much attention was paid to the terms of the offers, some of which amounted almost to commercial loans, and some of which were still undisbursed five years later. It is also worth remarking that the programme's heavy emphasis on reconstruction rather than transformation persisted throughout. Thus despite the centrality of the land issue, the category of 'land settlement and rural/agricultural development' was budgeted at only 21 per cent of total investment (pp. 21–2), and inside that category, resettlement required only 13 per cent (Z$103.5 million) or less than 3 per cent of total investment. Moreover, as a consequence of the

Lancaster House terms, half of the resettlement budget represented land purchase costs, not new investment.

The proclaimed government policy for social and economic transformation has rarely been opposed explicitly by aid donors; however they (and the IMF) have pressed 'sound' policies that have required, to put it at its lowest, going slow on such changes, or to be more accurate that were totally inconsistent with them. (For example see World Bank, 1987a.)

The highly publicized commitment to planning was manifested in the publication of the three-year *Transitional National Development Plan, 1982/83–1984/85 (TNDP) and the First Five-Year National Development Plan, 1986–1990* (FFYNDP) (Republic of Zimbabwe, 1983 and 1986). There is no space to analyse these in detail here, but as an example of the lack of real planning content in these documents, the latter depended on achieving an export growth rate of 7 per cent per annum (Zimbabwe having achieved about 1 per cent on average over the previous six years), without addressing the constraints in the domestic economy preventing the shift in gear implied. Another example relates to housing: the plan inconsistently projects a decline in the communal area (CA) population from 4.3 to 4.0 million, and a consequent rise in the urban population, requiring the building of 550,000 houses; yet it proposes to provide resources that would build at most 100,000 houses. The degree of overcrowding implied by a shortfall of 450,000 houses in an urban population of about 3 million is clearly unsustainable; as there will be a comparable shortfall in formal-sector jobs, it is clear that most of the people will be forced back on the already overcrowded CAs (see Chapter 19 of Stoneman, 1988, for a more detailed discussion).

Apart from the lack of realism of some of these targets, the process was in no sense one of 'central planning'. There have been no attempts to use physical balances, nor even to use 'indicative planning' techniques (on for example the French model) to ensure compatibility; there have been no mechanisms for ensuring compliance with plan targets beyond an implicit assumption that by maintaining tight control over foreign exchange and imports, the state can indirectly thereby control investment decisions. But this hope has not always been realistic, and any control exercised has not been part of a coherent strategy.

In conclusion, it is clear that actual development strategy has assumed a mixed-economy context, with no identifiable operational plan, and more specifically, no industrialization policy. There have been a few state takeovers of private companies (several of them South African), all with generous compensation. Beyond this it is also clear that although the strategy was modest in the extreme in structural terms, it was also absurdly overambitious in quantitative terms, with the TNDP calling for average GDP growth of 8 per cent, and the FFYNDP seeking over 5 per cent. The shortfall on the TNDP target was about 7 per cent, and in early 1988 the most favourable projections would yield an average rate of 0–1 per cent growth for the first three years of the FFYNDP. Of course there are excuses: the three-year drought of 1982–4; the world recession; the 'dissident' situation in Matabeleland, and the costs of fighting destabilization and guarding the Beira Corridor. If the TNDP may be excused for not taking account of these factors, the FFYNDP cannot, however. The outcome, as Kadhani has pointed out (in Mandaza, 1986, p. 111), is that the consequent effective abandonment of planning and resort to crisis management meant that the annual budget, with all the conservative consequences that are thereby implied, took over the role of resource mobilization and determination of economic policy. Zimbabwe, for all the high-sounding pronouncements, ended up cutting subsidies to the poor, restricting credit, and balancing its external payments, as if its economic structure was already satisfactory.

Income Distribution

The Lancaster House agreement, and ZANU's ensuing policy of reconciliation, effectively froze the pre-existing pattern of income distribution in which almost 60 per cent of income was earned by the 4 per cent minority. No radical restructuring of wage and salary scales occurred, for such risked causing an uncontrolled exodus of whites. But an equal cause of inertia was in the persistence of the patterns of wealth distribution and the associated income-generating and income-consuming consequences. Ownership of agricultural land and mining and industrial capital of course influenced how the surplus was divided not only between labour and capital but also between salaried workers (usually related by race if not family to the capital owner) and wage workers.

But it is also important to take account of the physical nature of white living conditions in urban Zimbabwe: these have always been extravagant in land use, but the relative unavailability of imported consumer goods and restricted opportunities for foreign travel under sanctions, further biased white expenditure patterns towards luxurious housing standards. The typical white-owned house was on a one-acre plot with swimming pool or tennis court (often both) and servant accommodation, resulting in towns and cities of very low density where bus services were uneconomic and car ownership was essential; about three-quarters of the total area of Harare is occupied by the elite, now racially mixed but still only making up about an eighth of the population; the other seven-eighths *and* the industrial areas occupy the remaining quarter. Reduction of high incomes would thus not impact primarily on consumption of goods but rather on property maintenance, especially in the context of the introduction of minimum wages for domestic workers. Indeed soon after independence 'low-density' house prices roughly halved in value as about half the whites left, but falls to a tenth would have been necessary to open the door to any significant redistribution to wage-workers, even at higher occupancy rates, so the fall merely provided bargains to the new black elite, a process which in the long run confirmed the inequitable distribution.

City-centre housing (requiring less transport) was very scarce, and there was no obvious way of acceptably or cheaply raising densities of occupation in the suburbs. Similar considerations applied to social services, health and education: fuller utilization of schools in former white areas was, however, possible, but required 'bussing' of children after 1980, but even this was expensive and many children spent up to two hours walking from the townships to school in the white suburbs.

It was in this context, as we have indicated in Chapter 4 above, that minimum wages were introduced and the Riddell Commission began work (Riddell, 1981). Minimum industrial wages were raised to Z$70 in 1980 and Z$85 in 1981, and were introduced at Z$30 for domestic and agricultural workers. Even the former were well below the poverty datum line estimated at Z$128 in 1981.

The Riddell Commission recommended the raising of minimum wages to 90 per cent of the PDL over a period of a few years, a job evaluation and upgrading programme, and policies to set a fair grading structure and to reduce differentials accordingly, but suggested that

In the short run rates of remuneration higher than those applicable to the new structured grading and consequent pay scale would be permitted ... where necessary for the maintenance and expansion of production. [Riddell, 1981, p. 132.]

These, it was thought, should be seen as contingency emergency payments renewable every six months before eventual elimination. Such a proposal mirrored the successful efforts to reduce wide disparities by new governments in China and Tanzania.

Although the report was accepted in principle, few of its detailed recommendations were: there has, for example, been no comprehensive attempt to evaluate the relative worth of jobs or to set up a new grading structure, although there has been a programme to upgrade existing skills. Minimum wages have been raised several times since 1981, and, following the report's recommendations, by more than has been allowed for salaries (in fact in 1981 salaries above Z$20,000 were frozen, as were salaries above Z$45,000 in 1988), which furthermore have been subjected to higher taxation. But as Riddell himself wrote in 1984:

Between mid-1980 and mid-1982 the ratio of average wages to minimum wages remained constant, the absolute gap widening by Z$890 a year. And since mid-1982 no policy changes have led to a narrowing of these gaps. [Riddell, 1984, p. 468.]

By 1988 the minimum wage had been raised to Z$100 for agricultural and domestic workers and to Z$182 per month for industrial workers. As the poverty datum line was then estimated at Z$320 per month, we see that the minimum industrial wage had fallen from 66 to 57 per cent of PDL between 1981 and 1988.

Aside from the fall in real wage rates, the need for the majority of people was still for a much greater number of job opportunities. So far as formal wage labour is concerned the retention of inflated salaries for an elite has in large measure made it impossible for these jobs to be planned for. So far as alternative employment is concerned, this waits on a central attack on the present pattern of land distribution. This, let us remind ourselves, was established for two inter-related reasons: to guarantee inflated incomes for commercial farmers and to promote labour migration from the 'reserves' to supply cheap labour to the formal sector; it continues to reproduce these consequences to this day (see the following chapter).

The level of formal employment in 1988 is probably hardly above that of 1980 when the total was 1,010,000 (*Quarterly Digest of Statistics*, December 1987); in 1984 it was 1,036,000, concealing a decline in the agriculture sector from 327,000 to 271,000; the increase of 82,000 in other sectors went entirely into services (mainly education and public administration), whilst a gain of about 10,000 in manufacturing and construction was more than cancelled by a decline of 12,000 in mining. The latest figures are for September 1986, but exclude agriculture; if employment in that sector has not declined further then total employment had probably reached 1,093,000, exceeding the peak 197 figure for the first time. Thus it is unlikely that formal employment has grown by more than 14,000 (1.4 per cent) per year since independence.

However, over 100,000 young, increasingly qualified, people are now coming on the job market each year, and the numbers are expected to peak at about 250,000 a year in the early 1990s, with no prospect, even on the (in the context) over-ambitious targets of the FFYNDP, to provide employment for more than a fraction of them. The total investment envisaged in the plan is about $7 billion over five years, or $1,400 million a year; of this at least 40 per cent will be needed to maintain existing capital, so we have perhaps $800 million per year for new investment. If all 100,000 people are to have jobs 'created' for them, this implies about $8,000 per head (or under (US$5,000). This is perhaps one-sixth of what is needed to create a job under conditions of modern technology: as a recent (extreme) example, the chemical firm Hoechst announced in 1987 investment in a chemical manufacturing plant in Zimbabwe to cost $4 million, creating 15 jobs — at $267,000 each! Even the current palm-oil project, which as an agricultural investment might be expected to be below the industrial average, is still expected to cost Z$180 million for the 10,000 jobs it should create, that is Z$18,000 each.

There is therefore *no* prospect of meeting the job aspirations of even a half of Zimbabwe's young people on orthodox policies. It is not just a matter of choosing more labour-intensive investment — it would be difficult if not impossible to bring the average down to $8,000 (or even $18,000) whilst still relying on Western technology, institutions and markets — but rather a question of the whole structure. This is for the following reasons:

— First, — the unequal income distribution pre-empts a large slice of potential investment funds for luxury and conspicuous consumption (and for that matter luxury *investment*, as in aircraft and conference centres).
— Second, — the market context would inevitably exert pressures for profit maximization which would in many (not all) cases point away from labour-intensive technology: if capital and its rate of profit is the bottom line, it will usually be more 'efficient' to employ fewer people and more capital, leaving the unemployed as a charge on the CAs. Putting it rather technocratically, only a socialist state would be able to insist on a wider accounting framework that brings such human and economic costs into the equation, over-riding the partial return to capital alone.
— Third, the above market constraints would be reinforced by openness to world market forces and the need to export high quality manufactured goods (using capital-intensive technology because of developed world tastes and demands for consistency of product). The vicious circle of a small internal market leading to a need to look outwards

leading to neglect (and impoverishment) of the internal market is not easily broken in this structure.

Foreign-exchange concessions to 'emergent businessmen'; the transfer of some existing commercial farms; and the newly arising access to high incomes and bribes for the new bureaucracy were other supposedly redistributive factors which however merely transferred income and wealth-acquisition opportunities from whites to blacks inside a small elite; they probably had no affect at all on overall inequality. But the main consequence of the strategy was a freezing not just of a pattern of inequality but of a whole economic system — or more strictly its reform and consolidation in free-market directions — through the promotion of blacks as new political buttresses to the structure. As the US *chargé d'affaires* said in 1986, 'Our support is tied to government's continuation of sound and successful policies that have provided incentives to producers and reduced or eliminated debilitating subsidies which previously distorted the fundamentals of this country's economy' (quoted in Sibanda, 1988, p. 258).

The Inherited Dual Structure

It became customary in colonial times to refer to two quite distinct sub-sectors of agriculture. Nowadays the distinction is between 'commercial' farms, sub-divided into large and small, and 'communal' areas. In fact today's 'Large-Scale Commercial Farm (LSCF) Sector' comprises what were the European-owned farms — an area of land exclusively reserved for white, private ownership. There were also the African farming areas — 'Reserves' or 'Tribal Trust Lands'. The boundaries of these two racially-exclusive preserves were modified periodically but in the last decades of colonial rule they each comprised almost exactly half of the usable land; the rest were forests, parks or wild-life preserves designated as National Lands.

The institutionalization of this dual structure began with the arrival of the whites, but at first they laid claim to land without making use of it themselves (they were still pre-occupied with minerals) and they only removed its indigenous occupants as this century progressed. In fact the first take-off into commercial agriculture was made by African peasants who supplied the early mines and town settlements with food. They were gradually but decisively elbowed out of the internal market and kept out of the later export markets by deliberate interventions by the settler state as this century progressed.

The large white farms thus came to occupy a high proportion of the better-watered and higher potential land in the east and north-east, as well as some mixed farms more dependent on ranching in the less reliably watered central areas, and some ranches in the semi-arid south and west. For decades, their technology, productivity and main crops were not markedly different from black peasant producers. But as the production of the latter declined under the unfair competition as a result of discriminatory marketing regulations and price structure, and increasing land shortage, its over-use and resulting deterioration, the white farms began a technological breakthrough after World War II b⸍   ⸌n the application of accumulated research that produced improve⸍ priate chemicals and detailed advice even to the extent of f⸍ was made possible by extensive support services and m⸍

credit. These inputs were not available nor often appropriate to peasant farmers. Except for a few privileged 'master farmers', and for a small group of black commercial farmers who were allowed to buy middling-sized holdings in the 'African Purchase Areas', productivity stagnated, the average holding size went down below the minimum level to provide subsistence, and the land and people were impoverished. The 'reserves' became more productive of migrant labour, much of it for the white farms, rather than of crop surpluses. The underdevelopment of the Communal Areas is thus related to the dualism and to the growth of the LSCF sector.

The Large Commercial Farms

In their heyday in the early 1970s there were some 6,000 large commercial farms, averaging some 3,000 hectares in size, but ranging from holdings of 100 or 200 hectares that might be irrigated, to ranches in arid areas of up to 1 million hectares. They produced 90 per cent of the marketed maize (the main staple) and cotton (the main industrial crop) and virtually all the tobacco and other exports, including almost all the other food crops — wheat, coffee, tea, sugar etc. They employed a labour force of 336,000 in 1974 — most of them permanent. But since then the number of white farms has declined, as a result of the war and then their leaving the country at independence, or selling their farms for resettlement. They also retrenched in face of minimum wage legislation, so that their labour force dropped to 271,000 in 1980 and was down to 21,000 by 1984.

Some at least of these farms use sophisticated techniques and equipment — overhead irrigation, combine harvesters for wheat, flue-curing barns for tobacco, specialist market gardening and vineyards, tea and sugar plantations and factories, pedigree dairy herds and breeding stock, and seed-producing farms growing indigenous high-yielding varieties. Yields are often high compared not only with peasant producers in general — although not so vastly greater on land of comparable potential — but also with producers in other countries. However, this is a high-cost agriculture with a high import content, it has not seen much overall growth in the last two decades and is less likely to be an engine for future growth. It is also relatively extensive and extravagant in its use of land. Only a small proportion of the land owned was ever cultivated — perhaps only 3 per cent of the total, although a higher percentage of the arable land (estimated at between 20 and 40 per cent by Weiner *et al.* (1985). But there was generous provision for fallow, the good arable land was used for light grazing, and there were low grazing densities on many ranches — often the result of finite limits of managerial capacities of the white owners.

Since independence the former white farm areas have been bought into by a few blacks and they have lost more of their land as part of the resettlement programme (see below). But they still retain over 12 million hectares, 32 per cent of the total land area. They now receive 70 per cent instead of almost 100 per cent of the agricultural credit, and still benefit from extension and other services, guaranteed, and, on the whole, good prices for their crops. Their importance to food security, export earnings and employment, though declining, still give them much clout and their actual influence is effectively orchestrated by the Commercial Farmers' Union (CFU) even though they have lost some, but by no means all, of their direct parliamentary spokesmen. Their weight is still decisive in annual price fixing, in resisting government attempts to jack up minimum wages, as in 1986, and in heading off more radical approaches to land redistribution and resettlement.

The Resettlement Areas

Almost 3 million hectares of LSC farms have been acquired to resettle African producers since 1980. On this land some 40,000 families have been resettled, most of them under a pattern, referred to as 'Model A', whereby individual householders receive 5 or 6 hectares of land for cultivation, plus access to common grazing areas for a small herd of cattle for ploughing and milk that varied in area depending on the differing potential of the agro-ecological zone. A few thousand have formed cooperatives (referred to as 'Model B') that received a large farm which they were expected to continue to run as a single operating unit. Some of these have done so quite successfully, but many have found it hard to overcome the lack of practical as opposed to rhetorical support from the government (see Hanlon, 1986), plus the difficulties of handling a large and sophisticated operation and at the same time of managing a large cooperating group with little training and no intermediate stages. Variants on these two models have led to experiments with a settlement of out-growers around a core estate, and with a system of using former ranching to provide extra, remedial grazing on a rotational basis for neighbouring Communal Area livestock owners.

There have been two related constraints to this programme, both stemming from constitutional provisions forced on the Patriotic Front at the 1979 Lancaster House Conference — perhaps the most serious compromise they were forced into swallowing. The Constitution's bill of rights specifies that, at least until 1990 when this provision will no longer be entrenched, the government can only purchase land against the owner's wishes if it is 'under-utilized', required for a public purpose, and only then if they provide prompt and full compensation in foreign exchange. This provision has effectively limited government to purchasing only the limited (and often poor quality) land that is voluntarily offered for sale to them, and further limits the programme (half of whose costs are for land purchases) to the funds made available by British aid and the government's own limited budget.

At this minimum level and confined to willing sellers' land, much of it the more marginal mixed farms concentrating on ranching in semi-arid areas, resettlement has been welcomed by the white farmers — it allows them to get rid of poor land and props up property values — and the Western diplomatic community that sees the sanctity of property as the litmus test of whether the Zimbabwean government is 'constitutional' and thus not socialist. Government has nevertheless tried to widen its access to land by the Land Acquisition Act (1986) that gives it the right of first refusal and some rights to acquire unutilized land. They are also tentatively exploring the options for a second stage of land redistribution after 1990. But so far, efforts to accelerate or expand this programme or improve the terms on which government, and in turn peasants get land, have been resisted by the CFU, white MPs and a few allies they can pick up, and the aid lobby. The argument around which opposition has been mobilized has been one of 'efficiency': that the target government set in 1982 of settling 162,000 families (four times the number actually resettled in seven years) would require, say, 60 per cent or more of the LSCF sector, and that this in turn would lead to a proportionate loss in production and employment, only partially compensated for by the production and family employment of those re-settled. The fallacies of this line of argument have now been revealed: the proportionate drop would in fact be far less insofar as the land taken over for resettlement is, as it has been, 'underutilized'; also the actual progress of resettlement shows that in more marginal, semi-arid areas (almost half of the resettlement areas) the number of resettled people outnumbers those formerly employed by factors of 5 or 10 (FAO, 1986). And evaluation of production on resettlement farms is already surpassing the long-term targets and in some instances is rivalling the yields of comparable commercial farms, and thus leading to net increases in production from the land. Resettlement is in fact leading to more intensive and quite productive land use. These facts notwithstanding, however, some elements in government, perhaps a consequence of their own private acquisition of land, may well be reluctant to pursue a vigorous resettlement policy in the teeth of diplomatic pressures from Western governments and aid agencies to slow it down.

Communal Lands

Some 4 million people live in the Communal Areas, and a sizeable additional migrant population are more or less frequent residents back with their households in the CAs. The adjective 'communal' does not apply literally but refers to a pattern of land holding whereby households occupy arable farms that have been allocated to them and in theory can be recalled by the 'community', which is also responsible for the common grazing land to which all livestock owners have access. In practice, pressure on the confined land area of the 176 separate units of Communal Lands has meant *de facto* permanent occupation by a household, with little fallowing possible. And as new families emerge, there is more encroachment onto less suitable and shrinking areas of common grazing land and some sub-division of household plots to provide for those for whom communal allocation can provide no further land. The system of land use is not met by any system of social control that can limit over-grazing and improve pastures. In addition, the communal authorities responsible for land allocation were weakened through successive changes. The chiefs' and headmen's authority was first removed then reinstated by the colonial authorities, then effectively undermined in many areas during the war of liberation. In the 1980s they have clawed back some *de facto* influence over land despite it being officially in the hands of local authorities, that are rather too remote from the village to have effective control.

Since 1980 many of the disadvantages facing CA agriculture have been reversed: credit has been provided, marketing channels opened up and discriminatory farm prices abolished, and extension services strengthened. There have been some dramatic results from these provisions and the simple removal of former restrictions. More than 90 per cent of peasant farmers in all but the most arid areas now use high-yielding varieties of maize and cotton, and the CAs now contribute more than half of deliveries to the marketing boards — from 10 per cent in 1980. However, the distribution of these advances and the benefits from them are not evenly spread. The maize surpluses are heavily concentrated (75 per cent in a good rainfall year, 90 per cent when drought affects arid areas) in the three Mashonaland provinces (out of eight) that have good quality land and reliable rainfall. Credit reaches far more than before but still only to a small minority (about 12 per cent) of all peasant farmers. Although there are a few even middle-size holdings, access to land is badly skewed — in the 0.5–12 hectare range. Significant also is the fact that in a farming system where timely access to plough oxen is crucial, perhaps 40 per cent have no oxen of their own and are thus dependent on hiring them. But rural inequalities depend perhaps even more on access to off-farm income for some members of rural families and this tends to amplify differences in agricultural resources. There is a large minority of poor peasants with little land, no oxen and without regular cash earnings — many of them women-headed households (as much as 20 per cent in some communities) that are the product of decades of labour migration.

The 'success' of peasant surpluses has tended to be trumpeted to counter arguments for more land redistribution and for any restructuring of the CA system of farming. But the underlying breakdown in some land use patterns and structures and the uncertainties of the land tenure arrangements, plus the great regional and intra-community inequalities within the CAs let alone *vis-à-vis* the LSCF sector point to the need for some reform. This difficult and sensitive nettle has not yet been firmly grasped. The government does seem to have set itself against those (usually non-Zimbabwean 'experts') who have advocated privatization of land titles to provide 'security' as an incentive to 'improve' and as a basis for credit. The more bureaucratic-minded officials seem to be inclined instead towards a form of leasehold occupation by households subject to government restrictions as to conservation and productivity. Others advocate some more effective communal management system suggesting that bureaucratic control of land use is likely to be authoritarian or unworkable — or both.

Manufacturing Industry

Zimbabwe has the most highly developed industrial sector in Africa south of the Sahara, apart from South Africa. There are two main factors that contributed to bringing this about: the relatively modest success of the mining and agriculture sectors, and the early attainment of a measure of domestic control of the economy. In contrast to the situation in Zambia with its copper, or Ghana with its cocoa, or a number of other economies in which one primary product was of dominating importance, Zimbabwe did not have a 'real business' that was manifestly the most profitable activity and from which manufacturing industry might be seen as diverting investment. On the other hand mining and agriculture were successful enough to make substantial and varied demands on industry for their inputs, from mining equipment for a dozen different sets of geological conditions to irrigation and tobacco-curing equipment, fertilizers and insecticides.

Since Arrighi's seminal paper (1967) the attainment by the white settlers of political power in 1923 has been seen as a crucial event. It is not clear that a desire for more domestic control over investment was a conscious aim of the colonialists at that stage, but political power immediately raised the possibility of investment for the long-term future of the colony, rather than the short to medium-run profitability for metropolitan shareholders, as tended to remain the criterion in other colonies.

Thus began a state-led process of industrialization favouring settler interests, in part at the expense of the economically dominant British South Africa Company which still controlled mineral rights and owned the Wankie Colliery and the railway. Local capital in the 1920s and 1930s was predominantly agricultural, but small-scale miners (up to a thousand in number) were competing with the larger foreign-owned mines, and manufacturing industry was beginning to supply a range of consumer goods to the settler population, and to seek protection against imports. The 1930s saw the Tobacco Marketing Act (1936), designed to strengthen the power of tobacco farmers against the monopsonistic United Tobacco Company, the establishment of the Electricity Supply Commission, and the setting up of the Roasting Plant, as a disguised subsidy to small-scale domestic goldminers. In the 1940s major state investments were made in the Rhodesian Iron and Steel Company (now Zisco) and in a cotton ginnery. Both of these provided a big stimulus to downstream private manufacturers (as well as to cotton growers in the latter case), and manufacturing industry began a steady rise from about 10 per cent of GDP before the war to 20 per cent in 1965, whilst agriculture declined in relative terms to about 15 per cent and mining to about 7 per cent. Isolation and the economic conditions of World War II and its aftermath provided natural protection, but during the years of the Federation of the Rhodesias and Nyasaland (1954–63), a complicated tariff structure was introduced, and after gaining preferences in their markets, Southern Rhodesian industry was stimulated by demand from its two less industrialized partners. A complex of opportunities and state responses not available to ordinary colonies thus allowed the development of an industrial structure with few if any parallels outside the independent dominions.

However these opportunities were never pursued unambiguously. As industrial capital grew it developed a need for a larger market, and as it was not yet internationally competitive this meant the internal (or federal) market. This in turn required the expansion of black purchasing power through restoring the viability of black agriculture, and thus it came into conflict with the politically more powerful agricultural capital, the white middle class and white workers, who combined to close off that avenue to expansion by the election of the Rhodesian Front in 1962.

Nevertheless, enforced protection during the UDI period gave an unexpected further stimulus to import substitution, and manufacturing's share of GDP reached 25 per cent by 1974, and with continuing protection after independence, over 30 per cent in 1986. Since 1966, tariffs have been relatively unimportant, with quantitative restrictions on imports being imposed so as to bring the total value of imports in line with export earnings. Because of the shortage of foreign exchange, initially arising because of sanctions on Rhodesian exports, any manufacturer who could demonstrate a capability for local production of any item has been very likely to gain protection. Thus it is important to appreciate that circumstances have played a major role in creating a climate conducive to the development of industry: although the state was somewhat interventionist as just discussed, 'natural protection', World War II, and UDI, have also played a major role. Indeed the professed ideology throughout was of a free-market, open-economy nature, having little in common at the rhetorical level with the command economy and interventionist, semi-autarchic policies pursued in states with Marxist governments, or even with the policies of the newly industrialized countries (NICs); in practice, however, the policies have not been vastly different from those of the latter. It is thus perhaps ironic that successful industrialization has followed from a policy that the dominant ideology would have prevented had circumstances not over-ruled it. Even after dependence, under a nominally Marxist regime, the government continues to make regular statements that its aim is liberalization of the foreign-exchange and trade regimes, although this may in part be in response to pressure from the World Bank and the IMF. Liberalization also appears to be an ideal for the business community, with a phased implementation of it gaining verbal support from the Confederation of Zimbabwe Industries (CZI) in 1987. In practice the members of the CZI are loud in their condemnation of particular breaches of protection, but they recognize that they benefit from state interventions, not only with respect to protection but also (for established firms) reasonably guaranteed foreign exchange allocations at a favourable exchange rate. Similarly, the continuing foreign exchange shortage and the fear of losing control of the balance of payments, has prevented any significant moves towards liberalization on the part of government.

Parastatals

Government has not hitherto played a large direct role in industry, although its catalytic effect in steel and cotton were probably crucial. Iron and steel were denationalized in the late 1950s, but government again increased its stake to a majority position in the UDI period after a major expansion resulted in high financial liabilities when the sanctions-busting of an Austrian partner was exposed. The main direct intervention was through the Industrial Development Corporation (IDC) which was set up in 1963 with capital of £1 million from government and private institutions, and charged with aiding development through strategic investments. These were, however, invariably minority investments, and the IDC appears to have acted without government interference as a minor investment company.

Things changed somewhat after independence, with the IDC both taking over a number of ailing companies, and becoming involved in a wider range of investments, sometimes of a majority nature; in 1983 it had total assets of about Z$40 million, under 1 per cent of total industrial assets. In 1985 it was expanded and became 100 per cent government owned, but remained self-financing. In early 1988 it was proposed to increase its capital again by tenfold to Z$100 million prior to a new expanded role. It already owns companies in general engineering, film processing, clothing, furniture, vehicle assembly, glass, stainless-steel products and pencils; it has investments in firms making aluminium products, hosiery, abrasives, chemicals, stoves and electronics. It has recently invested in joint ventures with local companies (making poly-propylene bags for agriculture) and foreign companies (an explosives factory with Swedish interests), and is involved in major new develop-ments which could lead to the production of chemical pulp and paper, caustic soda, plate glass and copper tubes. After the formation of the Zimbabwe Mining Development Corporation (ZMDC), however, it sold its mining interests, including the Kamativi tin mine. Government also has direct (usually controlling) investments in CAPS (pharmaceutics), Zim-papers (publishing), Heinz-Olivine (oils, fats and canned food), Zimbank, and it has recently acquired a controlling interest in the largest company of all, Delta Corporation.

A more formal state role in industrial development was promised in *Growth with Equity* in 1981 in the proposal for the establishment of a Zimbabwe Development Corporation. The terms of reference for the ZDC have not been published and it is not clear how it will operate, or indeed whether it will ever see the light of day. The failure to make progress in this direction is clearly associated with the more general failure to grapple with the problem of planning for industrial development, itself constrained by the context of continuing private ownership of the majority of industry.

Private Capital

Amongst the paradoxes in the political economy of Zimbabwe is that this state which proclaims Marxism–Leninism as its guiding principle (and unlike many a more avowedly capitalist state) has an active stock exchange, albeit with only forty-seven industrial companies and half a dozen mining companies quoted. The majority of these are under effective foreign control, and many are subsidiaries of transnational corporations (TNCs), which own a majority of the shares; since independence there has however been a trend to localization, with many foreign holdings falling below 50, or often 30 per cent, of the issued capital; at least one wholly-owned subsidiary (Dunlop) has gone public.

In 1987 the turnover of the forty-four companies that reported this figure rose 20.4 per cent to Z$2.69 billion (US$1.59 billion), and net earnings of all forty-seven companies rose 30 per cent to Z$175.5 million (US$104 million) (against an inflation rate of 15 per cent). As usual the top earner was Delta Corporation, then in the process of being transferred to government majority ownership by South African Breweries (which however intended to retain a 30 per cent stake), with earnings of Z$25.6 million (US$15.1 million). No other company made earnings above Z$10 million, but eight were around Z$7–9 million.

Four companies had turnovers above Z$100 million, Delta with Z$570 million (US$337 million) (however, only Z$360 million after excise duty), the locally controlled TA Holdings with Z$281 million (US$166 million), National Foods with Z$257 million (US$152 million), ZSR with Z$103 million (US$61 million), and Hippo Valley challenging with Z$98 million (US$58 million). The average ratio of net earnings to turnover was 7.4 per cent, with nine companies (led by local Tanganda Tea at 25.2 per cent) earning over 10 per cent of turnover.

The total net asset value of the quoted companies was Z$1.31 billion (US$775 million), with only three companies registering above Z$100 million, Delta (Z$168.0 million — US$99 million), Hippo Valley (Z$136.7 million — US$81 million) and National Foods (Z$104.5 million — US$62 million). The average return on net asset value was 14.8 per cent with eleven companies making over 20 per cent, including local Morewear at 26.8 per cent. Control of companies is not always clear, but in terms of predominant ownership, about eighteen are probably local and a similar number (generally somewhat larger businesses on average) are South African, with only about half a dozen clearly British.

There are also a number of large private companies, some of them local; the financial details of these are generally poorly known, but some clearly rival the larger public companies in size. One of them is the Thomas Meikle Trust, which began in hotels and retailing, but now extends into manufacturing, controlling not only the TM supermarkets, but also Zeco, a major (public) heavy engineering company, and Johnson & Fletcher (also public). A local private company largely involved in manufacturing industry is Tregers.

Foreign Capital

Most of Lonrho's and Anglo-American's holdings in the industrial field are wholly-owned subsidiaries, and the same is true of the holdings of a number of South African and British TNCs. Notable are large assembly and engineering plants owned by Lonrho, such as Dahmer and Zambezi Coachworks; the engineering works of Mitchell Cotts Engineering and South Wales Electric (GEC); fertilizer companies controlled by AAC and Norsk Hydro (local TA is also important); many oil and pharmaceutical companies, and Lever Brothers (Unilever) in soaps, fats and oils; Pigott Maskew (SA) and BTR are important in rubber, along with Dunlop. However, about half of the investment represented by foreign capital is probably still in public companies, notably: beverages, dominated by Delta, African Distillers and Schweppes; foods (with parent companies AAC and Tate & Lyle notable); clothing and textiles (Lonrho); cigarettes (BAT and Rothmans); electrical cables (BICC); and construction (Murray & Roberts). Recent estimates suggest that (including the state sector) local control of industry is much higher than for mining and is growing, so that it had probably reached a half of the total by the late 1980s, but with Britain and South Africa holding about 20 per cent each and the balance mainly American, Swiss, German etc.

The clear division of interest between foreign and domestic capital which began when the economy was still dominated by the British South Africa Company in the 1920s, was blurred considerably during the UDI period. Most subsidiaries of foreign companies continued operating under Rhodesian management, and after independence the parent companies often saw little reason to make fundamental changes, especially because the continuation of foreign exchange controls prevented full repatriation either of accumulated blocked funds from earlier earnings or even of new profits. There has therefore been little conflict of interest between foreign and local capital, with the former (even when South African) making efforts to show that they are 'good Zimbabweans' through publishing figures of the amount invested since independence, the number of workers upgraded, the numbers of blacks on the board, etc.

Nevertheless, government is increasingly pursuing what amounts to a national capitalist line. This has not produced a significant number of takeovers of foreign capital by domestic private capital, although as we have seen a number of rights issues have diluted foreign dominance of some quoted companies; rather government has encouraged the IDC to invest, or has invested directly, as in the pharmaceutical company CAPS, Zimbank or Delta Corporation (all purchased from South African parents at 'knock-down' rates). In fact a desire to 'Africanize' industry has sometimes taken precedence over a desire for merely local ownership which would usually mean white ownership. Thus faint echoes of Kenya's policy can be seen in the joint venture between the state and the US company Heinz, which took over the assets of the formerly domestically (but white) owned company Olivine Industries.

The Structure of Manufacturing Industry

Industry in small underdeveloped economies tends to be based on import substitution of the simpler consumer goods, mainly processed foods and drinks, and clothing. As we have seen, Zimbabwe very early developed some key intermediate goods industries like steel, but by the time of UDI in 1965 it was still very heavily biased towards consumer goods and simpler inputs into mining and agriculture, with a poorly developed chemical industry. There was, however a rubber industry, set up to supply the whole federation, and an oil refinery opened in 1964, destined to run for only about a year. Initially UDI stimulated rapid import substitution in consumer goods, followed by developments in a restricted range of intermediate and capital goods. Thus there were significant developments in the fertilizer industry, using cheap electricity, a major expansion of the iron and steel industry, and most important, rapid developments in engineering. The proportion of total gross output in manufacturing industry accounted for by the metals and metal products sub-sectors rose from 14.5 per cent to 22.1 per cent between 1967 and 1975. This is a major change in a key sector for self-sustaining industrialization, and depended on both state action in underwriting the expansion of the steel industry, and continued protection of a range of metal products industries that few developing countries have yet developed. It was claimed that by 1975 the number of products produced by industry had risen from 600 to 6,000. Clearly such a figure is mainly accounted for by relatively minor differentiation inside categories of goods already produced, but many new departures were also made, including the conversion of chrome ore to ferrochrome, the working of (imported) stainless steel, production of new basic metal shapes such as tubes and sheet steel, wider spare-part manufacture, and the beginnings of a capital goods industry which now produces a limited range of machine tools; many of these developments depended on 'pirated' technology used without licence or through the risky business of sanctions-busting imports of second-hand plant; the sheet steel mill for instance failed to produce consistent quality output. But many lines developed incrementally through successive phases of increasing local content: at one stage there were even plans to build a 'wholly Rhodesian' passenger car.

The counterpart of the expansion of engineering was relative contraction elsewhere, with foodstuffs, drinks and tobacco, and clothing and footwear, accounting for 42.5 per cent of gross output in 1967 but only 33.5 per cent in 1975. The large share of engineering was not, however, sustained in the decline from the 1975 peak, and one consequence of the partial opening of the economy after independence was to favour the more easily exportable textile and clothing sector.

The Construction Industry

The construction industry has declined in importance since the boom of the early 1970s when it commanded almost 5 per cent of GDP (it is now below 3 per cent). The number of 'high-cost' (i.e. for whites) houses built averaged over 3,000 a year, and 'low cost' houses numbered over 5,000 a year, rising to 10,000 in the late 1970s, with a peak of over 15,000. With independence and white emigration high-cost house prices collapsed and construction figures fell to around 300 a year, although a boom began in 1986 when almost 1,200 were built. As we have seen in Chapter 8, the unequal income distribution determined the extravagant character of white urban housing that persists to this day, and is now seen to be entirely inappropriate for a country at Zimbabwe's stage of development, let alone for one with socialist aspirations.

The counterpart to the luxury living for the whites was not shanty towns, but closely regulated townships, originally almost entirely for migrant labourers, and therefore consisting of bachelor quarters. Although family accommodation has long been accepted, the tradition of building only by authorized professional contractors has persisted, so that although conditions are extremely crowded in terms of houses per hectare and people per room, so-called 'low-cost housing' is still very expensive for lower-paid workers (unlike the common case in South Africa, township houses always have electricity, piped water and sewerage). Consequently it is not surprising to find that there is a disturbing trend in the building of low-cost houses, the construction of which almost stopped with the slump beginning in 1982 (hardly over 2,000 a year were built from 1982 to 1986); the FFYNDP projected 20,000 a year (we have seen above that its urbanization plans would have called for 110,000 a year).

Commercial building and civil engineering has held up better (although it too is down in real terms), with a number of major construction projects since independence (the Hwange thermal power station, irrigation dams, and hotel, conference centre and government office buildings), but although over a half of the work is still carried out by private sector contractors, the proportion done by or for the public sector has risen from two-thirds around independence to about 80 per cent.

Mining

Gold mining (along with copper and iron) was carried out by the indigenous Shona people of Zimbabwe for a millennium before the country's white settlement, which occurred in part in the expectation of finding a 'second Rand'. The now ruined site of Great Zimbabwe was one centre of a series of states with economies that flourished on the basis of gold-mining around AD 1000–1700. Although partly in conflict with Arab and Portuguese traders there is evidence that through them the trade reached as far afield as China. Rumours of this wealth attracted the German explorer Karl Mauch in the mid-nineteenth century, and he identified Great Zimbabwe with the biblical King Solomon's Mines, a potent mistake and one of the factors leading to the white invasion of 1890. In fact although there is significant mineral wealth, deposits are scattered and the pockets of minerals tend to be small (except for coal and chrome).

Except perhaps in the very early colonial days, mining has not therefore dominated the economy, although it contributed around 20 per cent to GDP before World War II; it has been at about 7–9 per cent for the last few decades. An expansion of the mining industry after UDI greatly contributed to the welfare of the other economic sectors by supplying foreign exchange (both from exports and from new investment income) and helping the manufacturing sector by stimulating demand. About 90 per cent of production is exported, so that in 1986 exports of minerals accounted for about 18 per cent of the total; however, this excludes effectively all of the chromium, copper and nickel, which are exported in the form of alloys or refined metal (technically counting as manufactured goods); if they are included, mining's share rises to about 35 per cent (similarly we might add in iron and steel, exported largely as billets, rods and sections, raising the total almost to 40 per cent). World economic recession severely damaged the base metal industry in the early 1980s and some large mines closed. The index of mining volume which had peaked in 1976 at 113.3 (1980 = 100) fell to a low of 92.8 in 1983, but recovered to just over 100 in 1987.

Gold, asbestos and nickel together account for 66 per cent of the new weighting structure used to calculate the volume of output in Zimbabwe's mining sector. Other minerals (in order of importance) are copper, coal, chrome, iron, silver, tin, phosphate, limestone, cobalt and lithium.

Gold. Output of gold declined from 574,000 fine oz in 1964 to 335,000 fine oz ten years later, when asbestos had long displaced it as Zimbabwe's most valuable mineral export. After 1972, however, the rise in price made gold-mining much more profitable (earnings rose twelve-fold in the 1970s with little change in volume) and from 1980 there has been an almost uninterrupted rise in output, reaching 478,000 fine oz in 1986 when gold production was worth over three times as much as any other mineral (although only marginally ahead of chromium after its conversion to ferrochrome). This recovery is due mainly to the opening by RTZ of the new Renco mine in the south-east of the country; the major producer overall remains Lonrho, with United Kingdom-based Falcon also significant; there are many 'small-worker' mines. Gold deposits are widely scattered and small in volume, with some evidence that reserves may run out within fifteen to twenty years; medium-term prospects are good, however, with some predicting a doubling in output over the next five years; Zimbabwe seems certain to remain amongst the top ten producers. Gold sales are handled through the Reserve Bank, which has established its own refinery, opened in April 1988.

Asbestos production has stagnated recently at around 160,000 tonnes under 60 per cent of the peak output of 1976; nevertheless Zimbabwe remains a major world producer (ranking between third and fifth after Canada and the Soviet Union); reserves amount to several centuries' supply at current exploitation rates, but poor world demand is the main problem. The industry is a monopoly owned by United Kingdom-based Turner & Newall.

Chrome ore is mined and converted to ferrochrome by two main companies: Zimbabwe Alloys, which is controlled by the Anglo-American Corporation of South Africa (AAC), and US-based Union Carbide. Zimbabwe is the world's third producer, and shares the bulk of the world's resources with South Africa, an effectively inexhaustible amount; it would thus stand to benefit from sanctions against South Africa if export routes can be assured.

Nickel is dominated by AAC, RTZ having closed its Empress Mine; its

Nickel is dominated by AAC, RTZ having closed its Empress Mine; its refinery however has reopened on the basis of nickel-copper matte imported from Botswana. Reserves were said to be adequate for fifty years' exploitation in 1980.

Table 10.1 Value of Mineral Production (Z$ million)

	1980	1981	1982	1983	1984	1985	1986	1987
Gold	144.9	117.4	122.8	193.9	214.1	241.3	292.8	349.9
Asbestos	70.2	91.3	76.6	69.3	80.8	84.5	85.8	97.9
Nickel	55.6	51.7	49.8	43.1	59.7	73.4	60.7	73.2
Coal	28.0	29.5	35.8	42.2	58.3	66.8	89.1	103.4
Copper	35.4	27.9	26.8	32.9	33.8	43.3	43.3	46.1
Chromite	18.4	20.4	19.9	26.1	29.7	33.7	39.7	44.2
Iron ore	14.8	14.8	13.9	14.6	14.5	18.9	21.1	28.8
Silver	13.0	6.0	5.3	10.6	9.0	7.9	10.6	15.8
Tin	9.9	11.3	11.6	16.2	18.5	22.6	10.7	11.5
Others	24.6	23.2	20.5	21.5	28.1	36.9	45.6	44.6
Total	414.8	393.5	383.0	470.5	546.5	629.6	699.4	815.4

Source: Quarterly Digest of Statistics

Table 10.2 Volume of Mineral Production, 1980–7 ('000 tonnes)

	1980	1981	1982	1983	1984	1985	1986	1987
Gold ('000 oz)	367	371	426	453	478	472	478	473
Asbestos	250.9	247.6	197.7	153.0	165.3	173.5	163.6	193.9
Nickel	15.1	13.0	13.3	10.1	10.3	9.9	9.7	10.4
Coal	3,134	2,867	2,769	3,326	3,109	3,114	4,047	4,639
Copper	27.0	24.6	24.8	21.6	22.6	20.7	20.6	18.8
Chrome ore	553.5	536.1	431.6	431.4	476.4	526.5	453.1	570.3
Iron ore	1,622	1,096	837	924	925	1,098	1,115	1,328
Silver ('000 oz)	949	857	918	935	895	799	840	814
Tin (tonnes)	934	1,157	1,197	1,235	1,209	1,207	1,079	1,038
Total index	100.0	95.9	96.4	92.8	97.0	96.9	99.3	102.8★

Source: Quarterly Digest of Statistics ★ Provisional

The main mining companies are all foreign owned: RTZ, Falcon Mines and Falconbridge in gold; Lonrho in gold and copper; AAC in nickel, chromium and coal; Union Carbide in chromium; Turner & Newall in asbestos. A recent entrant is Cluff Oil in gold, and a number of Australian companies are moving in.

In 1983 the government established the Minerals Marketing Corporation of Zimbabwe (MMCZ) to market minerals internationally. The intention of this was explicitly to rule out transfer pricing by the foreign-owned mining companies; although effectively all transactions are now through the MMCZ, over 95 per cent of metals are sold to the same intermediaries that were used before its establishment, with the final buyer being generally unknown; the MMCZ and its key personnel (some of whom were prominent sanctions busters who set up the sales chain) have therefore come in for much criticism, with suggestions that transfer pricing is still losing some Z$100 million annually. It has, however, also made some sales on its own account to China (steel), India (asbestos), and Tanzania (coal), but the total of such sales although rising rapidly was still worth below Z$1 million in 1987. The government also controls the Zimbabwe Mining Development Corporation (ZMDC), which is the controlling shareholder in the Mhangura mine (acquired from Messina of South Africa in 1984), the largest copper mine, and the Kamativi tin mine (the only source of tin in Zimbabwe). ZMDC has prospects of major gold developments and of establishing a world market for Zimbabwe's kyanite, which it has already exported to Japan, West Germany and South Africa.

Over 90 per cent of mineral production is exported, and effectively all of the gold, nickel, copper and chrome. Coal is largely used domestically, as is iron ore, and some asbestos is converted to asbestos cement products. There are now few opportunities for further beneficiation of minerals, as gold, copper and nickel are already refined in Zimbabwe, and nearly all the chrome is exported as ferrochrome. Even the latter counts officially in the trade statistics not as a mineral but a manufactured good, as of course do the iron and steel produced by Zisco, of which about 80 per cent is exported. As exports of the latter plus unmanufactured minerals amount to over 40 per cent of exports it is clear that the industry is of much greater importance than its 7 per cent contribution to GDP might imply. Unfortunately the benefits from mining are largely uncontrolled by Zimbabwe, whose output is too small in world terms for it to be other than a price taker (except possibly for asbestos and chrome), and effectively all the markets are in developed countries, with marketing outlets dominated by transnational corporations. Nationalization is not therefore an option likely to yield major benefits unless there is a prolonged boom in commodity markets; the government appears to have taken note of Zambia's unhappy experience with state control in the context of falling prices.

Zimbabwe has a highly developed and fairly efficient infrastructure by Third World standards. However, despite improvements since independence, it is still seriously maldistributed: the communal areas are still almost entirely without electricity, piped water, sewerage, and in most cases access to tarred roads or railways, which were built exclusively to serve white towns, farms and mines. The cities, by contrast, approach First World standards for provision of transport, electricity, water, retail distribution, sewerage and communications (although provision in the townships is very inferior to that in the commercial and 'low-density' areas).

Transport

Zimbabwe is a landlocked country, whose nearest access to the sea is the port of Beira in Mozambique, some 300 kilometres from the eastern border. Maputo (formerly Lourenço Marques) and Beira, carried the major part of Zimbabwe's external trade until 1975, when the border closure forced it to take the much longer routes (of the order of 2,000 kilometres from Harare) through South Africa. After independence, South African-supported terrorism severely disrupted the Mozambican routes, so that until recently over 90 per cent of external trade had to go through South African ports, imposing an effective 5 per cent tax (costing Zimbabwe some Z$100 million extra a year) and exposing Zimbabwe to continuous threats of blackmail. Only since 1987 has a significant proportion of trade been restored to Beira, through the protection of the 'Beira Corridor' (see Chapter 16) by up to 10,000 Zimbabwean troops (at a cost estimated to be at least Z$200 million), and in 1988 the start of rehabilitation and protection of the Maputo line brought hopes that soon dependence on South African ports might fall below 50 per cent.

The National Railways of Zimbabwe (NRZ) is a parastatal body which runs the internal railway system; the lines extend some 2,836 kilometres, linking all the major centres of economic activity, with a number of branch lines to mines and plantations. In 1988 Zimbabwe owned 249 diesel locomotives and about 160 steam locomotives. Of the 13 million tonnes of freight carried in 1981, about 45 per cent went over the border. The first stage of an electrification programme covering 457 kilometres of the Harare to Dabuka (near Gweru) line, was completed in 1983, but shortage of funds has suspended the programme with about thirty electric locomotives in operation. NRZ has also controlled the line through Botswana to South Africa, but negotiations in 1987 to transfer responsibility for this line to Botswana were stalled because South Africa tried to make recognition of the 'homeland' of Bophuthatswana (in which the line enters South Africa) a condition in the necessary new contract between it and Botswana.

Zimbabwe has 85,000 kilometres of roads, of which about 15 per cent are tarred and 54 per cent gravelled. Several main roads have been rehabilitated since independence, and heavy lorry traffic competes with rail freight; there are several haulage companies, some operated by mines and other industries, and there are also several rural bus companies and inter-city bus services. Much effort has recently been put into upgrading country roads, hitherto largely of earth in the communal areas.

Zimbabwe has eight airports, with Harare, Bulawayo and Victoria Falls classed as international. A new terminal is under construction at Harare. Air Zimbabwe operates an overseas service to London, Athens and Frankfurt, and has special agreements with British Airways and Qantas; about a dozen international airlines also operate services into Zimbabwe. Zimbabwe's airports handled 1.1 million passengers in 1985 (excluding transit passengers), about 10 per cent of which were international arrivals. Air Zimbabwe carried 453,000 passengers in all in 1985. Affretair, the state-owned airfreight company carried most of the 20,000 tonnes of airfreight in 1985.

Power

Zimbabwe has no domestic oil or gas resources but has huge deposits of coal, substantial natural and plantation woodland, and abundant hydro-electric potential, all of which are already major contributors to energy supply. The climate makes it one of the countries in which solar energy has significant potential, and a number of companies are active in this field. Government policy is for effective national self-sufficiency, and the recent expansion of thermal power generation has taken place in preference to the cheaper option of joint development of Mozambique's Cabora Bassa hydroelectric potential or continued purchases from Zambia.

Coal has long been mined at Hwange (Wankie) as a fuel for railways, industry and domestic use, for conversion to coke (primarily for the iron and steel industry) and for municipal power stations; it has recently become the centre of major thermal electricity generation at Hwange itself (see below). Estimated coal reserves are 30,000 million tonnes in some twenty-three fields, but the 3 million tonnes of annual production is entirely from the Hwange coalfield, although plans are advanced to open a new coalfield at Sengwa, south of Lake Kariba.

Imports of oil (entirely in the form of refined products) are used mainly for transport and lubrication; a pipeline from Beira in Mozambique (controlled by Lonrho) leading to a refinery near Mutare was opened just before UDI, and then remained inoperative until 1982, since when it is guarded as part of the Beira Corridor (the refinery was never reopened).

The Kariba dam and lake were constructed during the federal period to provide hydroelectricity to Zambia and Zimbabwe, and resulted in abundant cheap electricity for many years. Total installed generating capacity was 1,539 mw in 1984, of which thermal accounted for 906 mw and hydroelectric 633 mw; another 440 mw opened at Hwange during 1986–7. This represented the fruits of the immediate post-independence decision to go for energy self-sufficiency, something not achieved even by Rhodesia under sanctions. The decision appears to have been influenced by the World Bank and Western advisers: the Anglo-American Corporation of South Africa (AAC), with its equity stake and management contract in the Wankie Colliery found its position strengthened; the option to purchase surplus electricity from the Cabora Bassa dam in Mozambique was not even investigated; and the decision was taken to phase out electricity purchases from Zambia as new units of thermal electric power became available at Hwange. In 1987 Zambia started legal action after Zimbabwe stopped purchases ahead of the agreed schedule. Previously Zimbabwe had imported about 30 per cent of its electricity from Zambia; in addition the two countries cooperate (as they did throughout the UDI period) in regulating the generation of electricity from the two generating stations on the Kariba dam, which was built in the 1950s.

About 20 per cent of total electricity demand is made by just two concerns: Zimalloys in its ferrochrome plant and Sable Chemical Industries in water electrolysis as a source of hydrogen for the production of ammonia (a route that only makes sense when, as in the 1960s, the cost of marginal electricity is close to zero). Rural development plans envisage extensive electrification via growth points, with a first phase (involving 24 projects) about half completed in early 1986. The primary energy source for most of the population, supplying 29 per cent of national energy needs in 1979, is wood. Denudation of indigenous forests is a serious problem, and the World Bank has studied a Z$12.5 million tree planting scheme. However the concentration of development is on electricity supplies (unlikely to provide a realistic alternative to wood for some time to come), and it is estimated that per caput investment for non-wood sources is Z$75 per year compared with 17 cents for wood. It has been suggested that the most cost-effective approach would be to develop community-based schemes exploiting versatile bushes such as euphorbia that can simultaneously supply fuel, fodder and fencing material.

Water Supply

There are no natural lakes in Zimbabwe, but some 7,000 artificial dams. Much larger than the rest put together is Lake Kariba, containing some 160,000 million cubic metres. It is however low lying and primarily of use for electricity generation. The most important dam that is primarily for irrigation purposes is Lake Kyle (with under 1 per cent of Lake Kariba's capacity), but it primarily supplies the distant commercial sugar plantations in the south of the country, even though located in the heavily populated Masvingo province where in the drought years of 1982–4 and 1987 over a million people had to be provided with food from outside because of almost total crop failure. In all, about 10 per cent of arable land is irrigated including a high proportion of the higher potential commercial farming areas, which use many small dams and overhead sprinkler systems. This capital-intensive approach is ill-adapted to the needs of the communal areas, which are virtually without irrigation despite their much greater needs, given that 80 per cent of their area is in arid and semi-arid regions. Like Lake Kyle, Lake Macilwaine, one of Harare's two main water-supply dams, also has very attractive recreational uses.

Mass Media and Communications

There are state-owned radio and television stations (two channels, in colour) which take advertising. The press is free, but the two main papers (total circulation about 150,000 daily) are owned by Zimbabwe Papers in which the state has a controlling interest; there are also two Sunday newspapers and about a dozen weekly or monthly entertainment or specialist periodicals.

There were about a quarter of a million telephones in operation in 1985 through nearly one hundred exchanges; the service is quite good by developing country standards, although in the process of urgently needed rehabilitation. There is an internal STD service, and with the opening in 1984 of a satellite link there is now a fairly good international direct dialling facility. There are also almost two thousand telex terminals.

Finance

Zimbabwe has the most sophisticated money market system in black Africa, with a full range of institutions. The central bank is the Reserve Bank of Zimbabwe which acts as banker to government, issues currency and government loans etc., controls foreign reserves, acts as lender of last resort to the commercial banks, administers the exchange-control legislation and handles gold output. The main commercial banks are Barclays Bank of Zimbabwe, Standard Bank, Grindlays Bank, the Bank of Credit & Commerce (which came in after independence), and Zimbank (in which the government has a 61 per cent stake). In 1985 there were four merchant banks, two discount houses, five registered financial institutions, three building societies, an export-credit insurance corporation, and numerous insurance companies. The banking sector as a whole is not an important direct investor in the economy: out of total assets of Z$5,069 million in 1986, investments accounted for only Z$84 mn (1.7 per cent), whilst loans and advances made up 32 per cent and government stock 24 per cent of the total. Deposits (corporate and private) form 60 per cent of total liabilities, which are themselves equivalent to about 62 per cent of GDP, a high ratio for a developing country.

The Zimbabwe Development Bank began operations in March 1985 with authorized share capital of Z$50 million; it is 51 per cent owned by government, but has a number of foreign banks and developmental organizations in minority positions; it is concentrating its activities in the manufacturing sector.

Internal trade

Wholesale and retail trade are almost wholly in the private sector and are well developed in the urban areas, but less well so in the countryside, where communication and the low-level of spending power are serious constraints; indeed many rural areas are less well served by shops than is the case in much poorer countries. The major towns have department stores and chains of supermarkets catering for the rich elite, which bear comparison with standards in Europe in that they are well-stocked and displayed; down market are equivalent chains which cater mainly for lower-paid workers, and many family shops and 'cafe's' stay open after the usual closing time of 5 p.m.

Tourism

Zimbabwe has a number of tourist attractions, with the Victoria Falls pre-eminent, followed by the ruins of Great Zimbabwe, the Eastern Highlands, and several lakes and game parks; it has the added advantage that tourism is not restricted to any particular season. The total number of visitors in 1986 was 433,372 of whom over 80 per cent were on holiday. Direct foreign exchange earnings were estimated at Z$50 million in 1985 (although the total is thought to be about twice this), and the industry is growing at 15 per cent per annum. Competition with other land use is not yet serious, as the large game parks are in low-lying areas with poor rainfall and infected by tsetse fly.

There are over fifty graded hotels, some of five-star standard, but overall bed-occupancy rates are in the 30–40 per cent range; despite this, however, new hotels are being opened. The Harare Holiday Inn, a joint venture between the government and Rennie Grinaker (Zimbabwe) Ltd, opened in late 1983, and the Z$100 million (US$60 million) Sheraton Hotel and International Conference Centre was opened in late 1985 this was built by Energoproject of Yugoslavia, and was jointly financed by the governments of Yugoslavia, France and Zimbabwe. In addition there are many state-sponsored national parks with basic accommodation and camp sites.

Basic Data

Considering its small size Zimbabwe is a relatively closed economy, with visible exports equivalent to 26 per cent of GDP, and imports to 20 per cent in 1986. Much of the cause of this was the sanctions imposed in the UDI period; in 1965 exports were 47 per cent and imports 36 per cent of GDP. Unreliable figures from the late 1940s suggest ratios over 60 per cent at that time. The trade surpluses had not been typical of earlier periods when deficits had been covered by large capital inflows, but by 1965 capital was flowing out rather than in, and the servicing of the existing foreign-owned capital stock, together with a large deficit on services, made trade surpluses essential. This pattern continued through the UDI period and after, with the exception of 1981 and 1982 when aid inflows financed trade deficits occasioned in part by the need to rebuild after the war. As the aid tailed off and repayments fell due, imports had to be cut severely again to well below exports to cure the balance of payments deficit.

The terms of trade improved dramatically with the end of sanctions: on a base of 1980=100, they rose from 80.9 in 1979 to 111.2 in 1981 and 123.4 in 1985, since when there are indications that a fall has occurred to about 115.

Exports are dominated by primary commodities, roughly 40 per cent each for agricultural products and minerals (including refined metals and alloys), with only about 20 per cent being manufactures (although about a half of the share of mining is conventionally classified as manufacturing). There were reports during 1987 of rapidly increasing exports of manufactures, particularly of textiles and clothing, under the impact of the new export-revolving fund. Tobacco, almost entirely an LSCF sector crop, is generally the main export earner, bringing in Z$3–400 million (US$180–240 million) in recent years, about a fifth of the total; gold is not far behind at around Z$200 million (US$120 million), although the high price in 1986 prompted sales from stock, and total earnings were Z$413 million; ferroalloys also earn around Z$200 million and cotton lint (more than half produced by peasants) Z$150 million, these four accounting for over a half of all earnings. Also important are sugar, coffee, meat, asbestos, nickel, and steel, all earning between Z$40 and Z$80 million; the first 'true' manufactured goods are textiles and clothing which together earned about Z$60 million (a rise of over 20 per cent) in 1986.

By contrast imports are almost entirely accounted for by petroleum and chemicals (about 20 per cent each) and machinery and transport equipment (40 per cent); steelplate is another significant item, costing about Z$40 million in 1986. Consumer goods and other 'non-essential' imports have thus been almost completely squeezed out over twenty years of strict attention to ensuring that foreign exchange goes first to providing essential imports that cannot be produced in the country. The only partial exceptions are one or two luxury items, such as whisky, which the Smith regime continued to import, it was said, to help keep up the morale of the whites. Whisky is still imported for similar reasons, as well as because tourists expect to find it, but it is also now consumed as a status symbol by the new black bourgeoisie. Colour television sets and video-recorders have more recently acquired a similar status, but in aggregate such imports are unimportant.

Britain was traditionally the most important trading partner, with Zambia rising in importance during the period of the federation. UDI and

Table 12.1 Directions of trade, 1981 and 1986.

Percentages	Exports to		Imports from	
	1981	1986	1981	1986
South Africa	21.6	12.4	27.5	21.4
United Kingdom	6.9	12.3	10.0	10.9
West Germany	8.2	8.6	7.2	9.9
Netherlands	3.0	6.1	2.3	1.6
Italy	5.0	5.9	2.1	4.3
United States	7.9	5.7	7.3	8.3
Japan	2.8	4.6	6.1	4.3
Botswana	3.2	4.3	1.7	4.7
Belgium	3.6	3.2	1.6	1.1
Mozambique	1.3	3.2	1.9	..
Zambia	4.0	2.9	2.4	2.6
China	..	2.8	..	0.8
Switzerland	1.9	1.3	2.1	2.9
France	1.7	1.2	3.6	3.3
Others	28.9	25.5	24.2	23.9

Notes: Exports exclude gold. Petroleum imports of unknown origin were 11.6 per cent of the total in 1981, 9.4 per cent in 1986.

sanctions established the present dominance of South Africa, although this has recently begun to be challenged again, partly as a result of President Mugabe's desire to reduce dependence and if possible to introduce trade sanctions without too much disruption. Statistics are not available for the UDI period, but Table 12.1 shows the shift away from South Africa that has occurred since.

It is noteworthy that no member country of the CMEA appears in the above table; there is however significant trade, mostly of a barter nature, and varying erratically from year to year but rarely exceeding 1 per cent of the total, with Bulgaria, Czechoslovakia, East Germany, Poland and Yugoslavia. Individual deals are also often reported with Romania and North Korea.

The low positions in the table of Zimbabwe's partners in the Southern African Development Coordination Conference (SADCC) is also misleading, in that together they take about the same share of Zimbabwe's exports as does South Africa; they are however much less important for imports.

Exchange-rate Policy

The exchange rate of the currency has not been an important instrument in achieving payments balance. UDI brought expulsion from the sterling area and a severe strengthening of foreign-exchange controls; in this way, as has been the case in many other countries, the currency became overvalued, with significant divergences arising between internal and external prices. The over-valuation was probably never serious in the case of Zimbabwe, partly because stringent price control prevented inflation, and partly because, despite sanctions, the economy thrived under the combined effects of import substitution and large investments from South Africa, particularly into the nickel and sugar industries, to take advantage of favourable world prices in the late 1960s and early 1970s. Thus the implicit discrimination against exports and the bias in favour of the manufacturing sector was beneficial in maintaining the momentum of industrialization.

After independence, when inflation accelerated into the range 10–20 per cent per annum, and two years of payments deficits occurred, a correction, followed by a new approach became necessary. The correction involved a 20 per cent devaluation, followed by the tying of the currency to a trade-weighted basket of foreign currencies; however, the constitution of the basket has not been disclosed, and the Reserve Bank continues to fix the exchange rate according to its own undisclosed calculations. A significant devaluation thus appears to have occurred, from Z$0.643 to Z$1.665 per US$, between 1980 and 1986; however in real terms (allowing for the much higher inflation rate in Zimbabwe), devaluation has probably only been about 25 per cent. Between 1986 and early 1988, the currency has remained more or less unchanged (within 4 per cent) against the US$, representing a real appreciation against it (though not against most other important currencies) as the inflation rate has continued in double figures.

Unofficial estimates claim that the Zimbabwe dollar was about 20 per cent overvalued (compared with a hypothetical free-market rate) in early 1988; if this is true, it is probably deliberate policy, designed to promote continued industrialization (through keeping capital goods and industrial inputs cheap); the implicit bias against the primary sectors and exports is partly corrected by the use of export-revolving funds introduced during 1986–7; but it is judged that world demand is the main constraint against raising primary exports, so that devaluation would merely give 'windfall gains' to already profitable commercial farmers and mining companies without increasing exports.

Protection

Direct quantitative controls have instead kept payments in balance. *All* international transactions require Reserve Bank of Zimbabwe (RBZ) approval, whether inflows or outflows, as repayments of loans, payment of interest, dividends or profits, payments for goods or services, and whether or not currency is involved. The reason for the comprehensive nature of the controls, extending to 'no currency involved' transactions, is to prevent the exploitation of loopholes; thus even receipt of gifts is seen as having a possible hidden foreign exchange cost: the logic is that if some Zimbabweans receive gifts of luxury goods, they may eventually attempt to make gifts in exchange that could have earned foreign exchange to import machinery.

The import controls took their present form in 1966, when the regime was faced with a 36 per cent drop in export earnings; importers were allowed to purchase (with local currency) foreign exchange only up to a quota determined as a proportion of their actual average expenditure in 1964 and 1965. The system has been severely criticized as rewarding conservatism and penalizing new entrants, but has been operated with some flexibility. The actual fund to which quotas are related is calculated twice a year, and is the balance left after certain essential imports, including petroleum, fertilizers, defence procurements, etc., have been deducted from available foreign exchange earnings. It is then divided amongst commercial importers, who import on behalf of traders and small businesses, and direct industrial allocations to larger firms.

But the system does not only operate at this quantitative level: importers cannot use their allocations to import what they wish, but have to obtain import licences; this has the effect of largely restricting imports to essentials. Policy decisions are taken in standing committees of the ministries of trade and commerce, and industry and technology, and are the closest that Zimbabwe comes to industrial planning. Each half-year these committees decide on variations amongst recipient industries and individual firms from the historical allocation; this introduces flexibility, but also the possibility of corruption, which has however not apparently become serious. Since independence, other sources of foreign exchange than the basic allocation have become important, complicating the system considerably; these range from 'ad hoc' allocations, designed to correct problems arising from exogenous factors (like unexpected rises in essential import prices) to commodity import programmes (CIPs), arising from aid or export promotion policies of other countries. Thus Dunlop, which needs to import most of its raw materials — natural and artificial rubber, carbon black and tyre cord, none of which is made in Zimbabwe — found itself in the mid-1980s receiving only a third of the necessary foreign exchange in the basic allocations, and having to present cases for 'ad hoc' and CIP allocations on the basis of the threat to the harvest if orders for tractor tyres were not filled, and similar arguments.

Other committees consider foreign investments and investment generally, inspecting the foreign exchange implications of the proposals. There are a large number of criteria, not always consistent, including the promotion of import substitution, export earnings, use of local resources, creation of jobs, especially through labour-intensive investment, and so forth.

Thus we see that what started out as purely a defensive measure to prevent payments imbalances, gradually became during the UDI period an instrument for promoting import substitution for its own sake, and after independence this meshed in comfortably with the regime's ideology which emphasized self-reliance, a reduction of dependence on South Africa and the imperialist powers, and promotion of internal, especially rural development. We have seen above that socialist rhetoric has not been operationalized into measures to effect radical shifts away from dominant capitalist structures, whether in industry or even in the racial domination of the best farmland, but where structures strengthening state control (such as this unusual form of quantitative import control) were already in place, they have been successfully defended and partially realigned to serve if not socialist ends, at any rate economic nationalist ones.

Indeed some have seen the physical import control system as a potential nucleus for a practicable form of planning — possibly the most practicable available in the Southern African context. It is doubtful if it alone could bear the full weight of a socialist transformation, but it is certainly important in the ordering of national priorities where non-market outcomes are desired. Certainly its significance has been perceived by anti-socialists. Thus as early as 1981 attacks began on the foreign-exchange allocation system, and on its supposed harmful effects on industry; these emanated mainly from the World Bank, as discussed in more detail in Chapter 13 below.

State Trading Organizations

One of the factors that has been identified as a major element in the exporting success of Japan and South Korea, is the existence of trading organizations that specialize in marketing. The argument is simple: manufacturers specialize in manufacturing and develop a competitive advantage in a particular activity; it does not follow that they are equally efficient in other different activities, and exporting may require entirely different skills. In the case of manufacturing the foreign trade of Zimbabwe is still largely in private hands, in fact the individual producers.

However, most agricultural products are exported through the Agricultural Marketing Authority (AMA) which falls under the responsibility of the ministry of agriculture, and coordinates the operations of four boards which operate under statutory control. These are the Cold Storage Commission (CSC: beef and lamb), the Dairy Marketing Board (DMB: milk and dairy products), the Grain Marketing Board (GMB: maize, wheat, sorghum, rapoka, mhunga, groundnuts, soyabeans, sunflower oil, edible beans, coffee), and the Cotton Marketing Board (CMB). The first two still cater almost entirely for the LSCF sector, and the GMB and CMB although also heavily involved in peasant production still retain biases towards the more accessible farmers in the more fertile areas. The boards are, with only minor exceptions, monopsonies paying guaranteed prices to producers, arranging collection from depots, processing, marketing and exporting. They are generally regarded as efficient, and in some cases provide a channel for guaranteeing credit recovery. Tobacco is marketed under separate statutes under the Tobacco Marketing Board (TMB) through an auction system using the world's largest auction floor. Similarly pork products are under Colcom. Sugar, tea, horticultural products, and poultry products, are left to private enterprise, although the first three are major exporters.

The agricultural boards were established before independence, and developed exporting skills under sanctions. Since independence, attempts have been made to extend the principle into mining with the establishment in 1983 of the Minerals Marketing Corporation of Zimbabwe (MMCZ) to market minerals internationally (see Chapter 10), and a State Trading

Corporation (STC). The latter was promised in 1981, although discussions took until 1987. The new STC is not intended to be a monopoly or in any way to substitute for private sector trading arrangements, however. Its main function is to seek out new markets and new exportable products and to provide a service to existing exporters. Its only monopoly is to be in the field of barter trade.

Zimbabwe as a Regional Industrial Power

Zimbabwe's future is as a fully integrated member of the southern African region. The implications of this obvious fact for the regime's policies is discussed in Chapter 16 below. To conclude the present discussion of trade, it is necessary however to relate regional opportunities to Zimbabwe's problems arising from its small internal market on the one hand and the poor prospects for internationally competitive export-led growth (the supposed NIC model) on the other. The region could clearly provide a larger market (as part of it did during the federation), but unless it can also supply a higher proportion of Zimbabwe's import needs the benefits would be largely in Zimbabwe's direction, leading to conflict and ultimately breakdown. The dominance of the Zimbabwean economy in the region is illustrated by the contribution to GDP of the three productive sectors in the following table.

Table 12.2 SADCC Gross Domestic Product by country and sector of origin, 1983 percentages.

Country	Manufacturing	Agriculture & forestry	Mining
Angola	n.a.	n.a.	n.a.
Botswana	7.7	7.3	27.9
Lesotho★	5.5	18.4	2.7
Malawi	n.a.	39.0	12.8
Mozambique★	9.0	41.7	25.9
Swaziland	23.5	25.3	2.6
Tanzania	9.3★	51.5	0.6★
Zambia	19.8	14.2	15.3
Zimbabwe	30.0	12.8	6.2

Notes: n.a. Not available   ★ Data for 1982
Source: SADCC, *Macroeconomic Survey, 1986,* pp. 104 and 163.

The share of manufacturing in Zimbabwe is the largest by far in SADCC,

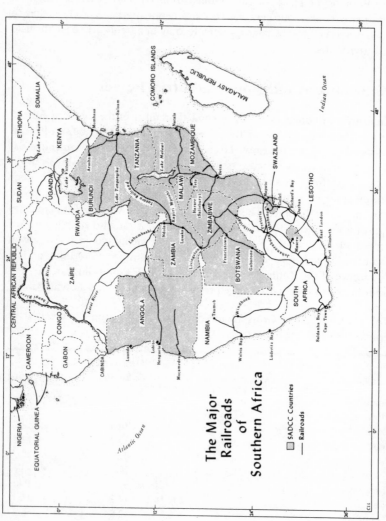

Map 3 Southern Africa: the communications network

including activities not found in the other countries on any scale, such as the small but growing capital goods sector. Further, Zimbabwe is the only country to have a fully integrated steel industry, with production right through from mining of raw materials to manufacturing of finished products. Manufacturing industry in Swaziland, although contributing a higher proportion than most, is much less integrated, being mainly agricultural processing plus assembly of parts and units imported from South Africa; it is even moving into the electronics assembly field for South Africa.

The static figures of the table do not reveal what is a serious trend, a growing polarization in the distribution of manufacturing. A principal consequence of the independence of Angola and Mozambique, followed as it was by sabotage and destabilization, was a realignment in the distribution of manufacturing activity within the region. These countries' share in regional manufacturing value-added (at 1975 prices) fell from 27 per cent in 1970 to 15 per cent by 1981 (and further after 1981) whilst that of Zimbabwe rose from 30 to 46 per cent. These disparities disclose a significant opportunity for Zimbabwe in aiding in the rehabilitation of the industrial sectors in Angola, Mozambique, Tanzania, and possibly Zambia, but Zimbabwe's increasing dominance and the other member countries' dependence on it could lead to serious consequences.

Zimbabwe also has the highest proportion by far of regional trade: almost half of all intra-SADCC trade originates there, and another 30 per cent of the trade are imports into it, so Zimbabwe is a partner to almost 80 per cent of total intra-SADCC trade. It also has a large trade surplus in the region. As the most natural market for promotion of industrial exports is the region, Zimbabwe and SADCC will have to find a way to balance the accounts regionally, or Zimbabwe's trade surplus will retard trade expansion. Indeed since 1984 a *reduction* of trade with Malawi has occurred, due to a combination of PTA regulations and Zimbabwe's foreign exchange shortage, and the same prospect with regard to trade with Botswana was only narrowly averted in negotiations in 1988.

Although disparities among the economies are real, what they share in common is also important. Zimbabwe exports manufactured goods but still relies heavily on capital goods imports; the other countries remain raw-material exporters and manufacturing importers. In all cases low wages stunt domestic demand, and foreign ownership and expatriates in skilled jobs reduce local control over economies. All would benefit greatly from any cooperation broadening the resource base for industries (see Thompson, 1988, for further discussion of this topic).

Part V
The Regime's Policies

13 Economic Policies

Domestic Economic Policies

It will be clear from earlier chapters that Zimbabwe's policies of economic management since independence show some continuities with those practised under sanctions. This is despite both socialist rhetoric on the one hand, and expressions of agreement with the World Bank on supposedly technical questions such as the desirability of 'liberalization' of the foreign–exchange and trading regimes on the other. The paradox may be partly explained through the common element of economic nationalism in a context of strong state control.

Also very important is a general attitude of caution. This was reinforced by the chastening experience of the severe balance of payments problems of 1981–3 which had been precipitated by the relaxation of controls in 1980–1. Decisions are taken only slowly after much discussion, and a consensus is usually sought prior to action rather than the 'rubber-stamping' of a centrally determined policy. One result has been a very orthodox monetary policy, with Zimbabwe priding itself on meeting debt obligations without rescheduling, and an exchange rate for the Zimbabwe dollar which has been regarded as only slightly overvalued for short periods. Likewise, despite the highly skewed wealth and income distributions discussed elsewhere, government has remained respectful of property rights, both for white farmers and for white and foreign capitalists. However, past practice reinforced by new ideology has made for significant state intervention, so that at a time when most developing countries are bowing to IMF/World Bank pressure to privatize, in Zimbabwe there is even a slight expansion of the public sector, with state involvement increasing in mining and manufacturing industry, and unchallenged in infrastructure and agricultural marketing. At the same time the state knows that the maintenance of output is still heavily dependent on the profitability of private capital, including foreign private capital, and avoids ill-considered or sweeping actions. However, a trend is now developing to buy out foreign, especially South African, capital cheaply. This is facilitated under present circumstances because repatriation of capital from sales is still strictly controlled, and can only take place slowly from blocked funds invested in government bonds at interest rates well below the level of inflation. Consequently, government is in a strong position to bargain with foreign shareholders who wish for immediate payment, with some deals recently (for instance the partial takeover of Delta Corporation from South African Breweries) gaining assets for the state at 30 per cent of current market values. Nevertheless, the state share in productive capital is still tiny and is likely to remain so for some time even on present trends. More generally, as summarized in Chapter 8, there is an attempt at state control of private industry, through import quotas, investment, price and wage control, and a comprehensive labour relations act.

There is a commitment to state expenditure on social programmes and prospectively to national insurance, and subsidies for some basic foods industries are thought to be inevitable if the producers are to be given sufficient incentives without raising prices to the lower-income consumer too much. The official position is that subsidies need to be reduced for budgetary reasons but that it is unrealistic (or undesirable) to attempt to remove them altogether: so government is explicitly opposed to IMF policy in this respect. A stand-by IMF programme negotiated in 1982 broke down in March 1984 following direct measures to control the balance of payments through the temporary freezing of dividend payments on pre-1980 private investment, the acquisition of the local stock of foreign assets, and a rise of the budget deficit to 10 per cent. Since then policy has been to continue to control payments by direct means, aided by an exchange rate declining slowly in real terms, and to squeeze public expenditure to prevent the budget deficit rising above 10 per cent, but making no attempt to reach the arbitrary IMF target of 5 per cent.

There is evidence from the growth of the share in net output of the manufacturing industry under sanctions, and within manufacturing of the key engineering sector, that before UDI the economy was too open, denying itself the protection needed to develop internal linkages. Sanctions, because they were not damagingly comprehensive (the outcome would undeniably have been severely negative had South Africa joined them from the start), forced a degree of healthy self-reliance, and a spur to initiative on the country's main economic actors.

Various speculative conclusions may be (and have) been drawn from this record. At one extreme it may be argued that the partial opening of the economy after 1980 was harmful, exposing it to a hostile world market, raising dependence on the export of primary commodities which were unstable (and generally declining) in price, opening up a capital outflow through repayments of loans and factor income from foreign investment, allowing in unnecessary imports, especially luxury cars (that then require a continuing stream of expensive spare part imports), and focusing attention on the external market at the cost of failing to develop the impoverished internal one in the rural areas.

At the other extreme, the World Bank and the IMF have been at pains to argue the inefficiencies caused by protection. Thus two studies on behalf of the former found sections of industry uncompetitive at world market prices, and recommended liberalization so that sub-sectors without a comparative advantage should be forced to improve efficiency or go under. The most startling conclusion from these studies, however, was that even in the World Bank's own terms the average efficiency (as measured by the conventional 'domestic resource cost' approach) was much higher than the Bank expected for a country after fifteen years of near complete protection, higher indeed than for its 'model' countries, like Ivory Coast or Kenya (Stoneman, forthcoming). Further, the Bank's own data showed that some key structural changes (in favour of the engineering sector for instance) had also occurred. Zimbabwe was thus able to argue that the World Bank case for liberalization was not economic but ideological, and so it has successfully defended its case for continuing comprehensive protection. However, during 1987, which was a year of economic decline, a widespread mood developed that 'something had to change', and promises to liberalize began to seem more serious. The World Bank elaborated its *Strategy for Sustained Growth* (World Bank, 1987b) which attributed low growth to low investment caused by the high budget deficit and the 'illiberal' foreign exchange regime. In 1988 a committee was set up to investigate both the desirability of liberalization and ways of phasing it in over a period. At the time of writing it is not clear how the committee will pronounce (it contains several members strongly opposed to liberalization), nor whether government would act on a recommendation for liberalization.

The above policies clearly do not fall into the free-market capitalist category advocated by the multilateral institutions, but equally clearly neither are they socialist. Zimbabwe's current course is a policy of moderate economic nationalism, which is attempting to redress, rather slowly, some of the worst distortions of the settler-colonial economy. Moderate but not exclusive use is being made of the state in this process, and private domestic capital (to some extent white as well as black) is also benefiting from the gradual decline of foreign capital, as well as from the continuation of protection and other controls. What also needs to be asked, however, is what overall policy for development is likely to emerge: are the current short-run methods of mild state management of a basically reactive nature likely to define a trajectory of continuity, or will a longer-term strategy for more thorough structural transformation be articulated and followed?

Alternative Development Strategies

At the same time as the liberalization option was forced on to the agenda by the economic slump of 1987, there were in fact also some tentative moves towards elaborating an alternative inward-looking strategy, which would reorient production towards the three-quarters of the population whose needs are very poorly expressed through market demand under the present system. One strand of this developed paradoxically out of a study on the possibility for the development of 'new NICs' by the Overseas Development Institute (ODI) in London; despite several advantages, Zimbabwe did not emerge as a plausible candidate, because of its disadvantages of small market size, landlocked situation, and geopolitical factors in relation to South Africa; world market conditions also reduced prospects (see Robinson, 1988, for a summary). So if such an export-led growth strategy was too risky, sources of growth must be sought internally, it was concluded, continuing the process (starting under sanctions) that had expanded the effective market from a quarter of a million whites to about a quarter or a third of the population — but extended now to the whole population. This would imply continuing protection, more labour-intensive and less import- intensive investment, realignment of investment to the rural areas, and industrial development restructured to be complementary to this process rather than to high urban living standards and exports.

Thus these economic arguments point towards a fundamental agrarian reform as a crucial mechanism for expanding the internal market. Aside from the equity considerations (which produced much of the impetus for peasant mobilization in the liberation struggle), and the increasing instability from rapidly rising numbers of educated unemployed, the economic argument for land redistribution is very basic: about half the good land is underutilized, and about half the poorer land is overutilized; therefore higher economic returns (and a larger market) will result from investment in the former than in the latter. Such economic common sense will not easily be applied, however, without further class struggle: the white owners of the underutilized land still have influence (and have persuaded many to continue to believe, quite wrongly, that significant redistribution would destroy agriculture's profitability); at the same time a significant number of black owners of commercial farms have arisen, and together these new allies threaten to precipitate a crisis of confidence in the running of the economy if they are seriously threatened. The consequences could clearly be a renewed white exodus, spreading to whites in industry, and the price of this would certainly be a freezing of international aid and credit from most Western countries and the multilateral institutions.

Given the opening that would also be provided for further South African destabilization (which would undoubtedly be ignored by the West in these circumstances), it seems clear that at present any sudden shif to alternative policies would run the risk of long-term structural damage to the economy's productive capacity. However, systematic structural change over a period, making use of existing state powers, and modifying and expanding existing programmes, could more realistically be attempted. A renewed and more vigorous resettlement programme, learning from the considerable experience already obtained, is indeed contemplated in some circles, but it would have to be coupled with constitutional changes, possible only after 1990, that could reduce costs, especially the prohibitive foreign exchange component of land acquisition. A significant underutilization tax on the LSCF sector would also be needed, so that underutilized land of high quality could absorb the landless and perhaps involve some of the qualified school-leavers in ancillary activities in more intensive settlement schemes; and the more marginal land that whites use for light grazing could be put to more intensive use as mixed farming by peasant households.

But there would also have to be a parallel expansion and restructuring of smallholder agriculture in the CAs if the twin goals of market expansion and reduction of poverty are to be met. What is needed is first an expansion of those services and inputs that have already generated notable increases in CA agricultural production so that they reach more than the better-off third of peasants. Second, some restructuring of the land-tenure system and of herding practices is necessary; and third, the building-in to the existing farming systems of redistributive measures and community or cooperative elements, will also be required if the resource-less and migrant widows are not to be sacrificed to immediate productive goals.

Although involving some government expenditure, such programmes would be less expensive than the alternative of depending entirely on rural relief-works programmes, and would represent a shift from recurrent to investment expenditure, a long-standing aim. If properly implemented, such programmes could soon become self-financing through the increased intensity of agricultural production, and could even be popular with the industrial bourgeoisie through the consequent raised demand for irrigation, construction and agricultural production equipment, let alone for consumer goods. Although other sections of the bourgeoisie and petty bourgeoisie might be expected to oppose such policies, there are overall benefits to the non-agricultural elements of this class. The measures could well be presented to them in nationalist terms, and as the necessary means of buying off the peasants and workers whose discontent is increasingly threatening.

At the time of writing the outcome is uncertain; we might hazard a guess that, as in the past, no real decision will be taken, for with the economy improving again in 1988, and the prospect of a fall in the debt-service ratio, neither the free-market nor more radical approaches will be deemed necessary, and continuity will be preserved with a mixed approach, which will not however prevent inequalities from increasing.

When ZANU came to power in 1980 it took over a country in which institutionalized racism and sexism had taken firm root (although the previous four years had begun a limited reversal). The economy was capitalist, although resistance to sanctions had brought increasing state intervention, but always in the context of safeguarding white economic privileges and the viability of capital.

The Lancaster House agreement limited the new government's power to reverse both racial and capitalist policies. This it did mainly through the guaranteeing of property rights, which made it prohibitively expensive to redistribute land, and residential or industrial resources. In the fields of health and education, it was made clear that most whites saw the preservation of high standards in these respects as a condition of their remaining. Within these constraints government policy therefore necessarily took the form of only very limited wealth redistribution whilst attempting to extend elite privileges to the majority, with some emphasis on the doubly disadvantaged position of black women. Given the limited resources available, this process could not go far, and consequently a vital ingredient from the whites' point of view was the ability to opt out of state education or health provision into the private sector, which therefore had to be allowed to grow.

Education

Before independence educational opportunities for black children were severely limited, and just as much in qualitative as in quantitative terms. The latter were bad enough: only 42 per cent of children of primary school age were at school in 1979, and less than 20 per cent of the primary school leavers were able to find secondary places, and even then to be faced with high exclusion rates after two and four years.

The result was a high level of illiteracy amongst black adults estimated at 45 per cent illiterate and 12.5 per cent semi-literate in a 1978 study. Thus at independence there were over 2 million functionally illiterate adults, over half of the economically active population, a potentially serious brake on plans for rapid development. But the large majority even of those who attained literacy, received inferior quality education designed to fit them for menial tasks in society. The few who filled the small number of academic places available attained better academic standards than their white counterparts, but effectively the only jobs open to them were in the black education or health services. (See Kadhani and Riddell, 1981a, for further details of the pre-independence situation.)

An effective democratization of educational opportunities at all levels was achieved within two years of independence, an undoubtedly major achievement of the new government. Free primary schooling was introduced, and enrolments for the seven years increased from 819,000 in 1979 to 2,260,000 in 1986. At secondary level there is a commitment to provide a four-year course for all primary school graduates (not completely free, however); enrolments in secondary school (four years to GCE O-level and two more to A-level) increased dramatically from a mere 79,000 (a high proportion of them white) in 1979 to 546,000 in 1986, a six-fold increase. This expansion was of course extremely costly, putting a heavy burden on the budget. State capital expenditure averaged about Z$18 million a year between 1980 and 1985, as compared to Z$8.9 million in 1979/80. Recurrent expenditure increased from Z$118.7 million in the latter year to Z$640.5 million in 1985/86.

Teachers' salaries, which take about 80 per cent of the education budget, are covered by government, even in private schools. The expansion required a huge increase in the number of teachers, and many untrained people were employed; thus between 1979 and 1985 the number of primary school teachers tripled to 57,000, but the proportion of untrained teachers rose from 9 per cent to 47 per cent; even in secondary schools, where the number of teachers increased five-fold, 32 per cent were untrained in 1985. A significant number of expatriate teachers, mainly from Australia and Britain, have eased the teacher shortage, and despite rapid training of new teachers, they will continue to be needed for about another ten years. By allowing the expansion of 'private' schools, government has been able to subsidize rather than carry the full cost of providing universal education. ('Private' schools include elite schools, mission schools, district council schools and farm schools.)

The desegregation of schools within two years of independence was aided by a policy of re-zoning. The colonial regime had practised a form of racial and class discrimination through a strict zoning system which prevented children from enrolling in schools outside their residential zones. However, by the simple procedure of placing a black township within the same zone as the former white only areas, and by double sessioning all urban secondary schools, racial integration was achieved. Although instruction is in the vernacular in the first two primary forms, by the end of the third year a transition is made to English, which thereafter becomes the medium of instruction.

One of the greatest forms of discrimination before independence, was through disparities in the teacher–pupil ratio. In 1982 this was standardized for all schools with prescribed ratios of 1:40 for primary and 1:30 for secondary schools (falling to 1:20 in sixth forms).

However, inequalities persist and may now be worsening. Part of the reason for this is that parents were given the right to charge themselves higher school fees by a simple majority vote. In rural private schools these fees may contribute to needed building. But in urban schools where the physical infrastructure already exists, the higher fees may be used to employ more teachers than the state paid quota under the policy of Management Agreements. Though fees are relatively high for lower income earners, they are not prohibitive, varying from Z$2 per year to Z$88 a year for day scholars.

Despite re-zoning the Management Agreement system has resulted in a widening of the gap between higher-income and lower-income schools: former white schools which are situated in more affluent suburbs are generally well staffed with qualified teachers, whereas poorer schools in distant rural areas and high density townships may be unable to find or retain qualified staff. Some township schools have however reached very high standards.

In the important area of adult education, the major feature has been a National Literacy Campaign, using indigenous languages, launched in 1983. This campaign has been beset by bureaucratic problems in that the major responsibility was given to the ministry of community development and women's affairs which is inadequately staffed and financed to carry out such a major programme. The 74,000 teachers and half a million secondary pupils under the ministry of education were not mobilized to support the work. The result was a low priority campaign with 28,520 participants in 1985, of whom about three-quarters were judged to have become literate. This small programme contrasts with the high priority given to adult literacy in other countries of socialist orientation, including Tanzania.

An equally serious problem has been the limited degree of change in the curriculum. Despite new syllabuses at primary and lower secondary levels, classroom practice obstinately remains set in a pre-independence mould. The reasons for this include the inadequacy of teacher training, and the consequent reliance on large numbers of unqualified and underqualified teachers. Another reason is inadequate supervision due to an insufficient number of supervisory staff and the use of an inherited supervisory system which is prohibitively expensive in terms of transport and subsistence costs.

Consequently despite an official emphasis on science, technology and education with production, actual classroom practice often remains tied to the rote-learning of facts. This has been caused not only by inadequate training and re-training of teachers, but also by insufficient investment in facilities and equipment for the more expensive practical and technical subjects.

Tertiary education has also expanded in response to post-independence demands, with the number of students in the university increasing from about 1,500 students in 1976 to over 4,700 in 1985; meanwhile polytechnic student numbers nearly doubled to 14,000, and students in teacher training colleges increased from under 2,900 to over 7,700.

In terms of enrolment of girls in the formal school system, Zimbabwe has a fairly good record with almost as many girls enrolled as boys (see Table 14.1).

Table 14.1 *School Enrolments by Sex, 1986*

	Boys	%	Girls	%	Total
Primary schools	1,157,065	51.2	1,103,302	48.8	2,260,367
Secondary schools	323,799	59.3	232,042	40.7	545,841
Teachers colleges	3,325	67.8	1,579	32.2	4,904
Total	1,484,189	52.8	1,326,923	47.2	2,811,112

Source: Ministry of Education Enrolment and Staffing Statistics, First Term 1986, mimeo. (Taken from Chung, 1988, which was the major source for this section.)

At tertiary level the proportion of women is significantly lower, at for instance only 23.4 per cent of the total university enrolment in 1985. By contrast the literacy campaign statistics for 1985 indicate that 84.8 per cent of the participants were women.

'Education with production' has been official government policy since independence, but has received low priority, depending on a non-governmental organization, the Zimbabwe Foundation for Education with Production (ZIMFEP) established by the minister of education in 1980. ZIMFEP has made substantial progress despite its limited brief to rehabilitate displaced Zimbabwean children who had returned from the liberation struggle; to establish schools where pupils are involved in both educational and productive activities; to experiment and propagate curricula involving education with production; and finally to ensure that the ex-refugee school leavers are placed in jobs. Several large schools have been built by ZIMFEP through self-help methods at one third of the established price. Large farms attached to the schools are successfully run by a combination of modern farm technology and labour-intensive methods involving the pupils. And job creation through the establishment of cooperatives has been a modest success. However, the good example remains marginal to the system as a whole.

The successes of educational expansion and democratization in Zimbabwe illustrate the contradictions inherent in its political economy. The racial system produced too few skilled people for the economy's needs; however a simple expansion of that system produced 100,000 secondary school leavers in 1987, half of them with reasonably good qualifications, and the figure rises to 150,000 by 1990, whilst the fundamentally unchanged economic structure is demanding at most 10–20,000 extra people a year. Zimbabwe, despite ample warnings, is repeating the mistakes made earlier by, in turn, India, West Africa and Zambia. Clearly the expectations of the educational planners was that, as in socialist countries, the schools would be hard pressed to keep up with the economy's demands for more highly qualified people.

Another problematic success is in the highly academic character of the skills imparted, raising unrealistic expectations amongst most pupils of a 'white-collar' job in town. This is due in large part to the disrepute into which many technical and practical skills were forced under the white regime, with its practical 'F2' secondary schools, manifestly inferior in funding and prestige to the academic schools that all white children went to. Government policy has not yet changed so as to relate schooling to the type as well as the number of economic opportunities now realistically available, but the growing budget deficit may force this before long.

Health

Disparities between black and white in the statistics for disease and infant mortality before independence show the magnitude of the task confronting the new government. Of equal importance is the fact that the provision of such health care as there was, was both fragmented under five authorities (the ministry of health, local authorities, religious missions, industry-based clinics, and private clinics), and highly concentrated on the urban areas. The two Harare (then Salisbury) hospitals took 31 per cent of the total health budget in 1979/80. Conversely there was very little attention paid to preventive medicine which was allocated 8 per cent of the budget for the whole country; people in the distant rural areas generally received no primary health care; if they became seriously ill, they had to move to an urban area.

In 1980 the infant mortality rate was 14 per 1,000 for whites (similar to developed countries), 50 for urban blacks and 140 for rural blacks. It is believed that conditions were yet worse on the white-owned farms where about a million people lived. Everywhere in the rural areas and townships measles, pneumonia, tuberculosis and diarrhoeal diseases were rife, as were parasitic diseases. Probably as few as 5 per cent of registered doctors worked in rural areas, most of them in mission hospitals.

With independence came a new policy, eventually reflected in a major policy document *Planning for Equity in Health* (Ministry of Health, 1984). This recognized that the causes of ill-health lay primarily in bad living conditions and inadequate nutrition and water supply, and it gave a blueprint for a comprehensive and integrated national health service, with primary health care as a core element. Immediate action was taken to give effect to reforms, with the introduction as early as September 1980 of free health care for all people (and their families) earning less than Z$150 per month (at the time the minimum wage was set at Z$70 per month). Provincial and district hospitals were upgraded, and by January 1987 224 rural health centres had been completed (Loewenson and Sanders, 1988, p. 140).

Other important changes since independence have been an expanded programme of immunization against the six major childhood infectious diseases and against tetanus in pregnant women; a diarrhoeal disease-control programme with emphasis on oral rehydration therapy, epidemic control, improved nutrition, prolongation of breast feeding, and improved hygiene through water supply and sanitation; a national nutrition programme involving a child supplementary feeding pro-gramme from 1981–5 covering the worst drought period and monitoring through growth cards; a village health worker programme, which by 1987 had trained 7,000 out of a target of 15,000 of these multipurpose basic health workers; and a programme of education in contraceptive practice through a parastatal National Family Planning Council, which has resulted in Zimbabwe having the highest rate of contraceptive use in sub-Saharan Africa (Loewenson and Sanders, 1988, pp. 140–1). The share of preventive services rose to 15 per cent of the (greatly expanded) budget by 1984/85. The number of doctors and nurses in government service rose substantially, but because of emigration of a high proportion of whites, primarily but not exclusively in private practice, overall numbers rose much less. For doctors there were 288 in government service in 1980 out of a total of about a thousand; in 1984 there were 468 out of a total of about 1,250. Nurses numbered about 5,200 in 1980 and 12,400 in 1986.

The cost of the changes has been considerable, and there has already been some backtracking under the pressure of the growing budget deficit. Real government health expenditure rose 27.5 per cent in real terms in 1980/81 and a further 47 per cent in 1981/82, but then fell slightly and has since more or less stabilized; as a proportion of the rising government budget this represented an increase from 4.6 per cent in 1979/80 to 5.9 per cent in 1985/86, but it was still only about 3 per cent of GDP (the total including private provision does not seem to have been calculated).

The impact of these changes has been real but limited, and there are signs of stagnation (and maybe even a reversal) of the trend. The overall infant mortality rate fell from 120 per thousand in 1980 to 83 in 1983 (Loewenson and Sanders, 1988, p. 146), and maternal mortality rates fell by 28 per cent. Overall disease incidence does not yet seem to have been significantly reduced except for immunizable diseases like measles, with pneumonia, diarrhoea and tetanus remaining major killers, and measles still significant. Partial surveys of nutritional status suggest limited improvements over 1980–3 with little change since (Loewenson and Sanders, 1988, p. 147).

The signs of a levelling off in improvement in health status corresponds both to the three-year drought (which caused hardship in the rural areas despite feeding programmes) and to pressure from the IMF and the World Bank to cut public spending and reduce the budget deficit. Although most people in employment were eligible for free healthcare in 1980, hardly any are now, as the minimum wage was raised to Z$158 per month (largely an inflationary adjustment) in 1986, whereas the Z$150 per month qualifying level for free healthcare has remained unchanged into 1988.

Despite some pressure for a democratization of the healthcare system through decentralization of planning and administration of health services, there are few signs that the struggle to demystify health planning is being won. Medical–professional decisions still dominate over programmes which might transform the social and economic relations which underlie ill-health. As an example we may take the introduction of village health workers, who although in principle representing their own communities and responsive to them in all matters affecting health (including social and economic factors), are increasingly selected and paid by district councils. Thus local accountability is declining and the health workers are changing in status from community workers into health service employees.

Moreover, class bias still persists, and the private sector continues to threaten the principle of a nationally integrated health system, propped up as it is by widespread medical aid funding which is increasingly being targeted at capturing the higher income sections of the working class, to the cost of the majority. The emerging divergence between declining death rates and static quality of life as reflected in nutritional status is indicative of the rapid expansion of health care provision on the one hand, and of the relatively static economic conditions for the majority on the other.

15 Spatial and Demographic Dimensions of Social Policy

Zimbabwe has a rapidly growing population but not one of the highest growth rates by African standards — or so it is thought. The last census in 1982 just after independence was accurate enough but the calculation of a growth rate of 2.8 per cent is obtained by working back from there to earlier censuses which may well have inaccurately assessed the black population. Whatever the real growth rate, population pressure is perceived as a problem by the government, to a lesser extent perhaps than its colonial predecessor, but it is nevertheless inclined to share to a surprising extent a view that sees 'population growth' as an underlying causal factor that generates a number of key problems. These include pressure on agricultural land, its consequent over-utilization with disastrous consequences for the environment, rapid urbanization, and the social problems and financial burdens that that generates. Although social policies in the areas of provision of land, the environment, urbanization and employment all need to be interrelated it is simplistic to see them as merely offshoots of a more basic population problem that policy must tackle. 'Population growth' can only be comprehended within the context of the inherited racially-defined institutional features of the society. Rhodesia's class–race structure had both demographic and spatial dimensions. Historically, the CAs were left, without any significant development but with frozen boundaries, as labour reserves, with the consequence that they became overcrowded and eroded. Urban growth was regulated by influx-control measures, so that black labour (which was predominantly male) could be treated as transient and glaring unemployment was kept out of sight. But these latter patterns began to change. In the 1970s part of the labour force became more settled; despite legal obstacles, blacks flooded to towns, shanty towns mushroomed, and the balance between male and female adults in the urban areas became more equal, suggesting a more settled population, but unemployment was no longer so disguised. The question after independence was one of determining what kind of further evolution from the Rhodesia spatial political economy and its demography should be fostered, an agenda that includes such interconnected issues as: how to tackle land shortage and environmental deterioration in the CAs; whether to retain some means of limiting the growth of the urban population; and how to cater for the growth that will occur. These policy issues relate in turn to that of how vigorously a stabilized (and hopefully fully employed), more completely proletarianized, working class is to be promoted as opposed to the migrant labour of 'worker-peasants'. Government has as yet only partially developed an appropriate perspective for tackling these areas of policy.

The most wide-ranging effort in government circles to address these issues was in the Riddell Report (see Chapter 4). Of relevance to this discussion is not the specifics of its proposals, but the general strategy that sought to tackle the poverty and such social problems as 'divided families' by providing more opportunities and more land so that a more stabilized peasantry would not need to be so dependent on migrant earnings; by significantly increasing wages and also, crucially, by social welfare provision so as to encourage more complete proletarianization. The criticism has been made elsewhere (Bush and Cliffe, 1984) that however desirable this is as a long-term goal, and even though the trends are inevitably towards a more settled proletariat, these proposals are unrealistic in the medium term. As we have shown, real wages have scarcely grown at all, and certainly no end is in sight to poverty or to the insecurity consequent on old age, sickness or unemployment, even for those workers currently in regular employment. At the same time unemployment has forced itself to a central position on the agenda of key social problems. The TNDP projected a 3 per cent growth in employment, premised on a 8 per cent growth of GDP, and neither were achieved. In fact employment in the productive sectors has tended to fall in the 1980s. This is all the more worrying in a context where great strides in education mean that by the late-1980s around 100,000 secondary school leavers each year are competing for only 10,000 new formal sector jobs. By the mid-1990s the annual shortfall will be of the order of 250,000 jobs a year on anticipated trends of employment creation, and a third of the labour force will be out of work.

Employment Policy

There has, however, been some concern to enunciate a strategy for employment creation. But up to 1987 this concern has in practice been translated into little more than the setting of over-optimistic investment and growth rates, plus 'encouraging self-employment by formalizing the informal sector'. This latter seems to mean providing training and advisory services (though 'formalizing' might well be a formula for reducing this sector's labour-absorption capacity!) and 'promoting the development of cooperatives in all sectors' (FFYNDP, 1986 — although this policy does not seem to be active, see Chapter 7 above). Some public works programmes designed on a more or less permanent basis to absorb unemployed youth, especially in the rural areas, have been initiated as an extension of temporary food-for-work projects in the most recent drought year of 1986. Recent public statements suggest that the employment issue has now been given an even more important priority. An inter-ministerial Task Force on Employment Creation was set up in 1987, and a major study of employment and growth prospects in industry and commerce was to be concluded in 1988. But if direct employment creation through industrial expansion and public works offer only partial solutions then rural development is one policy area that is crucial, and must be approached from a perspective that sees population and employment in social and not just demographic terms.

Population Policy and Rural Development

Government has also moved to limit population growth, but commitment has been somewhat muted. Certainly there is a nationalist reaction to what were perceived as racist attitudes in the colonial period that sought to curb black population, which makes some politicians suspicious of any population control policy. There was, for instance, an understandable and heated reaction to the widespread and often somewhat enforced use of the long-lasting, injected birth control drug, Depo-Provera, which had potentially dangerous side-effects, and its use was banned by Herbert Ushewokunze when he was minister for health. However, its use has once again been sanctioned, albeit in more carefully controlled circumstances and on a voluntary basis, as part of a Plan goal 'to extend family planning services to all parts of the country' (FFYNDP, 1986). The slight ambivalence which attaches to this policy does serve to limit the extent to which population control is seen as some kind of prerequisite to all other development policies, which is the simplistic orthodoxy preached by the international population control lobby. The alternative perspective, that sees voluntary limitation of births as a *consequence*, not a precondition, of the alleviation of poverty and social insecurity, points to the need to look at how far policies in other areas are geared not only towards aggregate growth but also towards income redistribution and the elimination of poverty and ill-health. It is now widely accepted that poor households where mortality rates are high, especially in rural areas, have every reason to have big families in the hope that some children will survive and eventually provide for the older generation. In circumstances where employment creation is not keeping pace with the numbers of job-seekers in the formal sector and there is no improvement in the wage-share or social security, the persistence of linkages between urban workers and work-seekers and their rural families, and of practices whereby migrants seek to retain land, livestock and homes in the countryside is not surprising. These attitudes further underline the lack of realism in many proposals like Riddell's for ending migrancy and separating out workers from peasants.

Such perceptions have not yet been fully integrated into government thinking. However, it is as well that policies over landholding have retained communal allocation of land in the CAs and have avoided the privatizing of titles which would have caused a major exodus from the land. But other dimensions of rural development policy run the risk of promoting the growth of production by a minority, as we have seen, and thus of generating a group of rural poor, with access neither to off-farm income nor enough resources (land, oxen, seed, inputs, labour) to farm, and who might therefore be easily dislodged to swell the ranks of the urban poor: the issues of rural development and urbanization policy must thus be inter-related in planning; how far they are will be discussed below. Rural policies must thus have as a central goal the gainful absorption for at least another generation of a rural population that will inevitably increase in absolute if not relative terms. This requirement is not always appreciated by agricultural planners whose task is often carried on without reference to overall national imperatives — particularly the first imperative that rural policies must avoid *generating* that poverty (resourcelessness), unemployment, and even more rapid urbanization that are seen as symptoms of a 'population problem'.

Environmental Policy

There is a tendency for agricultural planners in Zimbabwe, the knowledgeable and experienced, but blinkered, agriculturalists of Rhodesia and their protégés, to see their jobs in terms of planning optimal land use — another example of a naturalist rather than a social approach to environmental issues. One consequence is for them to think in terms of 'optimum' carrying capacities of land and of ensuring 'economic' sizes of farms, which in turn lead to proposals that a more 'rational' system of agricultural production is only possible if the farming areas shed an 'excess' population — regardless of the poverty-creation effects noted above. This tendency is enhanced by another strong current of thinking inherited from Rhodesian (and South African) environmentalists of a certain school. Their (proper) concern for a *sustainable* agrarian system, for halting over-use and degradation of arable and grazing land and of wilderness, is myopically translated into prescriptions of shifting people off the land (in fact 'people' who are black, and peasants, and whose land use practices are seen as incorrigible — at least without draconian enforcement) or limiting their access to wilderness or especially productive areas..

Again, a well-informed and 'scientifically' based school of thought, which is nevertheless premised upon a disguised racism in its view of the society that is interacting with the environment, has been partly absorbed or not seriously challenged by the incoming Zimbabwe planners. The strong conservationist lobby left over from Rhodesia days, drawing on international inspiration and resources from bodies like the World Wildlife Fund, promoted the drawing up of an official 'National Conservation Strategy'. A draft of this discussed at a 1985 conference saw 'abuse of the natural vegetation [as] the single most common cause of ecological deterioration', and called for restriction of animal numbers to match grazing-area capacities and for 'effective control over indiscriminate cutting of trees for house poles and fuelwood'. These measures show no appreciation of the very real socio-economic problems faced by rural dwellers, especially the poor. In a context where livestock are vital because no other source of traction power is economical or affordable, there is in fact a shortage of oxen for ploughing in some areas, and the poorest 40 per cent have no livestock anyway; and there is frequently no other source of fuel than trees that is available or affordable. The very way the problem is posed — to protect 'nature' — precludes seeking solutions to the human problems of poverty induced by limited resources in a manner that would be environmentally sustainable — and such possibilities do exist to be explored. In addition, the means that are proposed to achieve these controls are essentially statist and authoritarian: regulations about land use, orders to reduce livestock numbers; here the Rhodesian legacy can be discerned as wedded to some of the commandist notions held by some of the nationalist leaders and even those who find 'Marxism–Leninism' a convenient label for state direction.

Other policy-makers, including some Zimbabwean environmentalists, however, have been sufficiently worried about this approach to 'conservation' to engage in a behind-the-scenes debate. The document referred to had to go through five drafts before a form of words was sufficiently agreed to go public, and even then its status was downplayed. It was presented at the 1985 conference as a 'strategy' that might provide the basis for policy, and not as a policy paper as such. But here is another area of policy-making where there is only partial questioning of inherited approaches, and badly needed creative thinking about environmental issues within a Marxian framework has yet to develop.

Urbanization Policy

Urbanization is another policy area that ought to be approached as part of a broader social focus on issues of population and employment, for it is the other side of the coin of rural development and environmental sustainability; but here again there is a lack of a fully coherent alternative to colonial urban policy, which placed legal restrictions on black people living in towns, which were in fact classified as white areas originally. In the first half of the century they remained so and blacks were given temporary residence rights only as long as they were in formal employment. These men were provided with bachelor hostels; family dwellings were not provided, no unauthorized 'shanties' were sanctioned, and families and casual job-seekers were confined to the reserves by influx control measures. Later, as employment expanded, concessions were made to allow 'African Townships' where blacks could have some property rights and family housing was provided by local authorities — but all strictly segregated and controlled.

The actual complexion of town populations changed dramatically in the 1970s. The total grew rapidly — by 1980 Zimbabwe was 25 per cent urbanized — and despite restrictions, the black component rose as a percentage. Squatter settlements began to appear, and in the 1980s, when restrictions had been removed or were politically difficult to enforce, they mushroomed — one in Harare grew from 5,000 to 30,000 in the course of 1982. The only policy responses have been some limited formalizing of squatting by 'site and service' schemes, whereby residents are provided foundations and helped to build structures themselves on credit, but also a resorting to enforced clearances of 'illegal' squatters — a policy of desperation but a practice that might become more common if there is impoverishment as a by-product of rural policies and if there is no coherent urban strategy and spatial policy. Some draconian repatriation has been inflicted on those women who seemed to be on their own in towns — a male response to the great expansion in the number of women in towns. But although urban adult sex ratios are now more or less equal, only 15 per cent of those in paid employment in Harare are women. The influx of women does point to an increasing proportion of families who are no longer split between rural and urban residences, although it is suggested that the change from the inherited labour migrant pattern has not fundamentally altered even for these households — that although women no longer look after farms, their town occupations are still predominantly providing subsistence (cultivating spare plots, etc.) or concern with petty trade (Drakakis-Smith, 1986).

Policy towards South Africa

As Zimbabwe approached independence, South Africa was polishing its proposals for a 'Constellation of Southern African States' (CONSAS), which it hoped would link its Southern African Customs Union (SACU) partners (Botswana, Lesotho, Swaziland, and Namibia), Malawi and Zimbabwe (preferably under Muzorewa) and possibly Mozambique, with South Africa and its bantustans (thereby gaining them a measure of international recognition). The election of ZANU led by Robert Mugabe destroyed this hope, and Zimbabwe immediately entered the organization of the Front Line States. The successful collaboration of the FLS in helping to bring about a settlement in Zimbabwe was seen as a good example, and the Southern African Development Coordination Conference (SADCC) was established in 1980, attracting into its fold not only Malawi, but all the independent SACU members as well. That for the moment put paid to a formal CONSAS arrangement. However, South African *de facto* economic dominance remains considerable, with three SADCC members still also in SACU, and Mozambique's destabilized economy more and more dependent on South Africa and susceptible to a 'carrot and stick' policy.

Since 1980 Zimbabwe's policy towards South Africa has walked a narrow line, constrained on the one hand by a desire to aid the liberation struggle within South Africa and on the other by fear of the consequences of provoking open hostility and economic or military reprisals (indeed both of these have occurred in relatively minor ways as warnings). Despite its membership of the FLS, Zimbabwe has denied the ANC leave to establish bases on its territory, merely allowing offices in Harare; the ANC headquarters thus remain in Lusaka. In the light of the subsequent bloody raids on Botswana, Lesotho and Mozambique by South African commandos, aimed at the ANC but killing nationals as well, this may seem to have proved justified; the murder of ANC representative Joe Gqabi in Harare, and attacks on ANC offices there were warnings of how much worse things could be. And minor economic sabotage, like the withdrawal of leased railway engines, and curbing of the flow of fuel from South Africa after sabotage of depots in Mozambique, have given Zimbabwe a taste of the stick.

Zimbabwe's initial cool attitude towards the ANC is related to the split in the Zimbabwean liberation movement, which resulted in loose alliances between ZAPU and the ANC and ZANU and the PAC. However, after the 1985 election confirming Mugabe in power, it was clear that ZAPU would never be a serious political threat, and conversely that the PAC was declining relative to the ANC; a *rapprochement* also began between Zimbabwe and the Soviet Union (which had supported ZAPU).

As with some other foreign policy issues, Zimbabwe has gradually moved to a more radical position. The threat by South Africa not to renew in 1982 the long-standing trade agreement that allows some Zimbabwean manufactures into the South African market with reduced tariffs caused much concern, and some concessions were made. But trade negotiations have always been conducted at the level of officials, with Zimbabwe refusing demands that ministerial-level meetings should take place, for instance in the petrol crisis at the start of 1983 after South African commandos had blown up the oil-storage depot at Beira. Mr Mugabe's contempt for the US policy of 'constructive engagement' with South Africa led to increasingly outspoken criticism: the US ambassador left in April 1986, just before the independence celebrations, and, possibly in retaliation, a 4 July celebration attended by ex-President Jimmy Carter led to the latter's walkout when a speech by the foreign minister attacked US policy scathingly. When Mugabe refused to apologize, the US aid programme for 1986/87 was suspended. Mugabe's attitude to sanctions stiffened considerably during 1986, when Zimbabwe took the chair of the Non-Aligned Movement, and when it was represented at the Commonwealth 'mini-summit' which (with the United Kingdom dissenting) voted to impose sanctions. Promises were made by both Zimbabwe and Zambia that they would implement the sanctions package by the end of the year, but a series of dire economic consequences were pointed out, and postponements and further promises ensued until in July 1987 after Zambia refused to agree to a suspension of airlinks, and following a confused cabinet meeting, the minister of trade initiated a policy of denying the validity of most licences for imports from South Africa. Reports of misunderstandings at the meeting, of selective sanctions in January 1988 being intended, and of South African threats of an immediate and complete suspension of all trade, led to the withdrawal of the order after ten days.

It seems likely that Mugabe was in a minority in cabinet on militant action on sanctions, supported by Oliver Munyaradzi, Herbert Ushewokunze and few more. He is in a stronger position as President, but will almost certainly still listen to advice from his economic ministers. Trade with South Africa will continue to decrease as other sources of key imports (such as metallurgical quality coke and sheet steel) are found, and as the Beira route carries a higher proportion of overseas trade. But far from expecting Zimbabwe to take the lead in sanctioning South Africa, it is more reasonable to allow it to choose its own timing after further reduction of dependence, or even to be allowed to be a temporary exception, as was Zambia from 1968 to the early 1970s with regard to mandatory sanctions against Rhodesia.

Policy towards SADCC and PTA countries

Zimbabwe is clearly a pivotal state in the sub-region, just as much as South Africa in the region, and it sees itself as such. It therefore has played important roles in the FLS, in SADCC, and in the PTA, providing the first two executive secretaries of SADCC, and fulfilling its responsibility for regional food security competently. It also has a high degree of political sympathy with Mozambique and Tanzania, and recognizes the debt that it owes to the former for support during the liberation war, including the provision of bases for ZANU and the ruinously expensive border closure of 1975–80; there is a defence agreement and an active friendship society (Zimofa) between the two countries, and Mozambique has become militarily and economically dependent on Zimbabwe for keeping open the Beira Corridor. Although Zimbabwe provides it with one of its transit routes, relations with Zambia are less cordial (Zambia supported ZAPU, and detained and expelled ZANU members after the murder of Herbert Chitepo).

Unfortunately economic cooperation has lagged far behind political sentiment, and despite the formation of SADCC, the first two years of independence saw Zimbabwe taking strategic decisions (admittedly when inexperienced, and influenced by orthodox World Bank-type thinking) which reduced regional integration. One example of this was the decision to go for energy self-sufficiency, something not achieved even by Rhodesia under sanctions. The option to purchase surplus electricity from the Cabora Bassa dam in Mozambique was not even investigated, and the decision was taken to phase out electricity purchases from Zambia as new units of thermal electric power became available at Hwange.

In addition Zimbabwe with its significant industrial base has tended to see the region as an alternative market to South Africa, but has been less keen to import from it (see the table); accordingly its surplus has grown, the PTA's clearing house has become underutilized as other countries have had to settle in hard currency, and trade has stagnated. Likewise although the main rationale of SADCC in the field of investment is to help prevent wasteful duplication, Zimbabwe sees the usefulness of this larger market for its existing industry; however, if it is to benefit in this way it will have to make concessions so that other SADCC countries get a share of the planned industrial growth — a policy which the government has not yet been far-sighted enough to adopt. It has, for instance, insisted on proceeding with a chemical pulp and paper mill despite the existence of a major SADCC project with excess capacity in Tanzania; and it has been in dispute with Botswana over the latter's textile exports. Clearly if Zimbabwe is to sell to the region, it has to abandon its apparent aim of self-sufficiency extending to almost every product that the region might be able to sell to it (see Table 16.1).

Table 16.1 Intra–SADCC trade, 1982–4 average

	Imports†		Exports‡	
	US$ m.	%	US$ m.	%
Angola	12.0	4.3	2.0	0.8
Botswana	51.0	18.5	47.0	19.2
Lesotho	0.3	0.1	0.0	0.0
Malawi	26.0	9.4	21.0	8.6
Mozambique	26.0	9.4	14.0	5.7
Swaziland	3.0	1.1	7.0	2.9
Tanzania	24.0	8.7	4.0	1.6
Zambia	48.0	17.4	35.0	14.3
Zimbabwe	86.0	31.2	115.0	46.9
Total	276.0	100.0	245.0	100.0

Notes: * Estimates

† As reported by the importing country.

‡ As reported by the exporting country.

Source: SADCC, *Intra-Regional Trade Study,* Final Report, Supporting volume I (Bergen, Chr. Michelsen Institute, January 1986), pp. 6 and 48.

The Preferential Trade Area (PTA) complicates analysis of SADCC trade: for example Zimbabwe could not offer preferential quotas for imports from Zambia without extending the offer to other members of the PTA to which they both belong; however, Zimbabwe can still offer preferential quotas to Mozambique and Botswana, which are not yet members. Although intra-SADCC trade was not initially a country responsibility, it was an early preoccupation, and worries about Zimbabwe's surplus and the need to clarify SADCC's relation to the PTA initiated several studies; in 1986 Tanzania was given the brief, and now operates the SADCC Industry and Trade Coordination Division.

Mozambique and the Beira Corridor

Zimbabwe's close relationship with Mozambique is reflected in a defence agreement and a flourishing Zimbabwe–Mozambique Friendship Association. The 1981 Zimbabwe–Mozambique Defence Agreement states: 'We have concurred that an attack against Mozambique shall be regarded as an attack against Zimbabwe' (quoted in Evans, 1988, p. 227). On this basis a Special Task Force (STF) was originally deployed to guard the Mutare–Beira oil pipeline in 1982 but its role soon increased. Zimbabwean military involvement in Mozambique has grown, with 7–10,000 troops guarding the Beira Corridor in 1988. In August 1985 Mr Mugabe gave an open-ended commitment to the survival of Mozambique by stating that Zimbabwe would deploy up to 30,000 troops if necessary; in the same month ZNA paratroops launched an airborne assault on the Gorongosa base at Casa Banana and in November 1985 it overran the MNR's territorial base on the Pungwe at Nyarunyaru. Nevertheless STF operations still remained limited and failed to prevent further MNR penetration into Zambezia and Tete provinces which virtually cut Mozambique in half.

In October 1986 when the MNR 'declared war' on Zimbabwe for supporting FRELIMO, Robert Mugabe dismissed the challenge with the derisive comment 'oh come on.' Yet in the 1985 elections ZANU lost only one seat among Shona speakers — in Chipinge, on the eastern border, to ZANU-Sithole and its Ndau supporters. The security risk this posed to Harare was highlighted at the end of 1985 when it was confirmed that MNR insurgents and former UANC auxiliaries had infiltrated eastern Zimbabwe with South African backing. The possibility of former Sithole auxiliaries beginning operations with the MNR cannot be ruled out, while the late 1987 flurry of attacks on villages and tea estates near the Mozambican border is an ominous development.

Samora Machel's death in an air crash in October 1986 however stiffened Mugabe's resolve to stand by the FRELIMO government, and in November 1986 he declared: 'Survival of Mozambique is our survival. The fall of Mozambique will certainly be our fall ... All and one stand together. All and one fight together' (quoted in Evans, 1988, p. 228). Zimbabwe then took the initiative in persuading the FLS to stand firm with Maputo, and as a result 2,000 Tanzanian troops moved into northern Mozambique in March 1987. Pressure was applied on Malawi to secure its border to prevent MNR infiltration. It was agreed between Britain, Zimbabwe and Mozambique that the number of Mozambican officers being trained by the BMATT (see below) would be doubled by mid-1987. In February 1987 the STF began a wider offensive against the MNR in Tete, pushing up to the Malawi border. The focus of Zimbabwe's self-interest in Mozambique is of course access to its ports. Suggestions that Zimbabwe should recognize the FRELIMO government's deteriorating control and negotiate with the MNR or press FRELIMO to do so are readily dismissed, partly because of the evidence that the MNR is at heart a destructive tool of South Africa with no coherent programme or even much ambition to enter government: its paymasters do not want stability in Mozambique. To date the cost of the STF has proved sustainable (at the price of widening the budget deficits), and the Zimbabwean business community has gradually become enthusiastic about the potential of the Beira Corridor, and indeed the reopening of the Limpopo line, providing direct access to Maputo. The Beira Corridor Group (BCG) was set up in early 1987 under the ex-minister of agriculture, Mr Dennis Norman, to publicize and campaign for the development of the link. It offered 200 debentures of Z$5,000 each to businesses, and despite making it clear that the BCG was non-profitmaking, the offer was oversubscribed; further debentures were later sold to companies in Botswana and Zambia.

Work has proceeded well on the railway line and fairly well on the port itself, with cooperation coming in particular from the United Kingdom, the Netherlands and Nordic countries. By early 1988 about 25 per cent of Zimbabwe's trade was thought to be taking this route, and there had been major shipments of containerized minerals, tobacco and tea. Transport costs from Mutare to Beira were said to be less than a third of the Z$1,640 incurred via Durban.

Military Policy

At independence Zimbabwe's defence problem had two key dimensions: the threat from the overwhelmingly superior forces of South Africa; and the existence internally of three hostile armies. The latter problem was solved with extraordinary success with the help of the British Military Advisory and Training Team (BMATT); by early 1982 the three armies of ZANLA, ZIPRA and the Rhodesian whites totalling some 80,000 combatants had been welded into a disciplined regular army of 40,000. The new Zimbabwe National Army held together despite violent clashes of rival ex-combatants at Entumbane in 1981, and the expulsion of ZAPU from the coalition government. The South African threat (aided by an ex-Rhodesian fifth column) was made manifest in the sabotage of the Inkomo barracks and ammunition dump and the virtually complete destruction of the strike capability of the Air Force of Zimbabwe (AFZ), including its new British Hawk jets, in 1982. It would seem likely, as Evans argues (1988, pp. 230–2) that any restoration of strike capability to the AFZ would again attract a South African attack, which is why (apart from the cost) many regarded the proposal in 1987 to purchase Mig-29s with considerable scepticism. A full-scale South African invasion could not be resisted by Zimbabwe alone, but is for the moment unlikely. More important is to have the means of defence against limited incursions and airborne sabotage and the threat of more widespread destabilization, both through anti-aircraft defence and an efficient army. The war most likely to be fought is already being fought, in Mozambique, and to a limited extent in eastern Zimbabwe. To deal with the MNR requires helicopters and troop carriers, not sophisticated airplanes or tanks.

The commitment to Mozambique discussed in the preceding section in fact opens up a serious risk for Zimbabwe. The SADF'S support for the MNR in spite of the Nkomati Accord allows South Africa the prospect of attenuating Zimbabwe's military capability by supplying and arming the MNR. Unless clear limits are placed on the extent of operations, the ZDF'S Special Task Force (STF) faces the prospect of being bled to death in the Mozambican bush by Pretoria without the SADF firing a shot. Some are already talking, only half-humorously, about 'Zimbabwe's Vietnam'. Zimbabwe's military resources are simply not sufficient to sustain large forces on extended operations, while according to Evans, 'STF headquarters will almost certainly require upgrading and expansion in what could become an excruciating command and control problem for the ZNA'. (1988, p. 229.)

Meanwhile the army has grown to some 46,000 in seven brigades; the Air Force of about 1,000 men has forty-three combat aircraft. In addition there is a National Militia of 20,000, a Police Support Unit of 3,000 and regular police numbering 15,000. National Service has been approved, but so far remains unactivated. The fifth brigade was North Korean trained, whereas the sixth and seventh brigades were trained in 1986–8 by Zimbabwean and UK instructors entirely from well-educated volunteers. In 1986 defence spending overtook the education vote as the largest ministry appropriation, an ominous indicator that immediate security considerations now have to outweigh developmental planning. Some Z$639.5 million of the Zimbabwean budget (19 per cent) is now devoted to defence, with Air Force procurement increasing from Z$38.6 million to $103.2 million.

Wider Foreign Policy

Outside the southern African region Zimbabwe has pursued a policy of non-alignment, indeed President Mugabe is the current chair of the Non-Aligned Movement (until 1989). This policy has resulted in opposition to the Soviet Union's involvement in Afghanistan, and Vietnam's in Cambodia, and also to US policy in Grenada (it co-sponsored with Nicaragua a UN Security Council resolution condemning the invasion) and in support for Nicaragua in resisting the United States; it abstained in the Security Council on a motion condemning the Soviet Union over the shooting down of a South Korean airliner. It is also strongly critical of US support for Unita in Angola, and its 'linkage' policy of Cuban troop withdrawals from Angola as a condition for Namibian independence. Indeed angec on US southern African policy generally boiled over in 1986 at a 4 July dinner in Harare attended by ex-President Jimmy Carter, who walked out in protest at a critical speech delivered for the foreign minister. When Zimbabwe refused to apologize, the US aid programme was suspended, and two years later despite discussions, no new programme has been announced. This is indeed a principled stand, given Zimbabwe's current foreign-exchange shortage, and given that the United States had been the main aid donor.

Relations with Nordic countries and most members of the Commonwealth are excellent, and they are cordial with Britain and West Germany despite disagreements over South Africa. West Germany, Italy and the Netherlands have become major trading partners. Diplomatic relations are maintained with effectively all countries with the exception of South Africa (and Namibia), Israel, Taiwan and South Korea.

Zimbabwe enjoys special relationships with certain socialist countries, with some of which it has signed friendship and barter agreements, including North Korea (which like Britain has aided military training),

Bulgaria, Cuba and Yugoslavia. Nevertheless this has produced little result in economic terms so far: the most important socialist country for Zimbabwe's exports in 1986 was China, only twelfth in overall importance and taking under 3 per cent; as a supplier East Germany was the most important, but only seventeenth overall and supplying less than 1 per cent. Yugoslavia and China have become important in several large construction projects (the former building the Sheraton Hotel and Conference Centre, the latter the national sports stadium).

17 Conclusions

This text has sought to present the main features of the social structure and the political economy of Zimbabwe, exploring the historical process of its (belated) achievement of independence and the roots of the particular political regime that gained power in 1980, and the policies it has pursued. We have seen that the literature on the country, including the writings of Zimbabwean analysts who claim to write from a Marxian perspective, question how far the regime's commitment to 'Marxism–Leninism' is more than just rhetoric. Certainly there has been precious little attempt so far to transform the socio-economic structure or to change the terms of the country's involvement with the world economy, in directions that would suggest a transition to socialism and that are differentiated from a more Africanist-oriented path of capitalist development after the decades of racial capitalism.

It could be argued, first, that it is too early to come to a definitive conclusion as to whether there will be any significant attempt to change the society in accordance with any kind of Marxist vision — the regime has only been in power a few years, and came to power in a war-ravaged situation, with advice ringing in its ears from the neighbouring front-line states that it should do nothing precipitate to lead to a white exodus and collapse of the one potentially strong economy in the region, or to upset too much the aggressive apartheid regime on which it was economically dependent. Moreover, that attainment of power was a compromise whereby the nationalists had to accept being hobbled for some years by constitutional niceties imposed by the United Kingdom precisely to inhibit any undermining of capitalism. Against an implied view that caution has tempered what remains of an underlying commitment to social transformation, one observer remarked at the outset that there was always the danger that patterns adopted as short-term tactics could be settled into as long-run strategy (Yates, 1980). And certainly there are powerful interests — not confined, we would argue to the rump of white settlers — that would settle for such a programme, some of them influential because of their access to decision-making either through 'corporatist' channels that persist from the colonial state, others through the party, with its mixture of committed cadres from guerrilla days, with their Marxist formulations, and old-guard nationalist politicians operating on a clientelist basis.

It can also be argued that a specifically socialist transformation is not only premature but in fact only possible after a first stage of transition of a more limited sort. There can indeed be found in some of Mugabe's utterances a formula that suggests that the strategy to be pursued (more wholeheartedly than has so far been possible) is that of a 'national democratic revolution'. However, there has been precious little spelling out of the possible content of such a revolutionary strategy by the party, nor by the radical analysts. The successful working out of such developments, either on paper as an explicit programme, or in actuality, whether consciously or spontaneously, will revolve around a number of choices or outcomes, all of which could be said to be in the balance in Zimbabwe at the current juncture. The land issue, for so long at the centre of shaping Zimbabwe's political economy, now depends on whether there is a significant second round of agrarian reform after some of the constitutional constraints come off in 1990 or whether a 'Kenya' pattern is followed. The overall trajectory will depend on the outcomes of the struggle (still observable in spontaneous peasant actions) for and against a major redistribution of white land, and the possible restructuring of peasant farming: whether purely individual production units are transcended, whether the state follows a too commandist role and whether productivity increases can be sustained. A second critical area of economic strategy is industrialization — what road (of national or regional import-substitution, or export-orientation?) is chosen to sustain the expansion of a significant industrial base, and how far this will involve a choice (and a battle) between foreign, indigenous and state capital. The choices made in these two strategic areas of the economy will affect, but themselves be the outcome of, contending social forces and the way these articulate their influence politically.

The kind of class cleavages and alliances that could emerge in this new period from 1990 are by no means clear cut, given the pattern of the colonial past and of the particular social structure it has produced. In the colonial period, the basic divide along which society was split was that of race, and there may still be a tendency for racial identities to obscure class identities and possible class alliances. In particular if a kind of national democratic strategy involving a degree of self-sufficiency, especially in industrialization, is to be pursued, active collaboration with locally based capitalists rather than with foreign capital may well be central. However, the attitudes and past political loyalties of these whites may stand in the way of a possible alliance between them, black workers and progressive party people, which might otherwise seize the opportunity of pursuing a common interest. But even in the past, the white ruling bloc was really a set of different class interests, as we have seen. The 1980s have seen changes in that racial definition of the class divide along two dimensions. First and most evident, the old alliances have broken up and the dominance of the white ruling groups has ended. But the present ambiguity about what trajectory will emerge is in part a result of the fact that new alliances are as yet still not firmed up. It is not yet clear whether Arrighi's projected bloc based on the commonality of interests of the black petty bourgeoisie and international capital has in fact emerged, or whether there has been an alternative leaning of the petty bourgeoisie more towards national capital. Nor indeed, in this end-of-the-century context is it clear that such distinctions between these two sectors (foreign and national) of capital are meaningful. The attitudes of the Zimbabwe government and South African state and capital towards each other, and how more generally the government manages its links with South Africa in the dangerous years to come, will surely be of equal if not greater importance.

At another level the backing of the ruling party by workers, unlike sections of the peasantry, has never been especially strong, but in neither case has it yet been withdrawn. But the contradictions are related also to a second dimension of ambiguity, not about the actual nature of the structured interplay of classes but in the plasticity of the very classes themselves. The changes before and after independence do not amount to a social revolution, but they have nevertheless involved significant changes in the position and composition of various groups: the agrarian capitalists are somewhat on the wane; the black petty bourgeoisie, and particularly its bureaucratic component, has grown considerably. However the latter has not yet decided whether its interests are better served by using the state to favour its own private accumulation, thus transforming itself into an actual bourgeoisie (the Kenya path), or by riding on the back of state capitalism and becoming what in Tanzania was termed a bureaucratic bourgeoisie. The broad class group of workers-cum-peasants based on labour migration is also in flux: at one end of this former continuum there is more thorough proletarianization, whilst some impoverishment of some peasants occurs at the other end, but workers and peasants cannot yet be regarded as distinct classes.

How these different social forces coalesce and pursue their interests, and in turn grapple or side with each other, remains to be worked out. In these circumstances Zimbabwe's prospects are still not completely determined. They are, however, limited — in the short term by South Africa's proximity, the circumstances of a negotiated independence, and the inherited social structure. A socialist transformation is not an immediate prospect, but it is still an open question whether in the long run the Marxist ambitions are likely to remain merely a camouflage for an unambiguously neo-colonial and capitalist project, or whether they can become the basis for some 'national democratic reforms'. If the latter occurs the reforms will be both protracted and strongly contested, and their character will depend on the kinds of social forces that emerge. The overt policy battle will mainly take the form of political infighting *within* the party and bureaucracy, and class interests will in the process be mediated and perhaps distorted within structures that reflect ethnic and other factional, as well as class, forces, and through the medium of an ideological rhetoric in which different brands of nationalism will probably be more significant than the official 'Marxism–Leninism'. Finally, the process will be deeply influenced by the way in which the regional conflict in Southern Africa is ultimately resolved, how far it impinges directly on Zimbabwe, and how far Zimbabwe continues to pursue its principled commitment to the security of the other front-line states.

Bibliography

Arrighi, G. 1967. *The Political Economy of Rhodesia*. The Hague, Mouton.
— 1970. Labour supplies in historical perspective: a study of the proletarianization of the African peasantry in Rhodesia. *Journal of Development Studies*, vol. 6, no. 3, pp. 197–234.
Astrow, André 1983. *Zimbabwe: A Revolution that Lost its Way?* London, Zed Press.
Baylies, Carolyn 1980. Imperialism and settler capital: friends or foes. *Review of African Political Economy*, no. 18, pp. 116–26.
Biermann, W. and Kössler, R. 1980. The settler mode of production: the Rhodesian case. *Review of African Political Economy*, no. 18, pp. 106–16.
Bratton, Michael 1980. The public service in Zimbabwe. *Political Science Quarterly*, vol. 95, no 3, pp. 441–64.
— 1987. The comrades and the countryside: the politics of agricultural policy in Zimbabwe. *World Politics*, vol. 39, no. 2, pp. 174–202.
Bush, Ray and Cliffe, Lionel 1984. Agrarian policy in migrant labour societies: reform or transformation in Zimbabwe? *Review of African Political Economy*, no. 29, pp. 77–94.
Charney, Craig 1987. Political power and social class in the neo-colonial African state. *Review of African Political Economy*, no. 38, pp. 48–65.
Cheater, Angela 1984. *Idioms of Accumulation: Rural Development and Class Formation among Freeholders in Zimbabwe*. Gweru, Mambo Press.
— 1986. *The Politics of Factory Organization: A Case Study in Independent Zimbabwe*. Gweru, Mambo Press.
— 1988. Contradictions in 'modelling' consciousness: Zimbabwean proletarians in the making. *Journal of Southern African Studies*, vol. 14, no. 2, pp. 291–303.
Chitsike, L.T. 1985. *A Report on the Review, Study and Effective Coordination of Cooperatives*. Harare, Government of Zimbabwe.
Chung, Fay 1988. In Stoneman, 1988.
Cliffe, Lionel 1976. Some questions about the Chitepo Report and the Zimbabwean movement. *Review of African Political Economy*, no. 6, pp. 78–80.
— 1979. The racial implications of Britain's sanctions cover-up. *Race Relations Abstracts*, vol. 4, no. 3, pp. 1–8.
— 1980. Towards an evaluation of the Zimbabwe Nationalist Movement. Political Studies Association Conference Paper, mimeo.

— 1984. Zimbabwe: political economy analysis and the contemporary scene. In Centre of African Studies, University of Edinburgh, *Southern African Studies: New Directions*.

— Mpofu, J. and Munslow, B. 1980. Nationalist politics in Zimbabwe: the 1980 elections and beyond. *Review of African Political Economy*, no. 18, pp. 44–67.

— and Munslow, B. 1980a. The 1980 elections in Victoria Province, Zimbabwe: a preliminary report. Paper for the University of Leeds Conference on Independent Zimbabwe, mimeo.

— and 1980b. The 1980 Zimbabwean elections and the politics of a future Zimbabwe. Paper for the University of Leeds Conference on Independent Zimbabwe, mimeo.

Cole, Barbara 1984. *The Elite: The Story of the Rhodesian Special Air Services*. Transkei, Three Knights.

Commonwealth Secretariat 1980. *Southern Rhodesian Elections, February 1980: The Report of the Commonwealth Observers' Group on Elections Leading to Independent Zimbabwe*. London, Commonwealth Secretariat.

Cowan, Michael 1981. Commodity production in Kenya's Central Province. In Heyer, J. *et al.* (eds), *Rural Development in Tropical Africa*. London, Macmillan.

Davies, Rob 1981. Foreign trade and external relations. In Stoneman, 1981a.

— 1988. The transition to socialism in Zimbabwe: some areas for debate. In Stoneman, 1988.

— and Stoneman, Colin 1981. The economy: an overview. In Stoneman, 1981a.

Day, J. 1975. The creation of political myths: African nationalism in S. Rhodesia. *Journal of Southern Africa Studies*, vol.2, no.1.

Drakakis-Smith, D. (ed.) 1986. *Urbanization in the Developing World*, editor's chapter on *Zimbabwe*. London, Croom Helm.

Evans, Michael 1988. In Stoneman, 1988.

FAO (Food and Agriculture Organization), 1986. Policy Options for Agrarian *Reform in Zimbabwe: A Technical Appraisal*. Paper submitted by FAO for the consideration of the government of Zimbabwe. Rome, FAO.

FFYNDP, 1986. See Republic of Zimbabwe, 1986.

Flower, Ken 1987. *Serving Secretly*. London, John Murray.

Green, R.H. and Kadhani, X.M. 1986. Zimbabwe: transition to economic crises, 1981–1983, retrospect and prospect. *World Development*, vol. 14, no. 8, pp. 1059–83.

Hanlon, Joseph 1986. *Producer Cooperatives and the Government in Zimbabwe*. London, mimeo.

Kadhani, X.M. and Riddell, Roger 1981. Education. In Stoneman, 1981a.

Kazembe, Joyce 1986. In Mandaza, 1986.

Kriger, Norma 1988. The Zimbabwean War of Liberation: struggles within the struggle. *Journal of Southern African Studies*, vol. 14, no. 2, pp. 304–22.

Ladley, A. and Lan, David 1985. The law of the land: party and state in rural Zimbabwe. *Journal of Southern African Studies*, vol. 12, no. 1. pp. 88–107.

Lan, David 1985. *Guns and Rain: Guerrillas and Spirit Mediums in Zimbabwe*. London, James Currey.

Leys, Colin 1959. *European Politics in Southern Rhodesia*. Oxford, Oxford University Press.

— 1978. Capital accumulation, class formation and dependency: the significance of the Kenya case. In Miliband, R. and Saville, J. (eds), *The Socialist Register, 1978*. London, Merlin Press.

Loewenson, R. and Sanders, D. 1988. The political economy of health and nutrition. In Stoneman, 1988.

Mandaza, Ibbo (ed.) 1986. *Zimbabwe: The Political Economy of Transition 1980–1986*. Dakar, Codesria.

Martin, David and Johnson, Phyllis 1981. *The Struggle for Zimbabwe: the Chimurenga Wars*. Harare, Zimbabwe Publishing House.

— and 1985. *The Chitepo Assassination*. Harare, Zimbabwe Publishing House.

MEPD (Ministry of Economic Planning and Development) 1981. *ZIM-CORD — Let's Build Zimbabwe Together*, Report on Conference Proceedings, Zimbabwe Conference on Reconstruction and Development. Harare, Government Printer.

Ministry of Health 1984. *Planning for Equity in Health*. Harare, Government Printer.

Minter, William 1986. *King Solomon's Mines Revisited: Western Interests and the Burdened History of Southern Africa*. New York, Basic Books.

Moore, David 1988. What was left of liberation in Zimbabwe? Struggles for socialism and democracy within the struggle for independence. In L. Cliffe, (ed.), *Popular Struggles in Africa*. Sheffield, ROAPE Publications, forthcoming.

Mpofu, Joshua 1980. The February 1980 Zimbabwe Elections: the Matabeleland North and South Provinces. Paper for the University of Leeds Conference on Independent Zimbabwe, mimeo.

Murray, D. J. 1970. *The Government System in Southern Rhodesia*. Oxford, Clarendon Press.

Palmer, Robin, and Parsons, Neil (eds) 1977. *The Roots of Rural Poverty in Southern Africa*. London, Heinemann; Berkeley, University of California Press.

Pankhurst, Donna 1986. Rural women, struggles in Zimbabwe. Paper for *Review of African Political Economy* Conference, Liverpool.

— 1988. Women's lives and women's struggles in rural Zimbabwe. *Leeds Southern African Studies*, no. 6.

Phimister, Ian 1988. In Stoneman, 1988.

Ranger, T.O. 1967. *Revolt in Southern Rhodesia 1896–97: A Study in African Resistance*. London, Heinemann.

— 1980. The changing of the Old Guard: Robert Mugabe and the revival of ZANU. *Journal of Southern African Studies*, vol. 7, no. 1, pp. 71–90.

— 1983. The invention of tradition in colonial Africa. In Hobsbawm, E. and Ranger, T.O. (eds), *The Invention of Tradition*. Cambridge, Cambridge University Press.

— 1985a. *Peasant Consciousness and Guerrilla War in Zimbabwe*. London, James Currey; Berkeley, University of California Press.

— 1985b. *The Invention of Tribalism in Zimbabwe*. Mambo Occasional Papers — Socioeconomic Series, no. 19, Gweru, Mambo Press.

Republic of Zimbabwe 1981. *Growth With Equity: An Economic Policy Statement*. Harare, Government Printer.

— 1983. *Transitional National Development Plan, 4 1982/83–1984/5;* 2 vols. Harare, Government Printer.

— 1986. *First Five-Year National Development Plan, 1986–1990*. Harare, Government Printer.

Riddell, Roger 1978. *The Land Problem in Rhodesia: Alternatives for the Future*. Gweru, Mambo Press.

— (chairman) 1981. *Report of the Commission of Inquiry into Incomes, Prices and Conditions of Service*. Harare, Government Printer.

— 1984. Zimbabwe: the economy four years after independence. *African Affairs*, vol. 83, no. 333, pp. 463–76.

Robinson, Peter 1988. Relaxing the constraints. In Stoneman, 1988.

Sachikonye, Lloyd 1986. In Mandaza, 1986.

Saul, John S. (ed.) 1985. *A Difficult Road: The Transition to Socialism in Mozambique*. New York, Monthly Review Press.

Shaw, William 1986. Towards the one-party state in Zimbabwe: a study in African political thought. *Journal of Modern African Studies*, vol. 24, no. 3, pp. 373–94.

Sibanda, Arnold 1988. The political situation. In Stoneman, 1988.

Sithole, Masipula 1980. Ethnicity and factionalism in Zimbabwe national politics, 1957–79. *Ethnic and Racial Studies*, vol. 3, no. 1, pp. 17–39.

— 1986. The salience of ethnicity in African politics: the case of Zimbabwe. In Paranype, A.C. (ed.) *Ethnic Identities and Prejudices: Perspectives from the Third World*. Leiden, Brill.

Smith, David and Simpson, Colin 1981. *Mugabe*. Harare, Pioneer Head.

Stoneman, Colin 1976. Foreign Capital and the Prospects for Zimbabwe. *World Development*, vol.4, no.1, pp. 25–58.

— 1980. Zimbabwe's Prospects as an Industrial Power. *Journal of Commonwealth and Comparative Politics,* vol. 18, pp. 14–27.

— (ed) 1981a. *Zimbabwe's Inheritance*. London, Macmillan; Harare, College Press.

— 1981b. Agriculture. In Stoneman, 1981a.

— 1981c. The mining industry. In Stoneman, 1981a.

— 1981d. Foreign capital in Zimbabwe. In *Zimbabwe: Towards a New Order: Working Papers, volume 1*. Geneva, United Nations, pp. 413–539.

— 1982. Industrialization and Self-Reliance in Zimbabwe. In M. Fransman (ed.), *Industry and Accumulation in Africa*. London, Heinemann; pp. 276–95.

— 1986. Zimbabwe: the private sector and South Africa. In J. Hanlon (ed.) *Beggar Your Neighbours: Apartheid Power in Southern Africa*. London, James Currey.

— (ed.) 1988. *Zimbabwe's Prospects*. London, Macmillan; Harare, College Press.

— forthcoming. The World Bank and the IMF in Zimbabwe. In Campbell, B. and Loxley, J. *The World Bank and the IMF in Africa*. London, James Currey; Toronto, University of Toronto Press.

Thompson, Carol 1988. Zimbabwe in SADCC: a question of dominance? In Stoneman, 1988.

TNDP, 1983. See Republic of Zimbabwe, 1983.

UNCTAD 1980. *Zimbabwe: Towards a New Order — An Economic and Social Survey*. Geneva, United Nations (report plus two volumes of working papers).

Ushewokunze, Herbert 1984. *An Agenda for Zimbabwe*. Harare, College Press.

Verrier, Anthony 1986. *The Road to Zimbabwe, 1890–1980*. London, Jonathan Cape.

Weiner, Daniel 1988. Land and agricultural development. In Stoneman, 1988.

—, Moyo, S., Munslow, B. and O'Keefe, P. 1985. Land use and agricultural productivity in Zimbabwe. *Journal of Modern African Studies*, vol. 23, no. 2, pp. 251–85.

Weitzer, R. 1984. In search of regime security: Zimbabwe since independence. *Journal of Modern African Studies*. vol. 22, no. 4, pp. 529–77.

Wood, Brian 1988. Trade union organization. In Stoneman, 1988.

World Bank 1987a. *Zimbabwe: An Industrial Sector Memorandum*. Washington, DC, World Bank.

— 1987b. *Zimbabwe: A Strategy for Sustained Growth*. Washington, DC, World Bank.

'Yates, Peter' 1980. The prospects for socialist transformation in Zimbabwe. *Review of African Political Economy*, no. 18, pp. 68–88.

ZNHSCP (Zimbabwe National Household Survey) 1984. *Demographic Socioeconomic Survey of Communal Lands, 1983/84, Reports 1–8*. Harare, Central Statistical Office.

Index